THE HANSA TOWNS AND THE HANSEATIC LEAGUE

BY

Helen Zimı

THE HANSA TOWNS AND THE HANSEATIC LEAGUE

Published by Wallachia Publishers

New York City, NY

First published 1900

ABOUT WALLACHIA PUBLISHERS

IN bringing before the public what I believe to be the first History of the Hanseatic League, it gives me pleasure to think that the impetus to write it came from the United States. The work was suggested to me by my valued friend, Mr. G. H. Putnam, of New York, a citizen of the country in which the principle of federation is best understood and most thoroughly carried out. The Hansa was one of the earliest representatives of that federal spirit which will, beyond doubt, some day help to solve many of the heavy and grievous problems with which we of the Old World are struggling; but that day is not yet, and meantime we have much to learn both from the successes and failures of the past

I have, of course, assumed in my readers some knowledge of German History, such as they can derive from Professor Bryce's inimitable "Holy Roman Empire," or from Baring-Gould's "Story of Germany," one of the earlier volumes of this series.

In conclusion, I desire to express my very cordial thanks to Dr. Otto Benecke, Keeper of the State Archives of the city of Hamburg, and to my uncle, Dr. Carl Leo, Syndic of the .same town, for the generosity with which they have accorded me valuable assistance in the preparation of this volume. I have further to thank Miss L. Toulmin Smith for help in revision of the MS., and for many useful suggestions. To my sister, Miss Alice Zimmern, and to Dr. Richard Garnett, of the British Museum, I am indebted for aid in proof-reading.

HELEN ZIMMERN.

FLORENCE,

March 1, 1889.

STORY OF THE HANSA TOWNS.

PROEM.

THERE is scarcely a more remarkable chapter in history than that which deals with the trading alliance or association known as the Hanseatic League. The League has long since passed away, having served its time and fulfilled its purpose. The needs and circumstances of mankind have changed, and new methods and new instruments have been devised for carrying on the commerce of the world. Yet, if the League has disappeared, the beneficial results of its action survive to Europe, though they have become so completely a part of our daily life that we accept them as matters of course, and do not stop to inquire into their origin. To us moderns it seems but natural that there should be security of intercourse between civilized nations, that highways should be free from robbers, and the ocean from pirates. The mere notion of a different state of things appears strange to us, and yet things were very different not so many hundred years ago.

In the feudal times the conditions of life on the continent of Europe seem little short of barbarous. The lands were owned not only by the kings who ruled them with an iron despotism, but were possessed besides by innumerable petty lordlings and princelets, who on their part again exercised a rule so severe and extortionate that the poor people who groaned under it were in a condition little removed from slavery. Nay, they were often not even treated with the consideration that men give their slaves, upon whom, as their absolute goods and chattels, they set a certain value. And it was difficult for the people to revolt and assert themselves, for however disunited might be their various lords, in case of a danger that threatened their universal power, they became friends closer than brothers, and would aid each other faithfully in keeping down the common folk. Hand in hand with princes and lords went the priests, themselves often worldly potentates as well as spiritual rulers, and hence the very religion of the carpenter's son, which had overspread the civilized world in order to emancipate the people and make men of all nations and degrees into one brotherhood, was—not for the first time in its history—turned from its appointed course and used as an instrument of coercion and repression.

Such briefly was the celebrated feudal system—a system whose initial idea that the rich man should protect the poor, that the lord should be as a father to his vassals, is wise and good, but which in practice proved itself untenable. Even to-day, after many centuries and generations, the only European nations that have wholly succeeded in casting off the feudal yoke are those in whose history an entirely subversive revolution, like the French, has taken place. In others, notwithstanding years of struggle and revolt, not only its memory, but some of its customs, still survive; for systems and institutions die hard, and continue to exercise mischievous power long after their original force is spent. To this survival can be traced a large number of the evils that are agitating contemporary Europe; for example, the wretched state of Ireland.

That the people of Germany, the country with which we have chiefly to deal in treating of the Hanseatic League, was not wholly enslaved and crushed out of all individual existence by the state of things that reigned from the Baltic to the Alps in the early years of its history is due to the two great factors of memory and heredity. Memory, because when Tacitus, that most dramatic of historians, wrote his famous book on Germany, one of the chief points he noted in this land was that there existed an equality among the freeborn, an absence of rank and concentration of power. Heredity, because a love of individual freedom appears as an inherent quality in the Teutonic race from their first appearance in historic legend.

> "Though the mills of God grind slowly
> Yet they grind exceeding small,"

sings the poet, and all the ages have confirmed the experience that might is not suffered to be right for ever, that vengeance falls and justice asserts itself, even though the wrong be not righted, or the evil avenged for many a long year after the sin has been committed.

"Whom the gods would destroy they first strike with madness," says the Latin proverb. It was so with the ambitious rulers of Germany. They were not content to be sovereigns of their own empire, they desired also to hold in their hand the reins of Italy; the bestowal of the title Holy Roman Emperor by the Pope Leo III. upon Charlemagne moved their longing and cupidity, so that gradually they grew more occupied with the business of the fair peninsula, "the garden of the Empire," as Dante calls it, than with the condition of their own ruder and sterner fatherland. Added to this they took to fighting among themselves, being divided into two rival factions which elected opposing rulers, the result being that often no one knew who was head or who was subject.

Frederick Barbarossa was the last to uphold the real authority and power of Germany. He was a true hero of romance, one of the noblest expressions of the mediæval character. When he died the real empire fell. What remained was but a semblance and a ruin, and it is little wonder that Germany plunged henceforth into yet greater anarchy, invented the legend that peace and prosperity would not return to her until Frederick Red Beard should come back to rule, that giant among men, falsely reported dead, but who, in truth, was merely resting, sunk in enchanted sleep among the mountains of Bavaria. There he was waiting the hour when the ravens should cease to hover around the cloud-capped peak to emerge surrounded by the trusty Crusaders who shared his slumbers and restore to Germany the golden age of peace and strength.

It is claimed by some that Barbarossa has so returned, that he came back as recently as 1870, but whether this be fact or no does not concern us here. What does concern us is, that in the reign of Frederick Barbarossa we find mentioned, for the first time as a power in the State, a few of the many German cities that had arisen under the fostering protection of Henry the Fowler. Barbarossa found it useful to encourage the growth of that third estate so needful to the healthy existence of the body politic. Thus he could pit them against the nobles when it pleased him to harass his sometime allies; he could also draw from them the moneys that are the sinews of war. In return for such loyal aid the emperor freely granted municipal institutions, rights and privileges, exemptions and favours, little realizing that in so doing he was creating in his own land that very spirit of independence, that breath of modern individual freedom, to quench which he was spending his best years and strength beyond the barrier Alps.

The policy therefore of the "imperial knights" and "knightly emperors" who preceded and followed Frederick, while in one way it tended to destroy the unity of Germany as a political state, in the other was the means by which the cities of Germany, as well as those of Northern Italy, acquired that remarkable independence, that rapid, splendid commercial and intellectual development that raised them to the condition of almost autonomous communities, and made them the wonder, glory, and pride of the Middle Ages. Citizens and burghers became freemen, and enjoyed the privileges that fell to this lot. Hence men loved to crowd into the towns, and these grew up and flourished apace, until they acquired such power and assumed such proportions as their first promoters little contemplated.

It was the Lombard league of cities that broke the might of the Holy Roman Emperors, as the rulers of Germany loved to style themselves, as they styled themselves, indeed, long after the Empire, to quote Voltaire, was neither Holy, nor Roman, nor an Empire.

Ignominiously driven forth from Italy, the German kings at last turned their steps homeward, where they looked to reign with their old strength and might, even though the range of their rule had been circumscribed. They came back to find that long absences, internal and external feuds, pretenders and usurpers, had so weakened their prestige that their subjects had learnt to trust to themselves rather than to their sovereign heads. And when they did return, at last, it was to find themselves confronted with such another league of cities, as had wrecked their power abroad, a federation founded for mutual protection and defence, under whose ægis alone could peace or shelter be found.

This was the irony of fate indeed. To be sovereigns of the world, the German emperors had staked their national existence; staked and lost.

On a murky and disturbed horizon had arisen a brilliant star, the star of municipal liberty, helping men to hope for and aspire towards those better things, to which it alone could lead them. The political anarchy of Germany, increased by forty years' interregnum, not only had given birth but strength to the confederation of cities directed against the brigandage of the princes and nobles, which we first meet with under the name of Hansa, in the year 1241, at a time when both the Papal and Imperial thrones were vacant, when in France St. Louis wielded the sceptre and was strengthening the power of nobles and the church; when in England Henry III. had enraged the barons by his fondness for foreign favourites, and when that outburst was preparing which led to the formation of a popular faction and upraised the patriot, Simon de Montfort; a time, in short, when the long struggle even now waging between the people and their rulers was first begun in modern Europe.

PERIOD I.

I.

THE DAWN OF A GREAT TRADE GUILD.

WHETHER it be that our forefathers were not so prompt to put pen to paper as we are, or that they purposely avoided written words and inclined to silence from motives of that combined prudence and love of mystery-making that distinguished the Middle Ages, the fact remains that of the real origin and founding of that great federation of industry and intelligence known to after-years as the Hanseatic League, we have no accurate knowledge.

We see the tree in full growth, with its widespreading boughs and branches; of the modest seedling whence it sprung we are in ignorance. We only know most surely that some such seed there must have been, and in this case may with certainty infer that the main causes of this unique combination were the alliance of the North German cities among themselves, and the protective and social alliances formed by German merchants who met in foreign parts.

It is obvious that there must have been much commerce, and that it must have played an important part before either of these circumstances could have arisen. Therefore in order fully to understand the importance and bearing of the League we must begin our story earlier than its history proper would seem to warrant; only thus can we thoroughly comprehend why the Hanseatic alliance in fostering its own interests, in aggrandizing and enriching itself, was working also for all humanity, since it created and enlarged the idea of public right, and thus sowed the seeds of principles then novel, but on which our modern civilization is largely founded and with which we are now so familiar that it is difficult to realize how matters could ever have been otherwise. Can we grasp, for example, a state of things when wrecking was considered a legitimate occupation; when the merchandise thus thrown on land became the possession of the strand dwellers and the ship's crew their legitimate slaves; when barons who deemed themselves noblemen lay in wait within their strong castles to pounce on luckless traders, and either deprived them wholly of their wares or levied black mail under the name of toll; in short, when humanity towards the weak and unfortunate was a word of empty sound? Yet so strongly is the love of enterprise implanted in the Northman's breast that even these obstacles did not deter him from the desire to enlarge his experience and to widen the field of his energies. He was the kinsman of those adventurous Angles and Saxons who had not feared to cross the boisterous German Ocean and to subjugate Great Britain to themselves; in his veins ran the blood of those Normans, the scourge and terror of European coasts, against whom the peoples knew no better protection than the prayer addressed to Heaven in their despair—"*A furore Normanrorum libera nos Domine*," a clause that survived in their litanies some time after the cause was no longer to be feared.

Indeed it is not easy to distinguish the earliest traders from corsairs. It would seem that as occasion served they employed their long narrow rowing ships to scour the ocean or to carry the produce of the north, above all the much prized amber. It is thought that they bore it down even to the Bay of Biscay, nay, perhaps yet further within the Roman Empire.

Under the intelligent rule of Charles the Great the activity of the Northman assumed a more pacific character, and we meet with the idea of merchant and trade guilds, though the latter were not much encouraged by the emperor, who feared lest they should contain in themselves elements of corporate union and political revolt. But he fostered the growth of cities; and in those days trade and commerce filled up even more than at the present day the daily life of a citizen. In the Middle Ages the expression "merchant" (*mercator*, negotiator) was on the Continent actually held as identical with townsman.

It is curious that the early Teuton regarded manual labour as unworthy a free man, but did not extend this feeling to commerce, and trading became more and more the occupation of the third estate. We find them on horseback or in ships traversing many regions to bring their wares to market and to enlarge their sphere of action, and gradually as their numbers increased they would meet each other at the various foreign ports, exchange news, perhaps even wares, and hold together in that brotherly spirit that men of one nation and one tongue are wont to feel towards each other on foreign soil. Disputes and difficulties with the natives must also have been of frequent occurrence, for though the merchant, as bringer of news and novelties, was usually a welcome visitor at a time when intercourse between nations can hardly be said to have existed, yet, on the other hand, he had to reckon with the prejudice that regards what is strange as equivalent to what is hostile. Hence the merchants very naturally combined among themselves at the different ports to protect their common interests, and endeavoured by all means in their power to enlist in their favour their own sovereigns and those of the lands they visited.

Thus in the lawbook of London, under the reign of Ethelred II. the Unready (978), we come across the phrase, "the people of the Emperor have been judged worthy of the good laws, like to ourselves." This phrase meant that, in cases of wrong done to the foreigner by the native, the foreigner should enjoy the protection of the native laws as though he were a citizen, instead of being treated as heretofore like an alien. "The people of the Emperor" meant in this case the Teutonic merchants who traded on the banks of the Thames long before the German cities had combined to form their famous league, long before they had founded their factories in Russia, Scandinavia, and Flanders.

London was their earliest foreign settlement, and already in the tenth century we find that the Germans enjoyed the same rights when their ships entered British ports as those possessed by the English. In return for this they had at Easter and Christmas to make a donation of two pieces of grey and one of brown cloth, ten pounds of pepper, five pairs of men's gloves, and two barrels of vinegar. The fact that they thus paid toll in kind and not in money is entirely in accordance with the ancient usage of guilds and corporations, and the conditions of mediæval tenures. Gloves as tokens of good faith and submission, and pepper, probably because of its rarity as an Eastern product, were forms of payment frequent in early days.

After this first mention we find that year by year the privileges of the German were extended in England. The kings desired that they should be treated as subjects and friends, and after Henry the Lion had married a daughter of Henry II. of England, the alliance grew yet closer. Thus special privileges were accorded to them with regard to the sale of Rhine wine, of the importation of which into Great Britain we now hear for the first time. It is evident that the commerce of England was largely in the hands of these foreigners, a circumstance the more remarkable when we consider that the English have now for some centuries been the great traders of the world.

What hindered the rise of the British in early days was the feudal system against which the Germans had rebelled. It was a system incompatible with burgher life, with independent industry and enterprise. For many years the English trade was practically restricted to the exportation of wool, skins, lead, and tin. For where there is no middle class there can be no real commerce, and this fact explains the widespread power of the German merchants in England. The lessons they learnt here they carried farther afield; appearing now as the vanguard of civilization, now as the pioneers of Christianity, everywhere as traders desirous to fill their coffers, bearing in mind the maxim that "union is strength," and clinging closely to one another for mutual protection and defence. We must remember that travelling in the tenth, eleventh, and twelfth centuries was not what it is to-day. Dangers lurked on all sides for the bold mariner who ventured forth in ships of small size devoid of compass, load-line, chart, and chronometer. It was slow work to make headway under the difficulties put in the mariner's path by the elements alone, such as the darkness of night, fogs and storms, shoals, quicksands, and rocks, to say nothing of the peril from pirates. The fact, too, that, owing to the want of maps, they kept as close as possible to land, increased the risks they ran. Arrived at his destination, the trader would often have to wait long ere he could find a purchaser for his wares, for in those days the merchant himself carried his wares to market; there were no commission agents at the various ports; there were no posts, nor was the art of remitting money understood. In the stormy winter-time, moreover, neither sailors nor merchants cared to venture upon the ocean; and owing to the brevity of the northern summer it often became needful for them to pass the bad season at whatever place they happened to be. Indeed the hazards connected with a winter voyage were so great, that in the very earliest days of union it was determined by common consent that no merchants should send their ships to sea after St. Martin's Day (November 11th), and that they should endeavour as far as possible to be in port by Michaelmas (September 29th). "To sail after Martinmas is to tempt God," writes an old chronicler. With the 11th of November the winter season commenced for the Baltic trading fleet.

Curiously enough a similar custom obtains in Greece to this day. The Greek coasters do not sail on the seas from December 6th till after the New Year; during this time the ocean is hallowed for new trips. The Hanseatics, of course, had to extend the time of exemption in the northern seas. In the year 1391 a Hanseatic Diet ordained that no Hanseatic merchant should sail forth from a western to an eastern, or from an eastern to a western harbour between Martinmas and Candlemas (November 11th-February 2nd). The climatic conditions of certain ports obliged this rule to be extended to St. Peter in Cathedra (February 22nd), if they were carrying "precious goods."

It is amusing, however, to find in the older records an exceptional clause to the effect that herrings and beer, two of the most important exports of the coast towns, could not possibly be subjected to these restrictions. The herring, that much prized fasting dish, to the preparation and distribution of which the Hansa attached such value, had necessarily to be despatched before February 22nd in order that it might arrive at its destination before Lent. A no less important reason determined the transport of beer, which was brewed in most of the export towns, and which might easily spoil in a more advanced season of the year. These reasons caused the cities to decide that a ship laden with beer, herrings, or dried cod, might go to sea on St. Nicholas Day (December 6th) if it were ready laden by that date.

But this was the exception. The rule was for the trader to winter wherever he happened to be. In the long, cheerless evenings men liked to associate with compatriots who spoke the same tongue, and had the same interests and customs. These men of the Middle Ages were specially distinguished by their social instincts. They were bound together also by the element of a common religion, by the desire to worship together, to fulfil, perchance, some holy vow made in an hour of great danger, to bury, with the familiar rites of his own Church and country, some less fortunate comrade who had expired on foreign soil. Thus were formed those Guilds, or Hanse, as they were called, of merchants on alien soil, clustering, as a rule, around a church erected by them, and having besides a general living and storehouse for the safe custody of their goods. There is nothing strange in the fact that such settlements should have been formed; what is strange is the power they acquired in the course of time, until at last, in some places, they dictated terms to the natives of the country; nay, they even made and unmade their rulers, until in the end their sway extended from Bergen in the north to Venice in the south, from Novgorod and Smolensk in the east to York and London in the west.

II.

FEDERATION.

THE free ocean, owned by no king or ruler, has from earliest times been the highroad of nations, and in the life and movement of the last eighteen hundred years the Baltic takes a scarcely less important place than the lovelier, more poetical, and oft-sung Mediterranean. Even to-day it is more frequented than most of the seas; the traffic through the Sound being second to that of no other strait.

The Baltic has had its singers too. We need only turn to the strong, rugged Norse Saga to find that sea extolled as the nurse of mighty heroes, or the scene of giant combats; and the wilder element that pervades these heroic tales is in keeping with the rugged iron-bound coasts that skirt its waters, which do not invite the cooing of idyls, nor lap the fantasy in luscious dreams. Here all is stern life and movement; here man must fight hand to hand with nature if he would extort from her even the bare necessities for his daily nourishment.

The contrast between the North and the South is nowhere more strikingly seen than in the different characteristics of the two seas, and the races they have produced. Nor could these characteristics be better illustrated than by a comparison between the great commercial Republics of Italy and the Hanseatic federation of Germany. The former, though individually great, never became a corporate body. Jealousy and rivalry were ever rife among them, and in the end they destroyed themselves. Where nature is kind men can better afford to be cruel, and need not hold together in such close union. Thus it was here.

But if the Baltic is at a disadvantage compared with the Mediterranean in climate as well as in size, it is not inferior in wealth and variety of its produce. Mighty rivers, watering many lands discharge themselves into its bosom, and produce upon their banks rich and needful products, such as wheat and wool. In the earth are hidden costly metallic treasures, while the sea itself is a well of opulence from the number and diversity of the fish that breed in its waters.

It has been well said that since the days of the Hansa, possession of the Baltic and dominion of the sea are synonymous terms. The Hansa, the Dutch, and the English have necessarily played the first rôle in the Baltic trade. But the trade dates from an even earlier time. Thanks to coins accidently dropped, and after long years unearthed, we learn that by way of the Volga the Northmen brought to their distant home the treasures of the far East—spices, pearls, silks, furs, and linen garments; and that following the course of the Dwina, the Dnieper, and the Oder, they found their way to Constantinople, the Black Sea, and even the Caspian.

Canon Adam, of Bremen, a chronicler of the eleventh century, in one of those farragoes of fact and fiction in which our forefathers read history, tells of a great trading city at the month of the Oder, "Julin, the greatest town of heathen Europe." "It is a famed meeting-place for the barbarians and Greeksof the neighbourhood, inhabited by Slavs and other barbarians. Saxons, too, may live there if they do not declare themselves Christians; for the town is rich in the wares of all Eastern peoples, and contains much that is charming and precious."

This town of Winetha, of whose exact site we are no longer sure, since it has been destroyed by the encroachment of the Baltic, was, and is still, a favourite theme of song and legend with German writers. It is fabled that it was destroyed like Sodom and Gomorrha, because of its sins; for its inhabitants had grown hard and proud and disdainful, trusting in wealth, and despising God. On fine and calm days mariners can, it is said, behold the city, with its silver ramparts, its marble columns, its stirring, richly-dressed population, leading, beneath the ocean, the life which they led while their city was still on firm ground. Every Good Friday this splendid city, with its towers, palaces, and walls, is permitted to rise from the ocean, and sun itself in the daylight, to be again submerged on Easter Day, by this annual fall recalling to all who might else forget it the severe justice of God.

The extract given above from the old writer impresses on us a fact we must bear well in mind, namely, that the Baltic mainland littoral at the time the Teutonic merchants began to ply their trade upon its coast was not a German possession, but inhabited and owned by a Slavonic people, who clung to their pagan creed long after their neighbours in the East and West had become converted to the new religion. And, as usual to this day, it was the trader who preceded the missionary, and gave the natives the first idea of a different code of ethics and morality. In the missionary's track, as at this day, followed the soldier, enforcing by the sword the arguments that reason had failed to inculcate. It was thus that German merchants had founded on Slavonic soil the various cities and ports that were later to be the pride and strength of the Hanseatic Union. Nor did they rest content with the coast that bounded their own lands. They traversed the narrow ocean, touching Finland, Sweden, and Russia, and they established on the isle of Gothland an emporium, which, in the first Christian centuries, became the centre of the Baltic trade, and in which "people of divers tongues," as an old writer calls these visitors, met to exchange their products.

A glance at the map will show why this island assumed such importance. At a time when the mariner was restricted to short passages, not liking for long to lose sight of the shore, this spot naturally made a most favourable halting-place on the road to Finland, Livonia, or Sweden. It is evident from the chronicles that the Germans soon acquired and exercised great power in this island, and that they were accorded special privileges. Thus Pope Honorius II. granted them his protection for their town and harbour of Wisby, in acknowledgment of the part they had played in the conversion of the pagan nations.

There are many testimonies to the ancient wealth and commercial importance of the island of Gothland; among them the amount of Roman, Byzantine, Anglo-Saxon, and German coins still found on its soil, as also the number of ruined churches, many of them of great size and architectural beauty, dotted over its area. To this day the island, impoverished and depopulated, owns a church to every six hundred inhabitants. The churches have fallen into sad decay, but yet remain to testify of past prosperity and glory.

As the number of travelling merchants from various cities increased on its shores, it was natural that they should hold together more and more in a tacit offensive and defensive alliance against the aliens, and that when they returned home from their voyages they should speak of the mutual benefits rendered and the help that lay in union. Some influential persons among them doubtless brought pressure to bear upon the rulers and magistracies of the various cities to give their informal union an official character. Thus much is certain, that after a time the merchants from various cities who traded with the Baltic had united into a federation having a common seal and conforming to a common law, so that by the middle of the thirteenth century the Hanseatic League was practically consolidated, although this name for the association only occurs later.

So far, however, the Union only exercised rights abroad. It was from Wisby also that the reaction was to come for union at home; but this was a little later, when its strength was well matured and established.

What really, in the first instance, led the Germans from their inland towns to the shores of the Baltic was the desire to benefit by the great wealth that lay hidden in its waters in the form of fish, which could be obtained in return for the mere labour of fishing. At a time when all Europe was Catholic, or of the Greek Church, and fasts as well as feasts strictly observed, the sale of fish was an important industry, and, above all, of salted fish, since our forefathers were ignorant of the art of preserving these creatures fresh by means of ice. Now, from the beginning of the twelfth century until the beginning of the fifteenth, when they once more altered their course, each spring and autumn the migratory fish, and especially that most prolific and valued of fish, the herring, came in great shoals to the shores of Scania, the isle of Rügen, and the coasts of Pomerania, tempting the inhabitants of the strand and near inland hamlets out on to the waters to secure these treasures. Nor had nature herewith ceased her bounties. At certain points of the littoral there were salt springs, in which the precious draught could at once be pickled; and it is certain that the art of preserving the gifts of the ocean from decay was familiar to the Slav inhabitants of these districts long before it was known to those of the German Ocean. Already, in the eleventh century, "salt Kolberg" was famed as an emporium for salted herrings; and the words of a Polish poem of rejoicing at a victory won over its inhabitants in 1105 are extant to this day. It has more historical than literary value. "Formerly," so jubilantly sang the conquerors of the harbour, "they brought us salt and stinking fish, now our sons bring them to us fresh and quivering."

Salted herrings became an acknowledged form of tax or tribute, as also a medium of exchange for inland produce, and it was the value of these small fish that really first roused the cupidity of the inland dwellers, and caused them to compete with and finally oust the pagan Slav. And Wisby for a time was their great emporium, whence they extended their power, founding among other towns Novgorod on the Lake of Olm. It was to Wisby that association dues were paid; it was in Wisby that common money was deposited. They were kept in the German Church of Our Lady Maria Teutonicorum. For the churches in those times were buildings as much secular as religious, being not only places of worship, but also banks, storehouses, market-places, and sanctuaries. Four aldermen, selected from important cities of the League, namely, Wisby, Lübeck, Soest, and Dortmund, had each a key to the common treasure. The rules laid down in common council, over which these aldermen presided, and whose execution they enforced, were stringent in the extreme. For example, according to an old principle of Teutonic laws, a city was made responsible if a trader suffered malignant shipwreck or was robbed of his goods within its domain, and if these things occurred they were bound to help the sufferers to recover their goods or safety.

That it was not always an easy task for the towns to execute this command may be gathered from the fact that in the earliest times even the Church looked on flotsam and jetsam as its legitimate dues; indeed, the revenues of some monasteries and churches were distinctly founded on this. Even Papal authority, even excommunication in later days, could not for a long while break the force of a barbarous and cruel custom. All the booty the waves cast on the shore was designated by the well-sounding term of *strandgut* (property of the shore), and was regarded as a gift from Providence. The dwellers on the Baltic shore held so naïve a belief with respect to this matter that in their daily prayers they innocently asked God to give them a good harvest of *strandgut.*

Lübeck in 1287, demanding from Reval, on the basis of its treaties, the restitution of stranded property, is told frankly by the governor of the city that "however many and long and large letters they may send him across the seas," yet his vassals would hold to the rights of their land, and "if," he adds, "on your letters or your prayers your goods are restored to you, I will suffer my right eye to be put out."

Still by steady persistence the German cities got their will, and of course they exercised it first on members of their union. The defaulting city had to pay a fine of something like two to three hundred pounds of our money to the common fund of the Union, and, in event of a recurrence, was threatened with expulsion from the community. This punishment was called *unhansing*, and it was inflicted several times, and was only atoned for by the heaviest penalties not only of money tributes, but often of pilgrimages to some distant sacred shrine, to wipe out the disgrace that the city had drawn down, not on itself alone, but also on its brethren of the League, by the fact that there could be such a black sheep among them.

Such, briefly, was the empire that, by the middle of the thirteenth century, was exercised by a community of German men of commerce, who had their seat of control, not at home, but on a foreign soil. Such, briefly, was the rise of these powerful merchants who not only dared to dictate terms to distant cities, but were absolutely obeyed. Such, briefly, was the transformation of bands of pirates and adventurous traders into a peace-loving and industrious association.

Let us now take a rapid glance at what had occurred meantime in the Holy Roman Empire and the towns.

III.

FOREIGN TRADE.

IT is of importance to the study of the Hanseatic confederation to remember that the settlements made by the German merchants in their various foreign and distant ports, though permanent in themselves, were inhabited almost exclusively by a floating and ever-changing population. True, the traders who had done good business in this spot would return season after season. But they did not form an established colony, they did not take up their permanent abode abroad, and hence the connection with their native towns was never broken; they remained ever in touch with home. Now the pettiest trader of one of the German cities enjoyed in the Steelyard in London, in the St. Peter's Court of Novgorod, in the factory of Bergen, in the church of Wisby, and many other places, a measure of personal freedom, a number of privileges such as were frequently absolutely denied him in his fatherland, or doled out grudgingly by his territorial lord.

When the merchants had first appeared abroad they were protected more or less by their suzerains. Thus Barbarossa had given them the assistance of his strong name, and extorted for them certain important privileges from the King of England. The same holds good with regard to the Duke of Saxony. But as the emperors grew to care less and less for purely German affairs, as the Saxon ducal power was broken, as the German-speaking lands became the camp of anarchy, confusion, and lordlessness, where rightful and unlawful sovereigns quarrelled with each other, where ruler fought ruler, noble robbed noble, where, in short, the game of "devil take the hindmost" was long played with great energy, the towns that had silently and gradually been acquiring much independent strength, perceived that if they would save their prosperity, nay, their very existence, they must take up a firm position against the prevailing social conditions.

Founded upon trade, with trade as their vital element, it was natural that traders also should have a mighty voice in the councils of these towns. The councillors indeed were chosen chiefly from among the leading merchants, most of whom had been abroad at some time or other of their career, and tasted the sweets of wider liberty. None of these were insensible to the pressure put upon them by their returning fellow citizens that they should struggle in their common interests to maintain a position of strength at home, a position which could not fail to increase the security of their settlements abroad. For owing to this long period of political chaos, the merchants abroad noticed or fancied that the name of the Holy Roman Empire no longer carried the same weight as formerly; that to threaten those who overstepped their licenses towards them with the empire's power had ceased to have any serious effect. Yet unless there was some real power at their back, how, at this lawless time, could the Germans feel sure that the treaties they had made with the aliens would be upheld? Well then, urged the foreign traders, what our emperors cannot or will not do for us, busy as they are with Italian matters, or with self-destruction, we must do for ourselves.

And quietly, unobtrusively, but very securely, they formed among themselves that mutual offensive and defensive alliance of whose exact date and origin we are ignorant, but of whose great power in later times the world was to stand in awe and admiration. The purpose of the union was to uphold the respect for the German name abroad by a strong association of cities willing and able, if need were, to enforce its demands by force of arms.

Mutual protection, moreover, was needed as much, if not more, at home. The highroads, never too safe from plundering barons, had grown yet less so during the lawless and fighting period that followed the fall of the Hohenstauffen dynasty. These, too, must be guarded, or how could merchandize be brought from place to place. Peace and security of property, being the very corner-stones of commerce, did the merchant seek above all to secure, and since nothing in this life can be obtained without a struggle, these cities had to fight hard, not only with moral force, but often with the sword, in order to extort from their rulers these elementary rights of civilization.

Thus the Hansa from its earliest origin, though organized for the ends of peace, was from its commencement and throughout its existence a militant body, ever watchful to punish infringement of its rights, ever ready to extend its authority, ever prompt to draw the sword, or send forth its ships against offenders.

It is indeed a significant fact, that never once in the whole course of its history did it draw the sword aggressively, or against its own members. In its domestic disputes it never needed to exercise other than moral pressure. But the cities as they grew in power almost assumed the proportions of small democracies, and it is well-known that democracies, save for purposes of self-defence, are not so ready to rush into wars as monarchies. War is the pastime of kings and statesmen; of men who have nothing to lose, and perchance much to gain in this pursuit; of men who do not stake life and limb, health and home and trade. The wars waged by the Hansa were never in one single instance aggressive. Like all confederations, whose life nerve is commerce, the Hansa ever sought to avoid war, and only seized the sword as *ultima ratio*. It is noteworthy that its ships were designated in its acts as "peace ships" (*Friedenschiffe*), and even the forts it built for protection were described as "peace burgs" (*Friedeburgen*).

The germ of manly independence once awakened in the burghers grew apace, and as they felt the benefits of this new spirit they learnt that with it they could cow their would-be despotic lordlings, and exact from them respect and even aid. Cologne was the first among the older cities to emancipate itself. It is hard for us to realize the enslavement of the middle class in former days. For example, a merchant might not wear arms, no luxury, but an absolute necessity in those wild times. Frederick Barbarossa permitted him to carry a sword, but in order that there might be no confusion of social castes, he decreed that "the travelling merchant shall not gird his sword, but attach it to his saddle, or lay it on his cart, so that he may not wound the innocent, but yet may protect himself against robbers." The inference in this clause, that only a member of the third estate would be likely to hurt an innocent person, is amusing in its *naïveté*. As for the peasant, if he were found with arms upon him, a lance or a sword, he had to suffer severe punishment. The knightly weapon was broken across the back of any serf who dared to carry it.

A further instance of want of personal liberty in Barbarossa's days is shown by his contempt for commerce and for the trader's knowledge of the commercial value of his goods. Thus he decreed that a merchant selling his wares in camp must offer them at the price fixed by the field-marshal, and if the owner asked more than was deemed just by this functionary, who probably knew as much of the value of goods as his trusty lance, he lost not only his market rights and his wares, but was whipped into the bargain, his head shorn and his cheek branded with a red-hot iron. At home his choice of dwelling-houses, of trade, even of marriage was interfered with. Is it astonishing, then, that with so little personal liberty at home, so much abroad, the townsmen aspired to change this state of things, and aided by political events did change them, and rapidly too?

Nor was it only the merchants returning from abroad who stirred the legitimate longings of their stay-at-home brethren. A liberating influence came from yet another side; from that very land of Italy, for whose sake the German rulers had suffered their own country to endure neglect. Travelling Italian merchants on their road to Flanders passed through Central Germany, and as they halted in the cities they would recount in the long evenings those travellers' tales eagerly listened to in days when reading for the most part was an unknown accomplishment, and when all information was acquired by ear.

> "... I spoke of most disastrous chances;
> Of moving accidents by flood and field;
> And portance in my travel's history:
> Wherein of antres vast and deserts idle;
> Rough quarries, rocks, and hills whose heads touch heaven
> It was my hint to speak."

These Lombards told of the prosperity of their cities and the liberties they enjoyed, narrations that sounded like fairy tales in the ears of the Northmen. And when the Crusades broke out, and many of them saw with their own eyes the glories of the southern cities, when German merchants who had followed in the train of the emperor's Roman campaign returned, confirming all they had heard from the Italians about commercial liberties and privileges, their determination not to be left behind was strengthened.

Freiburg (Free City) was the first town founded as the outcome of the new liberty, an enlightened prince lending his help and means to that end.

Further individual aid was given to the new idea of personal liberty for all conditions of men by an apostle of freedom, Arnold of Brescia. This eloquent pupil of the French monk Abelard, the enlightened philosopher, the lover of Heloïse, himself a priest, was the most powerful opponent of the clerical ideas in the twelfth century, which tried to keep down the people in order that through their ignorance and dependence they might be ruled with absolute and unquestioned sway—ideas by no means wholly extinct to this day among this class of men. Banished by the Pope as a political and ecclesiastical heretic, Arnold fled to Southern Germany, where he preached his doctrines to eager ears, and roused an enthusiasm that laid the train for a later Church reformation, and helped towards the development of a new social state. He awakened or fostered the thought of personal liberty, a liberty not only consistent with corporate union, but part and parcel of the same; a condition alone worthy a rational human being, who, while doing whatever pleases him best, never loses sight of the fact that he has only a right to follow this desire so long as his liberty does not trench upon that of his neighbour and brother man.

John Stuart Mill had not yet defined the meaning of the much abused term, liberty; Madame Roland had not yet ejaculated upon the scaffold her true and piteous cry, "Liberty! what crimes are committed in thy name!" but Arnold of Brescia understood the meaning of the word, and what was equally important, he made his hearers understand it too. He did not merely preach vague doctrines, he preached sound political economy and social ethics.

And thus the Germans learnt from the Italians both the true meaning of liberty and the virtue of municipal institutions, which latter had, in the first instance, sprung up in Lombardy from a Germanic root; its essential features being a free choice of the civic rulers from the fittest elements, a right to govern themselves, and if need be to form alliances, and the right to tax themselves. Further, they learnt to recognize the principle that the final decision should not rest with one person, but with the mass of the inhabitants. This autonomy in all inner affairs, founded on Italian models, became in the course of several generations the most cherished possession of all those German cities whence sprang the Hanseatic League. There was, however, this difference that, unlike the Lombard cities, the Germans ever acknowledged the supremacy of the emperor, and never developed either into complete oligarchies or democracies, though in their statutes when they were at the height of their power, it was distinctly stated that decisions in important matters did not rest "with the general council, but with the people."

In the thirteenth century municipal privileges grew and extended, for though the townsfolk were supposed only to elect their own magistrates under the sanction of the bailiffs of their respective territorial lords, these functionaries, who generally lived in a strong castle within the city or just upon its walls, became only too ready to be bribed into compliance with the burgher will as the distresses of the empire caused their lords to require more and more of the hard cash and other solid assistance which the rapid progress of the cities in wealth could furnish. Of course circumstances were not the same in all places. In many there was open warfare between the lordlings and the townsmen, and many a sacked and gutted castle remained to testify to the successes of the third estate.

As the baronial strongholds were razed, the towns built up on their sites strong citadels, walls, and moats, which they defended by a burgher militia hardened to fatigue, brave, determined; who not only dared to face the resentment of the barons, but often extorted from them by force what they could not up to that date buy from them or obtain as a meed of justice. It was no infrequent event in the thirteenth century for a town to be besieged by its territorial lord; and these sieges, like that of Troy, would last many years, for the art of reducing strong places was but little developed, and wars, even if they lasted longer, were less terribly destructive than in our day.

The cities, having the wealth, were most frequently the victors, and it would even come about that as terms of peace their enemy would hire himself out to his vassals as the legal and bound defender of his own subjects, for a stated number of years. Further, the cities often bought from these princelings the lands outside their walls; the forests, mines, brine springs, even the highroads and streams, thus drawing into their power anything that might assist in diminishing the danger from all that could impede their commerce. They would also ask the cession of villages, of tolls; next the right to coin money. In a word, they made use of every means that came in their way, in accordance with local and momentary circumstances, to extend and consolidate their power.

What wonder that the burghers feeling their strength and seeing the weakness of the empire turned its dissensions and disorders to profit, and began to make among themselves, quietly and unostentatiously, alliances for maintaining peace in their immediate vicinities, for keeping the roads cleared of robbers, for opposing the black mail levied by their feudal lords, and anything else that offended against "the common freedom of the merchant."

Curiously enough such alliances were in direct contravention of the existing laws of the German Empire. At the Diet held in Worms, 1231, the princes had expressed marked disapproval of such leagues, in which they clearly recognized a dangerous rival power. But the cities seemed little troubled by this interdict. They, on their part, recognized that the time had come for a firm union, and adhesion of the weak against the strong, and more and more, as they saw that the empire threatened from within and from without was visibly falling asunder. For what respect could be felt for a crown which was at last actually put up for sale to the highest bidder, and acquired by the rich but otherwise impotent brother of the English Henry III., Duke Richard of Cornwall?

The towns of the Rhine were the first to form themselves into an alliance, a fact that can scarcely surprise us when we remember how thickly set is that lovely river with the now ruined strongholds of what erst were robber lords. And the Baltic towns were not slow to follow in their wake, forming a League "for the benefit of the common merchant." These cities even settled the contingent which each town had to place at their common disposal, a great stone of possible stumbling being skilfully avoided by a phrase which occurs in a contract of 1296: "If the fight goes against a prince who is lord of one of the cities, this city shall not furnish men, but only give money." The Rhenish section alone was able to put into the field some eleven hundred crossbowmen and six hundred stout galleys; no mean army in those days.

In a word, the times were out of joint, and the people had to help themselves, and did so. Sprung from modest sources, having its origin in true neighbourly feeling, what was at first a mere association of merchants had developed into an association of cities. The banner under which they had grouped themselves bore the device "freedom for the common merchant at home and abroad," and this device became the elastic but durable bond, which, keeping them together, made them a mighty power. Its very elasticity was the cause of its strength, giving it that facility of expansion and freedom from rigidity which in more modern times has made the glory and the might of England, whose constitution is distinguished by a like principle of flexibility.

A naïve North German chronicler of the thirteenth century telling of the various alliances formed, writes: "But the matter did not please the princes, knights, and robbers, especially not those who for ever put forth their hands for booty; they said it was shameful that merchants should rule over high-born and noble men." Undaunted, however, by such objections, the cities continued to form alliances, to make contracts among themselves until these contracts assumed the extent, dignity, and importance of those made by the towns with their foreign settlements.

Thus, by slow degrees, cautiously, but very surely, the Hanseatic League took its origin, and thus it grew until it became an independent popular force, a state within a state. Like everything that the Christian Middle Ages called into life, the Vehmgericht (Vehmic Tribunal), Gothic architecture, the knightly orders, it bore strongly the impress of individuality.

The origin of the name of Hansa is wrapped in some mystery. The word is found in Ulfila's Gothic translation of the Bible, as signifying a society, a union of men, particularly in the sense of combatants. He applies it to the band of men who came to capture Jesus in the Garden of Gethsemane. Later on Hansa occurs as a tax on commercial transactions, and also as the sum, a very low one, which the various cities paid as their entrance fee into the association.

But our League did not yet officially bear that title; it acquired it from the date of its first great war with Waldemar of Denmark and the peace of Stralsund (1370). Then it won name and rank at the point of the sword, and after this it came to be classed among the most redoubted powers of the period, being thus by no means the first, and probably not the last, example of the lift given to civilization by so barbarous a thing as the powder cart.

IV.

THE HANSA FIGHTS.

WHOEVER looks on the old Schütting at Lübeck, the building whence the herring fishers were wont to start upon their voyages, and notes its armorial bearings, three herrings upon a plain gold shield, should go back mentally a few centuries and call to mind the fact that the badge of this fish is the emblem of a might which many a time set forth from this spot bent upon commerce or needful warfare, and which for generations exercised great power over Northern Europe.

The district of Scania, which forms the southernmost portion of the present land of Sweden, was until 1658 almost exclusively the property of Denmark. The Danes, a turbulent and maritime people, had in the early times of our era been converted to Christianity at the point of the sword by the emperors of Germany, and during the 10th and 11th centuries these emperors exercised a recognized suzerainty over the Danish kings. Hence German traders easily obtained privileges among a people who were by no means inclined to commerce themselves, but who welcomed none the less eagerly the products that the strangers brought, above all, the heady ale brewed by the Easterlings.

But as the might of the empire declined and the Danes had grown strong, thanks to wise rulers, the people grew restive under the restrictions imposed upon them, and tried to secure their independence. Under Waldemar the Great (1157 to 1182), the country had acquired an important position, which his successors strengthened. This increase of might coincided with the German depression and with the change of course at spawning time that the herring suddenly took in the twelfth century.

Strange that a little fish should have had such great power over mankind; yet it is not going beyond the strict truth to state that the mysterious wanderings of the herring determined throughout several centuries the whole course of northern commerce. During the Middle Ages, upon the appearance of the herring now on this coast and now on that, the wealth and prosperity of the whole districts depended. Herring fishing became a branch of industry that decided the fate of nations. To it the Hansa owes a large portion of its riches and its power; in the herring fisheries, when in the year 1425 the fish began to spawn in the German Ocean, the Netherlands found the foundation stone of their wealth and dignity. Indeed, it was said later, with scant exaggeration, that Amsterdam was built upon herrings.

Now, as masters of the Belt and the Sound, the Danes were able, if they chose, greatly to harass the Hanseatic traders and fishermen. For many years they had not put forth their power, or rather the Hanseatic towns, with the diplomatic astuteness that greatly distinguished them, had averted the possibility of such danger by wise concessions of tributes and privileges. Still disputes would arise, things did not always go off peaceably, and in 1227 the Hansa towns won their first military laurels, defeating the Danes in the battle of Bornhöved and permanently weakening the power of their troublesome neighbours in Northern Germany.

A few years later Lübeck, almost unassisted, threatened in its independence by the Danish king, won a great naval victory over its neighbours; and gained yet another in 1249, when Eric II. had ventured to attack some of its ships upon the open seas. On this occasion the merchant townsmen even seized and sacked Copenhagen and planted their flag in Zealand.

It was no very easy position which the Baltic cities (for it was they who were chiefly threatened) had to maintain against the Danish kings as the power of the latter increased. For with their power, their rapacity and cupidity increased also, and this made them look on the rich commercial towns with a longing desire to absorb them into their own possessions. These, though extensive, were poor, and their inhabitants neither industrious nor prosperous. Further, the Danes, Norwegians, and Swedes were in constant feud with one another, and each of these states turned an eye of greed towards the flourishing Baltic cities, whose possession they coveted. The two Scandinavian powers, in particular, constantly harassed the German merchants by their scanty comprehension of treaty rights, their breaches of faith, and it was not easy work for the cities to steer clear between the three kingdoms, that were now at deadly feud with one another, now convulsed by civil wars, now united in a policy of rapine.

It would be tedious to enumerate the quarrels, jealousies, and feuds that agitated these kingdoms during the early years of the fourteenth century; to note in detail the trouble they caused to the Hanseatic traders, and the need they awoke among them of holding together in as close an alliance at home as they had hitherto done abroad. It was necessary to be ever wakeful and mistrustful; and to watch jealously for the faintest signs of an infringement of privileges.

In 1326 a lad of some twelve summers, whose memory was destined to be handed down to posterity as that of a hero of romance, ascended the throne of Denmark. In allusion to the famous fable about the election of a king of the frogs, an old writer speaks of this event as a choice by the frogs of the stork as ruler instead of the log. For Waldemar, as he was called, proved indeed no log and no puppet in the hands of his ambitious barons. As a mere youth he gave evidence of his strength and determination, and under his ægis Denmark acquired great wealth and consideration, and would have attained to yet more had not Waldemar, with mistaken judgment, drawn the reins too tight, until from a wise ruler he became a despot. It was his aim and policy to nationalize his country, to drive away the foreigners who utilized it for their warlike and commercial ends. He found it small and distracted with dissensions; after twenty years' rule he could point to marked success and change, for he had made Denmark respected and feared at home and abroad. History knows him as Waldemar III., story and song as Waldemar Atterdag, a nickname that well expresses the salient points of his character. For the name of Atterdag, which means "there is yet another day," refers to the king's constant habit of using this expression in the sense that if to-day a goal is not reached, it is not therefore unattainable, that a man must wait, never despair, and never lose sight of his aim.

And Waldemar for his part never did. He pursued his purposes with a strenuousness and a patience, which contrasted favourably with the vacillating attitude of his princely northern contemporaries, and which was only matched and finally surpassed by the same strenuous and patient policy on the part of the Baltic towns, and especially on the part of Lübeck, their astute and diplomatic leader.

Nor was it only good aims that the king followed with such persistence. He was an implacable, a relentless enemy, who never forgot an injury, and who waited with cruel calmness the day of vengeance.

In Waldemar's state policy there often appeared mixed motives; considerations of the most personal character were blended with care for the welfare of his state, and when one should alone have been considered, both frequently played a part. It was this that led to his ultimate ruin; like too many clever people he overreached himself. Therefore, while the early years of his reign were really a blessing to distracted and impoverished Denmark, of the latter part a contemporary chronicler complains that—

"In the times of Waldemar, every tradition of our ancestors, all paternal laws, all the freedom of the Danish Church was abolished. The rest of the soldier, the merchant, the peasant, was so curtailed, that in the whole kingdom no time remained to eat, to repose, to sleep, no time in which the people were not driven to work by the bailiffs and servants of the king, at the risk of losing his royal favour, their lives, and their goods." In a word, Waldemar worked his subjects hard, and even the most patriotic singers cannot present him as a wholly attractive figure. He is rather a character to be feared than loved.

The Hansa was not slow to recognize this. It saw that it was face to face with a man whom no obstacles could deter, to whom even treaty obligations were not sacred, and who was liable to be swayed by incalculable caprice. That it was right in its estimate and its fears Waldemar was not slow to make known, so soon as his power at home was fully secured.

The first attack upon the Hansa towns was made by the Danish king in the shape of interference with their fishing rights on Scania, breaking the contracts which his predecessors, and even he himself, had made, and demanding extortionate fees for the renewal of the time-honoured privileges. Diplomatic negotiations were entered upon, but Waldemar befooled the deputies from the cities, wasting their time with idle discussion of irrelevant matters, and refusing to come to a real agreement. After long and fruitless debate the ambassadors of the Hansa towns departed home anxious and discouraged. Ten weeks after their return the cities were startled by the terrible news that Waldemar, in a time of perfect peace, without previous warning or declaration of war, had suddenly invaded the island of Gothland, and seized, sacked, and plundered the rich city of Wisby, the northern emporium of the Hansa's wealth.

Such a blow was aimed not only at Wisby, but at all the Hanseatic towns; from that moment diplomatic negotiations with Waldemar were no more to be thought of. This act meant war; war at all costs and at all risks.

"In the year of Christ 1361 King Waldemar of Denmark collected a great army, and said unto them that he would lead them whither there was gold and silver enough, and where the pigs cat out of silver troughs. And he led them to Gothland, and made many knights in that land, and struck down many people, because the peasants were unarmed and unused to warfare. He set his face at once towards Wisby. They came out of the town towards him, and gave themselves up to the mercy of the king, since they well saw that resistance was impossible. In this manner he obtained the land, and took from the burghers of the town great treasures in gold and silver, after which he went his ways."

Thus the contemporary chronicler of the Franciscans of St. Catherine at Lübeck. By a skilful *coup de main* Waldemar had indeed made himself master of Gothland, then under Swedish suzerainty, and of the wealthy city of Wisby. His aim had been booty, and he had it in rich measure in the shape of gold, of fur, and silver vessels.

Legend tells that the year previous to the attack Waldemar had visited Gothland disguised as a merchant, securing the love of a goldsmith's daughter, whose father held an influential position in Wisby, and who, in her loving trustfulness revealed to him the strength and weakness of the island and town, thus helping him to secure the spot that was rightly regarded as the key to the three northern realms.

The inhabitants, unprepared, unarmed, had been unable to offer much resistance. It was a terribly bloody fight this that raged outside the walls of Wisby; the site of it is marked to this day by a cross erected on the spot where 1,800 Gothlanders fell.

"Before the gates of Wisby the Goths fell under the hands of the Danes," runs the inscription.

As was the custom among the conquerors of olden days, Waldemar, it is related, entered the city, not by means of the gates that had been forcibly surrendered to him, but by a breach he specially had made for this purpose in the town walls. The gap too is shown to this hour.

When he had plundered to his heart's content, aided in his finding of the treasure by his lady love, after he had added to his titles of King of the Danes and Slavs, that of the King of Gothland, Waldemar proceeded to return home in his richly laden ships. But it was decreed that he should not bring his booty to port. A great storm arose in mid-ocean. It was with difficulty that the king escaped with his life; his ships were sunk, his coveted hoards buried in the waves.

There are still shown at Wisby the two fine twelve-sectioned rose windows of St. Nicholas' Church, in which, according to tradition, there once burned two mighty carbuncles that served as beacons to light the seamen safely into harbour in the day of the town's prosperity. These stones, it is said, were torn from their place and carried off by Waldemar. The Gothland mariner still avers that on certain clear nights he can see the great carbuncles of St. Nicholas' Church gleaming from out the deep.

As for Waldemar's lady love, whom it is said he abandoned as soon as his purpose was attained, she was seized on by the infuriated townspeople and buried alive in one of the turrets of the city walls, known to this day as the "Virgin Tower."

It is difficult to decide whether Waldemar foresaw the full danger and bearing of his high-handed step; whether he knew what it meant to plunder a city like Wisby, one of the strongest arms of the Hansa. He had certainly thrown the gauntlet down to the towns; he was quickly to learn that the power which some years ago had successfully beaten his predecessors had but grown in strength since that date.

On the first news of Waldemar's treachery, the Baltic cities laid an embargo on all Danish goods, and then called together a hasty council in which it was decreed that until further notice all intercourse with Denmark should be forbidden on pain of death and loss of property. Then they put themselves into communication with Norway and Sweden in order in the event of a war to secure the alliance of these countries, an assistance that was the more readily promised because their sovereigns were at feud with Waldemar. To defray the war costs it was determined to levy a poundage tax on all Hanseatic exported goods.

A fleet was got ready with all possible speed, and when everything was in order, the towns sent a herald to Waldemar with a formal declaration of war.

In May, 1362, their ships appeared in the Sound, and brilliant success at first attended their arms. Copenhagen was plundered, its church bells carried to Lübeck as the victor's booty. At Scania the cities looked to meet their northern allies, in order in conjunction with them to take possession of the Danish strongholds on the mainland. Here, however, disappointment awaited them. Whether lack of money or fear had deterred the northern kings from keeping their word is unknown; at any rate, they did not put in an appearance with their armies.

The Burgomaster of Lübeck, Johann Wittenborg, who commanded the Hanseatic fleet, saw himself forced to use the men he had on board for the land attack. He held himself the more justified in doing this since he deemed he had so thoroughly routed the Danes, that from the side of the sea there was nothing to be feared.

This decision was rash, and Wittenborg was to atone for it with his life. Already it seemed as if the stronghold Helsingborgs was in his hands—he had been besieging it sixteen days with great catapults—when Waldemar suddenly appeared with his fleet upon the Scanian coast, surprised the Hansa vessels that had been left with but a feeble crew, and carried off twelve of the best ships, and most of their provisions and weapons. The consequence was that Wittenborg saw himself obliged to return with the remnant of his army to Lübeck.

He found the city embittered against him in the highest degree for his defeat; though it saw that the main guilt of the disastrous end of the war lay with the faithless northern kings. The stern free city deemed it right, not only towards itself, but also to its sister towns, to punish heavily the unsuccessful leader. Wittenborg had hardly landed ere he was arrested, chained, and thrown into a dungeon. Here he dragged out a weary year of imprisonment. In vain some of the cities pleaded his cause, in vain his friends tried to obtain his deliverance. Lübeck was a stern mistress, who knew no mercy, and could brook no ill success. In her dictionary, as in that of youth, according to Richelieu in Bulwer's play, there might be no such word as "fail." Wittenborg had, of course, been at once deprived of his burgomagisterial honours; a year after his defeat his head publicly fell under the executioner's axe in the market-place of Lübeck. Burial in the councillors' church was denied him. He was laid to rest in the cloisters of the Dominicans the spot where all criminals were interred in Lübeck during the Middle Ages; the spot where, down to our own era, all criminals passing that way to execution received from the pious monks a soothing drink as last farewell to life. Further, Wittenborg's name is absent from the record of the burgomasters; an omission in this place, which doubtless has the same meaning as the absence of Marino Falieri's portrait among the long row of Doges in the Venetian Palace.

The election of a burgomaster as leader of the troops is quite in character with the spirit of those times. Such trade warriors are not uncommon in the history of the Hansa. Within the roomy stone hall that served as entry and store-room to those ancient dwelling-houses, it was usual to see helmet, armour, and sword hanging up above stores of codfish, barrels of herrings, casks of beer, bales of cloth, or what not besides.

To this day the stranger is shown in the marketplace at Lübeck the stone on which Wittenborg sat before his execution, and in the collection of antiquities is the chair of torture in which he was borne thither. So sternly did the Hansa punish.

There exists an entirely unauthenticated fable that Wittenborg had betrayed his trust in return for a dance with the Queen of Denmark, promising her as a reward the island of Bornholm. That the fable had some currency is proved by the fact that for a long while there survived in Lübeck the expression, "He is dancing away Bornholm," when some one light-heartedly did an unjustifiable deed. The story has given one of the younger German poets, Geibel, the theme for a famous ballad. Further, it was fabled that twice a year the Burgomaster and council of Lübeck solemnly drank Hippokras out of silver cups made from Wittenborg's confiscated property, repeating the while a Low German distich that reminded them of their stern duty and their predecessor's sad fate. Modern accurate research, pitiless in the destruction of picturesque legends has discovered that these cups were not made till the sixteenth century, and were paid for by a tax levied on Bornholm, then in rebellion.

After the cruel defeat due to Wittenborg, the cities concluded an armistice with Waldemar, an armistice that might easily have been converted into a permanent peace, for the towns were not eager to fight. It was too great an interruption to trade. Moreover, the war expenses had exceeded their calculations, times were bad, harvests scant, food scarce, and, to crown all, the Black Death had reappeared in Europe and was devastating whole districts.

But Waldemar had resolved to break entirely the power of the Hansa. Once more he befooled it in diplomatic negotiations, and in the midst of the truce attacked its herring settlements at Scania, and captured some merchant vessels that passed through the Belt.

The towns held council, Waldemar was offered terms. Yet again he befooled them, and when he soon after married his only child Margaret, celebrated in history as the Semiramis of the North, to Hakon, heir to the thrones of Sweden and Norway, thus preparing the union of the three northern kingdoms under one crown, the towns, alarmed at the mere prospect, felt that now or never they must secure their independence.

In November, 1367, deputies from the Baltic and inland towns met in conclave in the large council chamber of the Town Hall of Cologne, a meeting that became the foundation act of the recognized and open constitution of the Hanseatic League, and on which account the hall still bears the name of Hansa Room. It seems certain that here for the first time was drawn up an Act, modified, renewed, altered in course of time, but yet always the fundamental basis of the League. There is no older Hanseatic document than this of the congress known as the Cologne Confederation, when the deputies of seventy-seven towns met to declare most solemnly that "because of the wrongs and injuries done by the King of Denmark to the common German merchant, the cities would be his enemies and help one another faithfully." It was decided that such cities as were too weak or too distant to help actively in the war, should do so by the contribution of subsidies. It was further enacted that such cities as would not join in the war should be held as outside the League, with whom its burghers and merchants should have nothing more in common, neither buying from, nor selling to, them, nor allowing them to enter their ports, or unlade goods in their domains.

Waldemar was warned of what the cities had resolved against him. He replied with an untranslatable pun, in which he likened the Hansa to a flock of geese, who deafened him with their cackle. Warned once more, Waldemar threatened the cities that he would complain of them to their spiritual and temporal lords; among them the Pope and the emperor. The cities had forestalled him. They had sent copies of a letter, stating their grievances against a king whom they denounced as "a tyrant and a pirate," to some thirty spiritual and temporal lords. In the letter to the emperor, Lübeck, whence all the letters were dated, excused itself in particular for not responding to Charles's recent invitation to join his Roman expedition on the plea of its home difficulties, while humbly giving thanks for the honour done it by the offer. It also justified itself for not paying during the past year to Waldemar a tax decreed by Charles, since this king, it wrote, "seeks to withdraw your town of Lübeck from the emperor and the empire." It grieved to state that the emperor lived too far off to shield by his arms his weak and neglected flock in the northern region of the empire. Therefore the emperor's most gracious majesty must not take it amiss if the cities, with God's help, did something towards their own protection.

Worded with all the servile language of the period, Lübeck yet in this letter made it pretty evident to its supreme ruler that it meant to stand on its own feet, as it knew too well how unsteady were its sovereign's.

Yet, again, Waldemar was warned of the growing strength, the earnest purpose of the League, and this time he seems to have been alarmed, for he tried to detach from it many of its members, and to win them over to his own cause. He received from the towns with whom he opened negotiations, the following reply, which proves how perfected and tightly secured were already the reciprocal engagements of the League.

"The Hanseatic League," they said, "having resolved on war, they must submit themselves to that general resolution which bound them all."

The cackling geese whom Waldemar had despised seemed to have grown into formidable eagles overnight. Lordlings and princes too, many of whom had private injuries to avenge, had joined the League or promised their support. The Hansa had set up a rival and successful king in Sweden, and it now proposed nothing less than to dismember Denmark, and to distribute its provinces to its own friends and allies. It did not desire to retain possession of it. It was ever its policy to restrict actual possessions, but to seek that these should be as far as possible in the hands of friends who would grant it the concessions and privileges needful for commerce. Thus could be applied to it what a Roman said of the peoples he subjugated, "I do not ask for gold; I only desire to rule over those who have gold." With this difference, however, that the Hansa, without wishing to conquer provinces, wished to draw to itself whatever profits could be found therein.

It was on the Sunday of Quasimodo, April 16, 1368, that all the Hansa ships were to meet in the Sound for a combined attack on Zealand. The Easter days approached. All Northern Germany awaited anxiously the moment for the decisive combat to commence; when suddenly the cities learnt that on Maundy Thursday Waldemar had secretly fled from his dominions, alarmed by the decision and strength shown by his enemies. In a ship laden with much treasure he had landed on the Pomeranian coasts to go further east and avoid the impending squall, leaving a viceroy in his stead, whom he authorized to conclude peace or carry on war.

Waldemar's cowardly attitude could not of course alter that of the cities. In that same month of April the war began and raged all the summer, the Hansa meeting with but little resistance. With the winter came a truce, after the fashion of those times, but in the summer war was renewed and for two years the Hansa ships harassed the Danish coasts and waters, sacked their cities and plundered their treasures. The treacherous attack on Wisby was avenged with interest, and the war proved so profitable to the League that it settled in congress that it should continue until the Danes sued abjectly for peace. Its leader was once more a Lübecker, Brun Warendorf, the son of the Burgomaster. He died in battle, but the memory of his gallant deeds remains in the stately monument the town erected to him in the choir of St. Mary's Church. Thus Lübeck honoured those who contributed to her honour.

By the close of 1369, Denmark was exhausted and the people weary of war. They pleaded for peace. On this the seventy-seven cities, whom Waldemar had derided as geese, dictated their terms. It was indeed a peace such as few kings have signed in the deepest degradation of their empire. For the term of fifteen years they claimed two-thirds of the revenues of Scania, the possession of its strongholds, the free passage of the Sound, and the right for the same fifteen years to veto the choice of a Danish ruler, besides a number of other valuable concessions and privileges; terms, in short, as humiliating for Denmark as they were glorious for the League. The last paragraph of this remarkable Treaty of Stralsund, which put the Hansa in the position of a first-class power, ran thus:

"Our king, Waldemar, shall seal to the cities the above terms of peace with his great seal, if he would remain with his kingdom and not give it over to another ruler. If it should be that our lord and king, Waldemar, desires to abdicate his land of Denmark during his lifetime, we will and shall not suffer it, unless it be that the cities have given their consent, and that he has sealed to them their privileges with his great seal. Thus, too, it shall be if our lord and king, Waldemar, be carried off by death, which God forfend. Then, too, we will accept no ruler but in council with the cities."

It is evident from this paragraph that the Hansa still mistrusted Waldemar, and feared he would by some subterfuge evade the treaty obligations made in his name by his appointed viceroy.

And they had probably not gauged him falsely.

It was further settled that Waldemar must sign this document within sixteen months: if he did not do so within this period, the Danish council and kingdom would nevertheless be bound to keep its terms "even if the king did not seal."

But abject though these stipulations were, complete as was the submission of Denmark to the League which they implied, Waldemar signed them within the appointed time. He saw that he was defeated, friendless, and alone. In vain had he scoured the mainland, and recounted his woes to all who would listen, in vain had he begged or bribed for help against his enemies. He had made himself too much hated, and even those who promised aid failed at the last to keep their word.

With the signature of peace Waldemar also signed away his position, nay, perhaps his life. Broken in hope and spirits, his health gave way. Four years later (1375) he died, after he had just appealed in vain to the towns to restore to him his castles in Scania.

With the peace of Stralsund the German merchants had established the supremacy of the Hansa over Scandinavia, and laid the foundation for that power over the northern kingdom, which, in the words of King Gustavus Vasa, places "the three good crowns at the mercy of the Hansa."

Thus ended the Hansa's great war against the King of Denmark—a war that marks an important era in its history and development.

The League henceforth took a changed position, not only in its own fatherland, but in the face of all Europe, for nothing succeeds like success. Flanders, France, and England, had all to recognize that a new power had arisen in the north of Germany. For the war had proved, not only how valiantly the League could fight if need arose, but also how well organized it was; how it held together for the common weal; how it would be not only unwise, but dangerous to resist its demands for trade privileges and concessions.

A curious juxtaposition of events was afforded by this chapter of history; a German emperor was busy in the interests of Rome, striving to bring back the Pope from his long exile at Avignon, and obtaining dubious victories over the great Italian family of the Visconti; while meantime a league of cities in his own empire was carrying on a successful war against the kings of the north, dethroning and defeating them. And so far from raising a hand to aid them, the emperor, on paper, at least, and by word and protestation, was taking part with Waldemar against his own subjects. A curious, a unique condition of things truly.

And herewith we have brought the history of our League to the close of what is known as its first period, dating from its origin to the peace concluded with Denmark.

PERIOD II.

THE HISTORY OF THE HANSEATIC LEAGUE, FROM 1370 TO THE PUBLIC PEACE OF 1495, DECREED IN GERMANY BY MAXIMILIAN I.

I.

LÜBECK RECEIVES AN IMPERIAL VISITOR.

THE great war ended, the Hansa, in true merchant spirit, instantly busied itself making up its accounts. The poundage toll, instituted to cover martial expenses, was at once abolished; credit and debit carefully balanced. Examination of its books showed that, notwithstanding the long duration of the war, the Hansa had been as little a pecuniary, as it had been a military, loser, in its struggle against Waldemar's assumptions.

While thus engaged, Lübeck was startled by the intelligence that the Emperor, Charles IV., intended to honour "his beloved free Imperial City of Lübeck" by a personal visit. Since Frederick Barbarossa no emperor had ever passed the city gates, and the town councillors were probably not far wrong when they perceived in this proposal a tacit imperial acknowledgment of the Hansa's great military victories, victories in which Lübeck had played the part of leader. For twenty-eight years Charles had worn the imperial crown, and all that time his chief efforts had been directed towards extending the power of his family, and the home influence of the emperors. He was a shrewd and wily old man, who saw the dangers Italy presented to the empire, and wished to avoid them. At first, however, he had no proper comprehension of the great power that had sprung up within his own domains in the shape of the Hanseatic League, nay, indeed, he had sided against his subjects and with Waldemar. But now the scales fell from his eyes, and he appreciated, as all Europe did, the greatness and the strength of the Hansa.

Of course he did not admit this in words, yet there is little doubt that he wished to gain the goodwill of this League, and hoped thus to get from it both pecuniary and military support for his dynastic plans.

It was, however, "diamond cut diamond;" the worthy councillors of Lübeck were no less shrewd and wily than their imperial master.

Needless to say that, in accordance with the usage of the age, they indulged in the most servile and hyperbolical expressions of their joy and unworthiness to be so honoured, but like true merchants they had a good memory, and knew that Charles had not so long ago pawned his coronation cloak and some of his tolls to one of their federation, and they suspected in their heart of hearts that ulterior motives were probably not absent to account for this unwonted event. Still, with the wisdom of the serpent, they let nothing of this appear, either in their replies to Charles, or in their treatment of him. Like their Lombard predecessors, even when in open warfare against the emperor's authority, they ever protested in words their submission and fidelity to the imperial crown.

It was in the autumn of 1375 that Charles the Fourth entered the gates of Lübeck as the city's guest. It is a curious fact that his visit coincided with the death of Waldemar on the island of Zealand; but in those days of slow communication the news did not reach the emperor till after the festivities were over.

On October 22nd, the Emperor, accompanied by the Empress, the Archbishop of Cologne, prince-bishops, dukes, earls, and suzerains many and mighty, halted before the closed gates of Lübeck. His suite, his armed retainers, and those of his party, made such a numerous host that Lübeck hesitated awhile ere opening its gates to so great a multitude, not feeling wholly sure whether their mission were indeed one of peace, or whether an affectation of peace was meant to cover a deceitful attack. For such things were not uncommon in those days.

After some preliminaries it was however decided to let them all in. A halt had been made outside the walls. Here was situated the Chapel of St. Gertrude, patron saint of strangers. The chapel was the property of the municipal council, and to obtain relics for it the town had spent many sums of money. Among other matters, they boasted of possessing some bones of Thomas à Becket, and it is curious to note that they sent over to England to buy these at the very time Chaucer was superintendent of tolls in the harbour of London, and was writing his immortal "Canterbury Tales," in which he derides the frauds constantly practised upon the purchasers of such wares; as in his "Pardonere's Tale." Now Charles IV. had a great fancy for objects of this nature; he was in the habit of making tours in his kingdom in order to collect them, begging them from churches or monasteries, and giving in return privileges and sanctions. It is possible he also had an eye to St. Thomas's bones, but among the rich booty he took with him from Lübeck, we find no mention of such relics.

It was before St. Gertrude's Chapel, then, that Charles and his great suite halted, and here he and his empress put on their imperial robes previous to entering the city. This done, they were greeted by a procession that came forth from the gates to welcome them. It consisted of the temporal and spiritual lords of the town, the leading men, and the most lovely and notable of its women. They carried before them a crucifix and a casket containing relics. Both the emperor and his consort kissed these with great fervour. Then two stately horses, richly caparisoned, were brought before them, upon which they mounted. That of the emperor was led by two burgomasters, that of the empress by two town councillors. Eight young patricians carried a baldachino of rich stuffs over the heads of the imperial pair. In front of the emperor rode a councillor, bearing aloft on a pole the keys of the city; while he was flanked by two imperial dukes, carrying respectively the sword and the sceptre of the empire. In front of the empress rode the archbishop, bearing the imperial globe. Behind followed all the nobles, the suite, the men-at-arms.

Such was the procession that moved from St. Gertrude's Chapel on the morning of October 22nd. In the space between the outer and inner walls of the city the women of Lübeck awaited them ready to greet the guests with cheers and song and waving kerchiefs. It was through the stately Burg Thor that the great train passed and entered the streets of the city, gaily decked out with arras and banners and verdure to bid them welcome. They rode the whole length of the town, through the Breite Strasse, to the sound of fife and drum, and then made for the cathedral. Here they halted, dismounted, and entered. A solemn thanksgiving service was held, and the choir sang the Introitus for the feast of the Epiphany: "Ecce advenit Dominator Dominus" ("Behold the Lord, the Ruler is come"), and then the second verse of the Seventy-second Psalm, "Give the king Thy judgments, O God." After this the party once more re-formed, and rode along the Königstrasse, till they came to the house that was to harbour the imperial guests.

Contemporary chroniclers tell us that all along the route of the procession and both by night and day the sounds of military and sacred music never ceased. Night was as light as day, thanks to the general illumination prescribed by the council; a prescription that, in a city thus overcrowded by a martial train and by curious spectators from far and near, was as much a matter of safety as of compliment to its guests. In those times street-lighting was an unknown luxury, and nocturnal brawls of constant occurrence.

The house where Charles halted exists to this day, as also that where the empress lodged. They are both corner-houses and boast gables, which according to contemporary writers was an indication of an aristocratic building. The lodging of the empress was opposite to that of the emperor, and a covered way was built across the street to connect them. Such road-bridges, springing from the projecting gable windows, were not unusual things in the narrow streets of those times. The condition of the unpaved roads made them requisite, as these could not be crossed on foot with safety or cleanliness.

For the space of eleven days Charles and his train halted at Lübeck, and the town spared neither cost nor trouble to entertain him right royally, and to impress him with its wealth and importance. Feasts, tournaments, rejoicings, followed upon one another; time was not allowed to hang heavy upon the emperor's hands. But neither was he allowed to carry out his ulterior objects. With great politeness and fulsome flattery Charles was made to understand that the Hansa was sure of its own strength, and since he had not helped it in the hour of need, it did not propose to make great sacrifices to assist him in his troubles. All however was done with perfect courtesy, Charles even being permitted on one occasion to be present at a meeting of the municipal council when both sides exchanged pretty compliments. He even went so far as to address them as "Lords." With great modesty they disclaimed this appellation. But the emperor insisted on it: "You are lords," he said; "the oldest imperial registers know that Lübeck is one of the five towns that have had accorded to them in the imperial council the ducal rank, that they may take part in the emperor's council and be present where is the emperor."

These five cities were Rome, Venice, Pisa, Florence, and Lübeck.

When Charles left Lübeck he was delighted with the hospitality he had there received, but disappointed in his political aims. It is certain, however, that he rode out richer than he rode in; to this the account books of the city bear testimony, of this the taxpayers told a tale for many a long day. Indeed the expenses incurred through this imperial visitor were to lead later on to some serious riots of the guilds against the municipality.

It was through the *Mühlen Thor* that Charles departed with his train and by order of the town council this gate was walled up for ever behind him. It was meant as a piece of subtle flattery to the emperor, a suggestion that no mortal was worthy to step where he had stepped, but it is not out of keeping with the astute sense of humour that distinguished these commercial princes, that the act also covered a secret satisfaction in having outwitted their imperial guest and in being once more the victors in an encounter with royalty. Certain it is that Charles' visit proves that the Hanseatic League had reached the apex of power, and that the city of Lübeck was regarded in Europe as the head of this organization. Charles' visit was one of the proudest moments in her story, and the memory survives in local chronicles.

It also survives in an old picture preserved until quite recently in the house where he lodged, and now removed to the rooms of the Municipal Antiquarian Society. In this canvas we see the Emperor Charles IV., seated on a large throne-like chair. On either side of him is a leaded window. A carpet lies before his feet bordered with black, red, and gold cords. The emperor is clothed partly in imperial, partly in episcopal robes: a not uncommon mode of representation in those days. He wears his hair long, has a long moustache, and his full beard is parted in the middle, showing the costly clasp that closes his mantle. His head is surrounded by a golden jewelled crown, in his right hand he holds a long sword, in his left the imperial globe. The subscription runs: "Anno Dni. 1376 ipse Sevori Dn. Carolus quartus imperator invictissimus decem diebus hac in domo hospitatus est."

II.

THE TOWNS IN THE FOURTEENTH CENTURY.

OUR League had attained its maturity. As we have seen from its origin and as we shall see until its decadence, security and extension of commerce was its one aim and solicitude. The Hanseatics were at all times desirous to extend their markets abroad, to obtain, if possible, the monopoly of trade, and it must be admitted that they succeeded admirably in achieving the end they had in view. When we look back and consider the disorganized state of the empire and the slight support they received from their nominal liege lord, it seems strange that they did not take this occasion to constitute themselves also into a political union, forming independent states after the pattern of the Italian commercial republics. In general, the towns in pursuing their policy took as little real notice of the authority of the emperor, as the emperor of the interests and doings of the towns.

Even our shrewd Hansa merchants, it would seem, were afraid outwardly to present a bold front to their rulers, though secretly they defied them and circumvented their laws. The very existence of the federation was illegal, and in direct contravention to one of the chief clauses of the Golden Bull, which forbade all associations and unions within the empire. It is no doubt on this account that the Hansa, like the Venetian Republic, kept its organization so secret. Even in its own day people were but vaguely informed as to the working of its government, and as to the number and extent of its dominions.

The very natural question arises now that our League is mature, How many cities did it count in its federation? but it cannot be answered with precision. Nay, this question can receive no final reply in any period of the Hansa's history. The towns that joined did not always do so permanently, or were not able to maintain their place, and to fulfil their duties. Often, too, they proved restive and were "unhansed," and it was no easy or inexpensive matter to be readmitted. The ban of the

Hansa was more potent than that of pope or emperor. A town that fell under it lost its commerce at one blow. Thus, for example, Bremen, headstrong and stiff-necked, anxious to play an undue part in the Hansa League, saw itself shut out in 1356, because one of its burghers had traded with Flanders at a time when such trading was forbidden. The municipality, called upon to punish him, took his part, with the result that for thirty years the town was "unhansed," thirty miserable years, during which "the city was impoverished, grass grew in its streets, and hunger and desolation took up their abode in its midst," so writes a contemporary eyewitness. Reinstated at last, Bremen had to take up heavy responsibilities in atonement for its misdeeds.

On another occasion Brunswick fell into the hands of discontented artizans, who headed a revolt of several towns against the League. A fulminating decree was issued by the Hansa with the same results as in the case of Bremen. Misery and hunger in this case also proved persuasive, and at last, after six years, this proscribed town was readmitted. It had to send deputies to Lübeck, who craved pardon in the most abject terms, and who had to accept the most humiliating conditions. Besides questions of internal management, the Brunswickers undertook to build a votive chapel in the town in memory of their bad behaviour, and to send pilgrims to Rome who should crave the Papal pardon for the murders of councillors committed by the rioters. Two burgomasters of Brunswick, and eight of the chief citizens walked humbly in procession, bare-headed, bare-footed, carrying candles in their hands from the church of our Lady at Lübeck, to the town hall, where in the great council chamber of the League, before an enormous crowd, they had publicly upon their knees to confess their repentance for what unruly passion had caused them to do, and to implore their confederates to pardon them for the love of God, and the honour of the Virgin Mary.

More and more did Lübeck come to take the leading place among the cities. Her laws ruled at the Hansa diets. They were reckoned the wisest ever framed by an autonomous community, and are still quoted with respect. The right to use Lübeck law was as eagerly craved by distant cities as the Greek colonies craved the holy fire from native altars. No wonder Lübeck's merchants loved to quote the proud couplet:

> "Was willst begehren mehr,
> Als die alte Lübsche Ehr?"
> ("What more will you desire than the old Lübeck honour?")

Æneas Sylvius Piccolomini, afterwards Pope Pius II., when travelling through Europe as Chancellor of the Emperor Frederick III., visited Lübeck, and writes of it as the town which surpasses all others in the wealth and magnificence of its buildings and churches. The same praise is echoed a little later by a rare guest, the Metropolitan of Moscow, who passed through Lübeck on his way to Florence, to be present at the great church council held there by Eugene IV. Æneas also visited Danzig, and says it was so well equipped for land and sea warfare, that it could call under arms at least 50,000 men.

The prominence of the cities varied greatly. Circumstances which at one time might be to their advantage, might at another time prove adverse. Thus Wisby, after its sacking by Waldemar, was the victim of an accidental fire, which destroyed all that the Dane had spared. In consequence it fell at once from its position of importance, and its very site, once the source of its strength, became the cause of its downfall, for it proved a most convenient station to pirates. Where the merchant had safely halted, he was now in peril of life and goods.

To the question put at various times to the Hansa's ambassadors "which are the Hansa's cities?" evasive replies were given, either "those towns that fought the Hansa's battles;" or a few were enumerated, and the list closed with a colossal etcetera, etcetera. For they were not easily caught napping, these worthy burghers, and had ever in view "the interests of the common German merchants," which they feared might be endangered by too much publicity. Still, they had become a power that could not be hid, and seeing how well they realized this in most respects, it is the more curious that they did not avail themselves of their chance of attaining political autonomy. The more curious too, because, as a rule, the Hanseatics, like the modern Italians, knew so well how to draw profit out of all the dissensions and disorders that agitated Europe.

It was indeed a vast dominion that stood under the sway of the Hansa. In the course of less than a hundred years there had arisen on the Baltic coast, within the area of two hundred and fifty miles, no fewer than fourteen cities of first-class importance, not to name those that already existed there. Thus the merchants held in their possession the mouths of all the great Baltic rivers, on all of which they founded harbours and depôts. Germany in that epoch evinced a power of colonization which in its successes recalls the most brilliant moments of the extension of Greek life in the Mediterranean. In more modern times only the North American soil has exercised an attraction similar to that of the Baltic coasts, and has shown an equal power of upraising cities within a brief space of time. Many of the towns boasted a far larger population than they have at this day. Thus Lübeck in the fourteenth century counted eighty thousand inhabitants, as against forty-eight thousand in 1870.

An interesting contemporary opinion on our merchants is extant from the pen of a learned and travelled Italian, Marino Sanudo, a pious Venetian, who set forth early in the fourteenth century with a mission to stir up the Christian world, and organize a new Crusade, for Askelon, the last stronghold of the Romish Church, had fallen into the hands of the unbelievers. His first purpose was to gauge the fighting power of the various European maritime states, for it was a fleet rather than an army that was required. In his journeyings he ventured as far north as the Baltic, and thus reports in his letter to Pope John XXII.:

"In Alemannia live many peoples that could prove most useful to us.... I have seen with my own eyes that these coasts of Alemannia are quite similar to the Venetian. The inhabitants, strong of limb and practised in arms, are mostly warriors; others well skilled in dyke-making; besides, they are rich, and what is yet more commendable, they show a warm zeal for the affairs of the Holy Land."

After enumerating other advantages to be gained from these allies, he is however obliged to draw his Holiness' attention to a serious drawback on their part, namely, "that the Germans are enormous eaters, which arouses anxiety in respect to supplies when the fleet shall find itself in the hot regions."

A love for feasting meets us repeatedly in the old chronicle reports on the German merchants, and shows that in those days there also held good what Hawthorne has more recently expressed, that the Germans need to refresh exhausted nature twice as often as any other peoples. Then, as now, they were an upright, thorough, massive race, not made of too fine a clay and wanting rather on the æsthetic side; a want sure to strike the more finely strung senses of an Italian.

It is certain that the fourteenth century was in many respects the epoch when the Hansa cities flourished most actively. Neither before nor after did they have so many sided an importance for the whole life of the German nation. It was a stirring period in the history of the European continent; when the Minnesingers gave place to the Mastersingers; when learning, hitherto stored up jealously in the monasteries and the libraries of the princes, had found its way out among burghers and laymen; when protectors of art and science were more often simple merchant princes than noble-born beggars. In a word, it was an epoch when the middle class sprang into full being, and took its due and proper place as a link between the nobility and the common people.

Towards bringing about this state of things the Hansa had greatly contributed. If it failed to emancipate itself entirely from the empire, it was yet ever keenly desirous of emancipating itself from its petty suzerains. Thus the burghers of Lübeck, Cologne, Goslar, and other cities were early forbidden to hold posts under the lord of the domain, no matter how lucrative such posts might be. Wismar, engaged on one occasion in a dispute with the Dominican monks concerning the repair of the town walls, and obliged to cede to these ecclesiastics because the lord of the land was favourable to the Church, carefully recorded the occasion in its "town book," "in order," as it wrote, "that it might remember the circumstance on some future and more favourable occasion." "To pay them out" is implied though not expressed in the phrase.

With the same insistence and energy the towns made good their claims when it was requisite to protect the burgher in his commerce, this source of life to all the cities. Formerly, it is true, the German merchants had appeared in the foreign markets as "the men of the emperor," but now the emperors had no longer might wherewith to back their right, and more efficient protection was called for. This each found in his own city. Hundreds and thousands of treaties and letters of freedom attest to the fact that the towns recognized their duties towards their citizens and practised them most strenuously. Sometimes these were written out in the name of a princeling, whose signature it was always possible to buy for hard cash; but as time went on the towns gradually took an entirely independent stand, so that from France to the Russian districts of Smolensk the whole continent was overspread with a network of diplomatic and commercial contracts eagerly supported and extended by the towns.

The first thing sought for from the territorial lords, was protection for person and property from the gang of banditti who dwelt in every castle under the leadership of some titled robber; then protection against the cruel rights of wreckage and salvage, which declared all such goods the property of the territorial lord; further, release from imprisonment for debts and other misdemeanours incurred within the jurisdiction of the city and to be dealt with by itself alone; assistance in obtaining payment of foreign debts; freedom from the so-called "judgments of God" in the form of torture, walking on red-hot irons, &c.; regulation and diminution of local taxes and tolls on the lading or unlading of vessels, the weighing of merchandise; permission to fell wood to repair ships; in a word, one and all of the necessary permits to render more easy and profitable the intercourse between towns and nations.

In each foreign country the Hanseatics had always their permanent settlement, known as the Kontor, and for these they had early obtained a species of autonomy that permitted them to exercise jurisdiction according to their native laws over their own country people. Defaulters were judged by Hanseatic rules, and the "common merchant" found a help and support against the foreigners among whom he for the moment resided and with whom he traded.

The shrewd towns knew well how to estimate the value of such foreign settlements, and it it is noteworthy that they never accorded reciprocal rights. In vain foreigners pleaded permission to found similar settlements in the Hansa's dominions; the towns always skilfully declined such requests. Thus in Cologne foreign merchants were not allowed to reside longer than six weeks at a stretch, and this only three times in the year; therefore only eighteen weeks in all. Similar and even more restrictive regulations prevailed in the other cities.

It is curious to note that, until the end of the thirteenth century, it was chiefly the inland towns who were the great traders, but when they needed for their trade the highway of the ocean, gradually the maritime ports had taken the place of importance. One of the chief lines of sea traffic was that between Bruges in Flanders and Northern Russia. On this route hundreds of ships sailed annually, all owned by the "Easterlings," as the Baltic merchants were called to distinguish them from the inland traders. It was not until the fifteenth century that we find Dutchmen, Zealanders, and Frisians striving to come into serious competition with the Hansa.

A decree that no German merchant might go into partnership with a Russian, Fleming, or Englishman, no doubt aided greatly this exclusive possession of the Baltic Sea. In Russia waterways led them as far as Smolensk; and, later on, they penetrated even further inland, by utilizing the roads that had been made by the German knights whose seat of might was Pomerania and Livonia. The Marienburg, the chief house of the Order, proved a welcome halting station for the merchant travellers, where they found safety and shelter. Furs were largely obtained from the inner districts of Russia. "They are plentiful as dung there," writes the pious chronicler, Adam of Bremen; adding, "for our damnation, as I believe, for *per fas et nefas* we strive as hard to come into the possession of a marten skin as if it were everlasting salvation." According to him, it was from this cause and from Russia "that the deadly sin of luxurious pride" had overspread the West.

Wax, that played so large a part in mediæval religious rites, and was required in great abundance, was furnished by the "honey-trees" of the virgin Russian forests. Leather, skins, tallow, and all species of fat, were also among the chief products of Russia and the exports of the Hansa. In return, they imported into that empire the produce of the looms of Germany, England, and Flanders, the fine Flemish cloths, the coarser English and German. Silk, too, and linen were valued goods. Important also were all manner of worked metal objects, and such wares as town industries manufacture. Beer, too, was a valued and most profitable article of commerce. This drink was brewed in superior excellence in Northern Germany, the hops being grown on the spot. Contemporary writers tell how outside all the northern cities hop gardens flourished. This beer was never wanting at any carouse in the whole stretch of land from Flanders to Finland; a heavy, heady beverage, which would now be deemed unpalatable and indigestible. Some specimens are preserved to this day in the Danzig Topenbier and the Brunswick Mumme. To this thirst for ale Hamburg largely owes its prosperity. For many long years it was the greatest beer-making town of the North, boasting in the fourteenth century no less than five hundred breweries.

From Sweden the Hanseatics fetched copper and iron; in many cases they had acquired the sole possession of the mines. Scandinavia also furnished skins, as well as the various forest products of wood, potash, pitch, and tar. From Blekingen, as at this day, the merchants brought granite, and from Gothland and Bornholm limestone, both stones being required for those building purposes for which the native material of brick did not suffice. Already the Baltic supplied the Netherlands with grain.

The Hansa carried in return to Sweden, Finland, and Russia the requirements of daily life, since these countries possessed neither manufactures nor skilled labour. Down to the altar shrines and the psalters of the Church the merchants brought the evidences of civilized workmanship to these lands. The very furs they had taken thence were returned to their northern homes; of course manipulated and worked up. Even the English, more advanced in handicraft, submitted to the same régime. It used to be said on the European continent in those days: "We buy the fox skins from the English for a groat, and re-sell them the foxes tails for a guilder." With England indeed the Hansa's intercourse was most active, as we shall show more in detail later on.

Danzig owes almost all its splendour to the English trade. This city dealt largely in Austrian and Hungarian products, which were distributed from out its harbour. English crossbowmen received all the wood for their bows from Austria by way of Danzig. They were made from the yew tree, which was considered especially adapted to this end.

What the German merchant obtained as produce from Russia, Scandinavia, and other parts of Europe, not to mention the special productions of his own towns, he distributed either at home or in the world-famed markets of Bruges and London, for the Hansa was then the only intermediary between East and West. For more than three hundred years Bruges maintained its place as the central market for the whole of Europe this side the Alps. Here could be met traders from all parts; the Lombard bankers and money-changers, the Florentine, Spanish, Portuguese, French, Basque, English, Scotch, North and South Germans. It was from Bruges that the Baltic merchant supplied his home and Northern Germany with the products of the East, which the South German had brought from Venice and over the Alpine passes along the Rhine. In Bruges he could buy the fruits of the Mediterranean, the silks of Florence, the oils of Provence, the wines of Spain and Italy. These meetings of merchants were wont to take place at stated times, intercourse being thus made surer and easier. This custom laid the foundation for those annual fairs for the exchange of wares, of which one yet survives in Germany in little diminished importance, namely, the great fair of Leipzig, where all the German publishers meet to exchange the intellectual productions of the year.

Another source of wealth to the cities arose from the circumstance that they not only supplied the requirements of the mass, but were also the purveyors to the princes and the aristocracy. We find in their books that these frequently owed them heavy sums for furs, Flanders cloth, and choice wines. They were also most often their bankers, for the towns and, above all, Lübeck, the centre of cash transactions, were held desirable places for money investments. Even in the distant districts of Sweden people knew no better mode of investing capital than to confide it to Lübeck merchants.

Of course the conditions of trade were vastly different from those of to-day. Above all, the merchant had to act more in person. Posts did not exist, orders and contracts, therefore, could rarely be made by letter, for it mostly required a special messenger to carry these. It was hence almost the rule that the merchant accompanied his wares "over sea and sand," as the phrase went. For the sake of greater security, and in order also to diminish expenses, many would club together to charter a ship. It was usual to interest the captains in the sales of the wares, it being held advisable that every one on board should have an advantage in bringing the goods safe to land and in their profitable disposal. This custom arose from the dangers that lurked from robbers, while insurance of goods in transit was yet unknown. By interesting captain and crew pecuniarily they were less likely to throw the goods overboard in a storm, or to allow pirates quietly to board and rob the vessels; both matters of common occurrence.

If it was dangerous to travel by water, it was yet far worse to travel by land. Not to mention that there were few roads, that the mud often lay piled wheel high, so that the strongest horses could not pull the carts; the presence of robbers was a constant cause of fear on the road. Many of these were, as we know, the lordlings of the land in disguise, and hence they naturally turned a deaf ear to the repeated petitions of the merchants to keep the highways in better order. Added to this, each lord had the right to demand toll for the passing of his dominions and the toll stations were often very close together. Thus, for example, within a space of fifteen miles from Hamburg the merchant encountered no less than nine. Fortunately the tables of tolls in those days were not too complicated. They were generally paid by waggon, or ship load, regardless of contents.

The Middle Ages were ignorant of protective taxes. These impediments to the useful exchange of international produce were reserved for the invention and practice of our more enlightened centuries. It is characteristic that the oath which played so great a part in all mediæval transactions, social and political, was also employed to settle the toll dues of the traveller. A crucifix was held before him; on this he swore that he was not defrauding, that the weight of his wares, as stated by him, was accurate, and herewith the transaction was completed. It was, however, necessary to be most careful not to diverge from the toll roads. If a merchant was found on a bye-road his goods were confiscated and he himself imprisoned. On this account, too, companionship was sought after, the leadership of some one familiar with the ground, and hence merchants and merchandize generally moved in caravans.

It is worthy of note that all the trade of that time was strictly legitimate, and what is known as real merchant's business. Speculation hardly existed. Commission and agency dues were not wholly unknown, but happily there was not existent that pernicious scourge of modern trade, the time bargains, which permit merchandize to be sold a dozen times over before it actually exists. It was honest, true trade, which only sold what it could show. Therefore, it could uphold and practise the axiom, "ware for ware, or for cash." In certain districts, for example Russia, barter was more common than money payments. Credit was absolutely forbidden in certain towns and in certain branches of trade.

If credit was allowed the borrower had to find a surety, and to go surety was a grave matter, of which the consequences might easily prove disastrous, entailing loss of property and often of personal freedom.

Payments were usually made in coined money, but bar silver was also employed, especially in Russia, and bills of exchange were not quite unknown. The bills were payable as a rule either at Lübeck or Bruges. Silver was the chief currency, but in the fourteenth century Lübeck was permitted to coin gold. It made guilders after the pattern of the Florentine ducats. The gold to coin them with was bought at Bruges. We must remember that money had a far higher value in those days than in ours, and that if we want to arrive at a just comparison with our own times, we must multiply the sums by seventy or seventy-five. The most common form of reckoning was the Flemish, *i.e.*, one pound, equal to twenty shillings at twelve groats each; in a word, exactly the reckoning that has survived in England to this day. The pound of money was originally a weight. The best money was that of Lübeck, and, above all, the English contracted to be paid in pounds of the "Easterlings," their generic name for the Baltic merchant. As a survival and abbreviation of this phrase we in England say pound sterling to this day. A bad light upon the morality and conditions of the period is thrown by the fact that the petty kings, seeing that their coins were often refused and mistrusted, did not hesitate to coin and give currency to false money bearing the imprint of the League. We come across frequent bitter and often useless complaints on this subject.

Putting out capital at interest was not wholly unknown in those days, notwithstanding the prohibitions of the Church which, founded on the text in St. Luke vi. 54, and the Fourteenth Psalm ("qui pecuniam non debet ad usuram"), forbade all usury business. The Jews early held this branch of trade in their hands. Rates of interest varied from 6 to 10 per cent. Loans, too, were made to princes, foreign and native, and to cities, upon industrial enterprises. Wholly erroneous is the notion that capital was inactive, kept in a strong box or an old stocking. That great riches were accumulated is proved by some of the old wills and account books.

Fortunes of a quarter of a million were not unknown. A single merchant would often own not only many farms in different and distant parts of the country, but whole villages and townships. As for the men themselves, we encounter them in every part of the continent, the artisan as well as the merchant. Thus, for example, Germans seem the favourite shoemakers; we hear of them in this capacity as far off as Lisbon. Then, as now, they were renowned as bakers, and no one knew better how to salt and preserve herrings and cod-fish.

In Livonia, Esthonia, Gothland, rich merchants died whose nearest heirs had to be sought in far off Westphalia. For instance: A worthy shoemaker became burgher of Lübeck; then visited Rome and San Jago di Compostella as a pilgrim, and afterwards being named shoemaker to the German knights, had as his chief debtor for goods supplied a cavalier who fought in Sweden. Thus diverse, many-coloured, and full of adventure were lives in those times, which we are too often tempted to think sleepy and stay-at-home.

It is difficult to gain an idea of the full extent and nature of mediæval trade, but this too was far more rich and varied than we suppose. Though there was no activity outside Europe, still it can well stand beside our modern commerce, and as regards honesty, thoroughness of produce and workmanship, it unhappily far eclipses it. Certainly the list of articles imported and exported in their variety of needful and needless objects, their luxury and magnificence, goes far to disprove our notions of the greater simplicity of life in the Middle Ages. For supply means demand, and meant this yet more emphatically with our practical forefathers.

Apart from the evidences of figures and statistics, the evidences of wealth and luxury can also be found in the yet extant monuments of the time, and, above all, in the churches. In the Middle Ages the one converging point of ideal life was the Church. Everything that went beyond the immediate practical needs of daily existence, every form of charity, every endeavour after culture, every striving of artistic and scientific activity had in those days a religious foundation. Imagination, too, came to the aid of this tendency in the shape of the possible and probable dangers encountered by "sea and sand," by the town traders. Thus in 1401 we find merchants and shippers at Lübeck founding "an eternal brotherhood and guild to the honour of God, of Mary His beloved mother, and all the saints; above all, the holy true helper in need, St. Nicholas, that they may aid and comfort the living and the dead, and all those who seek their rightful livelihood on the water, many of whom, alas! perish in water troubles, are thrown overboard or expire in other ways, dying unconfessed and without repentance; for on account of their agonies they could feel neither remorse nor penitence for their sins, and who have none who pray for them except the general prayers."

Such guilds were by no means rare. Legacies, too, were left for similar ends, by which thousands of our money were willed away: churches, monasteries, and holy foundations of all kinds raised or aided to pray for the benefit of the souls of the dead.

Nor were distant pilgrimages unknown. The merchant would go in person, combining business and religion on the road, or he would send a substitute, who for a certain sum would visit Rome, the Holy Land, San Jago in Spain, or Rocamadour in Guyenne. Such pilgrims by profession were frequent. St. Peter, St. James, after them St. John, then St. Nicholas and St. Clement as patron saints of merchants, shippers and fishermen, and among the women saints St. Catherine, were the chosen objects of North German piety. In no town was lacking a leper house, a refuge for those troubled with that plague of the Middle Ages, happily now almost unknown in Europe. These were dedicated to the Holy Ghost and to St. George, the slayer of dragons.

Above all, worship was paid to the Virgin Mary. All the municipal churches were dedicated to her. There is not a town that has not its church of "Our Lady." The municipal council were put under her especial protection. To this day the so-called Beautiful Door of the Mary Church at Danzig bears the inscription in golden letters: "Queen of Heaven, pray for us!"

These churches and religious buildings of all kinds, many of which survive to this day amid surroundings to which they have grown strange, speak more eloquently of the Hansa's might than piles of old parchment records. All Scandinavia can show nothing to compare with these architectural monuments, and we can well comprehend that the Northman entering the Elbe, the Trave, or other Baltic rivers, and seeing the lighthouses, churches, and mighty buildings of the towns, were awed by the Germans' wealth and power and strength, much as we are impressed now-a-days when we first set eyes upon Eternal Rome. These buildings resembled each other in externals; in each we find the same tall graceful steeples rising into the heavens, the same proud, defiant battlements and turrets, the same high-gabled many storeyed, small-windowed houses, the same tendency to employ bricks as building materials, and to use coloured varieties as ornamentation. Of this method of building and decoration the Holstenthor of Lübeck is a well-preserved example, as indeed these double gates to the towns were also a characteristic feature. One, a round tower, resembling greatly the Castel St. Angelo of Rome, situated on the south side of Rostock, was so strongly built that even the mechanical contrivances of our days found it hard work to demolish it when modern progress required its removal.

Art was then almost exclusively the handmaiden of religion, and hence it is also in the churches we have to seek evidences of what the Hansa could produce in this respect. Metal gravestones, rich bindings, cunning iron work, attest its taste. Evidence of a love of painting is found in many works now preserved in museums of the pre-Holbein day. And, incredible though it may seem, they were so famous for glass painting that early in the fifteenth century men came from Italy to Lübeck to learn perfection in the craft.

Of their domestic architecture little, unhappily, remains to us, the practice of building with wood having wrecked most of the cities. Such houses as survive, however, testify to the national love of cunning carvings and inscriptions of didactic purpose. For it is the keynote of that time to express in artistic form its ardent faith and activity, and its somewhat rough-and-ready philosophy. Theorizings and abstractions were little understood. Thus in old legal codes we see the punishments to be inflicted pictorially portrayed. Contempt and mocking also took tangible form, and the clergy were by no means exempted from such satire. Notwithstanding all the piety of the age, the people were ever on their guard against the encroachments of the wily priests. The deeds of Reynard the Fox—that favourite national comic epic, so wholly in keeping with the Hansa spirit of practical good sense and business cunning—was a favourite theme for weaving into arras and carpet; and it was common to give a distinct hit at the clergy in the person of the sly beast.

It was the custom to depict the Last Judgment in the court of justice of each guildhall. That painted in 1341 for Hamburg led to a long lawsuit before the Papal Court at Avignon, because the local dean and chapter saw in it personal allusions. Thus devoutness did not impede the townspeople from rigidly retaining their mental independence of view and action.

Science and literature—such as those ages could boast—were, like art, more or less pressed into the service of the Church. The only exception is to be found in the few popular folk-tales, all comic, like the deeds of Eulenspiegel, and in the town chroniclers who were in the pay of the municipal council; but activity was not great in this latter domain. In most cities, schools were attached to all the parishes, in which the children of the wealthy classes learned reading, writing, some arithmetic, singing, and a little Latin. These institutions were founded in defiance of the priests, who loved to keep the people in the darkness and enslavement of ignorance.

Nearly all the merchants and many artizans could read and write, even if they did not practise these arts with great facility. Business letters were indited either in Latin or German, for the latter tongue was more widely diffused for commercial purposes than in our day.

But if the wealth of the towns led them to encourage the gentler aspects of life, it also enabled them to give expression to less refined tastes, and refinement of taste was never a speciality of these rather coarse-grained and boorish Teutons. The Middle Ages were essentially a time of animal enjoyment and license; the people loved life and all life could offer on the material side. We come across constant records of carouses and feasts, at which the manners and customs were—to our ideas, at least—most gross. No occasion for merry-making, which meant largely eating and drinking, was allowed to slip by unheeded. Nor were these occasions few, for the Catholic Church, with its endless list of saints, furnishes easy and constant excuses for holiday-making, as we see to this day in Catholic countries.

When guilds, corporations, or associations met for convivial intercourse, this was pursued according to established rules, some of which survive in the student *corps* of German universities. Breaches of regulation were punished by extra rations of beer that were paid for by the delinquent. Entrance fees were defrayed by giving a feast to all members. In short, they ate hard and drank yet harder, with the result that nightly drunken brawls were frequent, the quieter folk often lodging complaints concerning disturbed sleep or rioting beneath their windows between the younger burghers and the watchman. Occasionally a man is banished for molesting the town guard, while intoxicated and disorderly, for undue license was not winked at by the town council.

This was also the epoch when flourished those civic games which furthered the sentiment of brotherhood, and served, besides, to improve the youth of the city in the use and practice of arms. Among these, the May games, May processions, May empires, took a foremost place. They had their origin in the pagan conception of spring as a fair youth, who, in victorious duel, overcame the treacherous winter.

The May emperor was usually elected from among the town council. The one who had obtained the wreath during the previous year delivered it up at the beginning of May or at Whitsuntide. He would ride out into a neighbouring wood "upon his good horse," accompanied by all the councillors clad in armour, to the sound of martial music and with the town's flag flying. This was called "going to fetch the May." A beautiful boy generally headed the procession. What ceremonies went on in the wood is not known, but when the procession returned, leading in the new May emperor, the boy would bear a flowery wreath upon his long pole as token of victory; while all the councillors and the huge crowd that followed in their train were decked with green branches and boughs. The newly-elected emperor was expected to treat the crowd. After a while this grew a heavy and serious expense, and we find it recorded that a certain burgher of Stralsund, who knew he would be elected to this honour, fled the city. He was, however, followed and brought back, made to accept the post and its expenses, and heavily fined into the bargain.

As in modern Switzerland, so in mediæval Germany, crossbow shooting for prizes gave another occasion for public holiday, the different guilds turning out, with banner and music, to do honour to their various patron saints. In such wise all adult men were trained to warfare, though the armies of the Hansa usually consisted in great part of hired mercenaries, easily obtained for ready cash in those days, when fighting was held a pleasure far beyond legitimate work. Many records survive to attest that these Hansa merchants were skilled in the use of dagger and axe. One, for example, a peaceful citizen and trader, with his own hand killed a noted pirate who had long rendered the Baltic unsafe. The merchant went his road, as the saying was, trusting to God and his own right arm. "Whosoever would be a good burgher at Danzig must be industrious both in commerce and arms," runs an inscription on the house of the crossbow shooters of that city.

Later on, as the towns grew more aristocratic in character, the gilded youth of the day had games of their own, from participation in which the artizan was excluded. These, in many cases, led to such riots and uprisings of the populace against the municipality as occasioned the "unhansing" of Brunswick and other cities. Foremost among them were the so-called "Popinjay Associations," who met to shoot down from a pole these bright-coloured birds with which travellers had become acquainted in the market of Bruges. It was usual for the winner to treat his comrades to a barrel of beer and cakes.

Indeed, without touching upon the innumerable institutions common to guilds, trades, patricians, and plebeians, a picture of those times would be imperfect. Some of these were instituted for purely hilarious purposes, others combined charity and mutual support with carouse and license. Thus in Cologne there was a society which met to drink wine, and presented to every honoured guest a medal having the inscription, "Bibite cum hilaritate." This society imposed on itself certain laws regarding the avoidance of bad language, of lawless living, of coarse speech and action.

In the North beer was the chief beverage, many companies were dedicated to Gambrinus, the "arch-king and inventor of brewing." Here, too, quaint rules attest the rudeness of contemporary manners. It was customary to exact a monetary fine from those who spilt more beer than they could cover with their hand. It seems that even women were not excluded wholly from these revels. At least a princely guest, harboured by Lübeck, expressed his disapprobation at the presence in the cellar of the town hall of patrician ladies, who under cover of their veils, which formed for them an incognito, drank hard and enjoyed themselves grossly.

Endless are the rules and regulations of the various calends, ghostly brotherhoods, companies, and other names by which they styled themselves. Thus, for example, they were forbidden to take the food off each other's plates, to call each other certain most injurious names, to throw knives and plates at each other, to appear at solemn drinking bouts bare-footed, to roll in the mud, to retain arms, hat, and cloak when in company, to tap a fresh barrel without the presence of an elder, and so forth. Their duties to each other combined social and religious obligations. Thus they were often bound to pray for those who, absent on travels, could not attend at mass. They gave decent burial to their poorer comrades, nursed them when sick, helped them when distressed. A pound of wax, half a hundredweight of tallow, a barrel of beer, were not uncommon fines for dereliction of duty. Games of chance were universally forbidden. Dancing and song were common forms of diversion. The shoemakers and tailors of Lübeck were noted for their skill in the sword-dance, a dance probably not unlike the Highland reel executed to this day by Scotchmen.

Wit, grace, imagination, were elements mostly absent from the lives of these rough Germans. This is nowhere more evident than in their amusements. The carnival practices furnished a notable example, practices so graceful, so pretty in the South, so rough and rude in the North. Two instances will suffice. At Stralsund it was customary to nail up a poor cat with which a man fought until he hit it to death, when he was mock-knighted by the burgomaster. In Cologne poor blind people were let loose in an enclosed space to hit a pig, which should be the prize of the successful candidate. The joy of the spectators reached its height when the poor blind men struck each other in place of their victim. The practices at weddings were too rude for description.

Luxury in dress was most pronounced, and sumptuary laws were repeatedly enacted. It seems strange that it was the men even more than the women who offended in these respects. Simple, nay, rude as the lives of these burghers were in their homes, out of doors they loved to make display, especially in the matter of costly weapons and brave horses. Young men returning from the wars or the great markets of London or Bruges, introduced new fashions and fantasies which changed far more frequently than we are apt to suppose. The most conservative dress was the headgear of the patricians, the councillors and members of the municipality. This consisted for many ages in a long cap of cloth, trimmed with fine fur. Before hats or caps came into fashion as coverings, the sight of these men in their long fur cloaks, with their heads enclosed in these curious hoods, must have had a stately, grave effect. So proud were the patricians of this dress that the councillors of Bremen actually forged a document early in the thirteenth century, according to which Godfrey of Bouillon, accorded to them, during the first Crusade, the permission to wear fur and gold chains. The dress, clogging the free action of the legs, necessitated a stately slow walk, and its length would seem often to have inconvenienced them in those times of unpaved streets and mud-coated roads. A certain Evart von Huddessen, the representative of Stralsund at the Court of King Erik of Sweden, gained the special favour of the monarch on an occasion, when, invited by the king to visit with him his pleasure gardens outside the town, he quietly walked through the puddles after Erik's horse, instead of waiting like the other representatives for their servants to carry for them their trains, which they feared to spoil in the mud. "Eh! what are we waiting for here?" he cried to his colleagues, "shall his royal highness ride alone? I reckon my masters of Stralsund are rich enough that they can make good to me my new coat."

Nor were they invariably simple in their homes, though usually so. A favourite German folk tale tells how Melchior, of Bremen, had his dining-room paved with silver dollars, and even if history or chronicle does not confirm this legend, it is thoroughly in keeping with Hanseatic modes of displaying wealth. There did exist, for instance, a certain Wulf Wulflam, of Stralsund, who sat upon a silver seat, and had his rooms hung with costly arras. When he married he, like a royal personage, caused the road from his house to the church to be overspread with a Flanders carpet, while musicians played day and night before his door. No doubt at his wedding appeared also the eighty dishes which at weddings was the highest limit allowed to burgher luxury by the Hanseatic by-laws.

It would seem, too, that the Hansa representatives when sent to "Hansa days" (the meetings of the various cities in common council) after a while indulged in great display to impress beholders with the power and wealth of their respective cities. This, after a time, assumed such proportions that poorer or wiser communities refrained, whenever possible, from sending members to the "Hansa days."

Such were the habits and customs of these old burghers. As we see, it was a time when men were occupied with the material rather than the ideal side of life. A curious medley it presents of egotism and altruism, piety and license, love of individuality and strict regulation, roughness of living and unbridled luxury, boorishness and civilization.

A word must be said of that important institution, the town council, to complete this sketch of the German towns during the fourteenth and fifteenth centuries. Its constitution varied somewhat of course, according to the size and wealth of the cities, but there were certain main resemblances. The number of aldermen varied from twelve to twenty-four. At their head were two or four burgomasters, who enjoyed no special privileges, except that in council they held the office of president. The appointment was for life, but they took it in turns to be on active duty. Certain limitations of choice as to aldermen existed. Thus for long in Lübeck no one could hold that office who earned his bread by handicraft. This regulation however did not last. Still merchants throughout filled the chief places; as, being travelled men, and knowing the requirements of their fellows, they were considered the most fit. Next to these, brewers and tailors took a leading part. The general constitution of the council may be regarded as in a fashion aristocratic, but it was checked in deliberations and decisions by a sort of second chamber, the common council. Under their rule the cities certainly flourished; the one chamber counselled, the other acted, and to be alderman was indeed no sinecure, but rather a post that imposed heavy labour. Honour it brought, but scanty remuneration.

Noblesse oblige was the proud motto these men acted on. The church bells called them to their meetings, which at first were held in the municipal church, later in the guildhalls. At Lübeck they always assembled first in their own chapel of Our Lady's Church, then went in procession to the town-hall. This was the centre of all national life. The market-place was built before it, around it were the chief shops. In the market-place justice was administered, either in the open air or under the open porticos of the guildhall. Civic feasts were held here, foreign guests received at this spot. No wonder, then, that the burghers spent great sums upon the building and decoration of their town-halls and surroundings. They were to them the palladium of civic independence, whence law and order, merriment and feasting took their origin. To this day the cellars of the town-halls in Germany boast the best wines and choicest foods, and though now let out as restaurants they still, many of them, show in fresco and carving the remains of ancient splendour. In the town-halls were preserved the treasure, the civic documents, and the great town books, called into requisition in all disputes. "No witness goes beyond the Book" was the axiom of the day.

The market-place was always the largest open place in a city. The streets were narrow and tortuous. This was necessitated by the circumstance that all towns at that date were walled, and hence their extension circumscribed. Each class of workmen lived together; shoemakers in one street, coopers in another, and so forth. Their houses being small, it was usual for them on fine days to do their work out of doors, which gave an animated appearance to the place. At night these streets were closed by iron chains drawn across them.

The town life was, in short, but the family life on an extended scale, and the municipality watched over the welfare of the inhabitants as a father over that of his household. To facilitate commerce and industry, and to look after roads and buildings, were among its chief cares. It is noteworthy that in some towns regulations existed compelling every one who had means to leave in his will a certain sum for repairing the highways and keeping the ports in good condition. Many fulfilled this provision, even without this order.

Another occupation of the aldermen was to superintend trade, and see it carried out on honest principles. Thus, at Novgorod, a bale of linen is discovered to be bad, so that "no honourable and good man could be paid in such ware." It is sent back to Riga, thence to Wisby, thence to Lübeck, where the aldermen had to find out who delivered these goods. Punishment for such fraud followed inevitably, and was so heavy that, on the whole, few attempted to play these base tricks. We also come across complaints that barrels of herrings had been packed fraudulently, good and large fish being on the top; small and inferior and even stale ones filling the rest of the barrel. As such perishable goods could not be returned, the aldermen instituted official herring packers, who were responsible for honest action.

In all difficult matters, the advice of the municipality was asked and given. It was held "that they knew what others did not know." Thus burgher and burgher ruler worked hand in hand, and each man felt himself a link of the whole chain. This feeling gave rise to an active patriotism, a warm love for their own town, of which instances abound in the mediæval chronicles. Many tales are preserved of brawls arising in the towns through the vauntings of rival citizens. Thus a certain Lübecker meeting a Bremener in a Hamburg inn, boasted so greatly of his native town's advantages and made such fun of his companion's aldermen that they all but came to serious blows. "You had better mind your words and drink your beer in peace," was the friendly advice of a bystander.

Such were these burghs which had grown free and strong through burgher industry, and were kept powerful by burgher unity and honesty.

III.

THE VICTUAL BROTHERS.

A serious interruption to the Baltic trade after the glorious peace with Waldemar arose from the notorious gang of pirates known to history as the Victual Brothers. Upon the principle that all is fair in love and war the Hansa, during its campaign against the Danish king, had openly countenanced and even abetted piracy, so long as the attacks of the robbers were directed against their enemies. The chance of plundering under protection was too tempting not to attract a large number of adventurers, who for some years carried on their black trade under the designation of "Victual Brothers," a name chosen because their ostensible aim was to supply with provisions that part of the Swedish coast which belonged to the Hansa.

It seems strange to us of to-day to find as the leading spirits among these Brothers the names of Moltke and Manteuffel, doubtless forbears of the famous modern German generals. These pirates founded masses and charitable institutions on the one hand, and robbed and sacked remorselessly on the other. Peace being concluded, the Hansa naturally had to clear the seas of these pests, but it had been easier to call them into activity than to suppress them. A large body of men had found profitable employment coupled with stirring adventure; this latter being a powerful incentive in those days, and were loth to quit their free wild life.

They continued their association, nay, even enlarged it, forming themselves into a corporation, after the pattern of the Knights Templars, and divided all booty equally among their body. In a brief space they became the scourge of all the commercial cities. "God's friend and all the world's enemy" was their audacious motto. Masters of both seas, the Baltic and the German Ocean, on one occasion they even seized, plundered, and burnt down Bergen (1392) and took prisoner the bishop. Gothland became their stronghold, and Wisby, once the Hansa's glory, was turned into a pirate's nest near which the merchant sailed with fear and trembling.

It seems strange, to our modern ideas, even to think that piracy was once a reputable calling. It was held as such, for example, in ancient Greece, as we may read in Thucydides, book i. chap. 5. No offence was in those days either intended or taken if one Greek asked another if he were a pirate. In the Baltic, like duelling in more polished climes, this practice long survived the positive laws framed against it. Pirates would even give back empty ships to merchants, wishing them a happy return with fresh and fuller cargoes.

In vain did Margaret of Sweden protest against the audacities of the Victual Brothers. She was helpless against them. The measure of her impotence can be gauged by the fact that she begged from Richard II., king of England, permission to hire three ships at Lynn for the protection of her kingdom. In vain, too, on the days when the Hansa met in council, was this theme discussed. For three whole years all fishing on Scania had to be abandoned. The result was severely felt throughout the length and breadth of Christian Europe, for herrings and other Lenten food became rare and costly.

Stronger and stronger grew these pirates, so that at last it was decided to send out an army against them. Once more recourse was had to a poundage tax to raise supplies and thirty-five large vessels with three thousand men were sent to sea in 1394. After long and arduous struggles they at last broke the power of the association, but for long afterwards separate bands of pirates, once members of the mighty gang, rendered the navigation of these seas a peril.

Legend took possession of these robbers from an early date, and we come across them in song and fable. Taking a foremost place were Godeke Michelson and Stortebeker, whose special mission it was to harry the traders with England. Stortebeker, it is said, was a nobleman, indeed noblemen were frequently found in the association. As a youth he had been wild and lived so riotous a life that all his property was gambled and drunk away. When finally the town of Hamburg, the scene of his carouses, in order to pay his debts, deprived him of his knightly armour and forbade him the city precincts, he joined the Victual Brothers.

At this time their leader was Godeke Michelson, who hailed the new confederate with joy, after testing his strength, which was so great that with his hands he broke iron chains like string. And because his new ally was also great at drinking—he could pour down huge bumpers at one gulp—he bade him lay aside his noble name and renamed him instead Stortebeker ("Pour down bumpers"). Once when the pair had plundered the North Sea clean they made a descent upon Spain. As was their wont, they divided their spoils with their comrades, only on this occasion they kept for themselves the holy bones of St. Vincent, stolen from a church, bearing them under their coats upon their naked breasts. Hence, says legend, they grew invulnerable, so that neither crossbow nor axe, sword nor dagger, could harm or wound them.

When the Victual Brothers were conquered by the Hansa and banished from the Baltic, these two chieftains with their followers found good friends in Frisia, where to this day memories of Stortebeker survive, and the chieftain Keno then Broke became his father-in-law, for his lovely daughter lost her heart to the doughty pirate, and followed him on to his ships and his floating kingdom. For Stortebeker was a king in his way. When he made captives who promised him a ransom he let them live. But if they were poor and old and weak, he threw them overboard relentlessly. If they were poor but strong, and so likely to be of use, he tested their strength in this manner. He caused his own enormous goblet to be filled with wine. If they could empty it at one gulp they were his peers, and he accepted them as comrades. Those who could not pass this ordeal were dismissed.

It is said that Stortebeker and Godeke Michelson sometimes had moments of penitence concerning the lives they led. In such a moment of remorse they each presented the cathedral of Verdun with seven glass windows, on which were painted cunningly the seven deadly sins. Stortebeker's "mark," two reversed goblets, is depicted in one of them, probably the one that treats of gluttony. They also founded a charity for distributing bread to the poor.

In 1400, the Hansa sent out a fleet to Frisia to combat these chieftains. It was in this war that the Hamburgers attained the honour of conquering the Victual Brothers, dispersing their crew and releasing their captives. Keno then Broke was carried off into confinement, for he had, against his oath and faith, contrived to aid the pirates. With Keno the town of Hamburg made a new treaty. It is said that just as it was signed and the councillors had left the council chamber, Stortebeker managed to slip out of a hiding-place, where he had heard all that passed, and joked with his father-in-law at the expense of the Hamburg aldermen who had once more put faith in him. Whilst so engaged a certain Councillor Naune, who had forgotten his gloves, returned to the hall and overheard them. Hence the war broke out afresh. Once more many Victual Brothers were captured and beheaded in Hamburg. Their heads were stuck upon poles for the warning of all beholders, while the account books prove that the executioner received eight pennies per trunk decapitated and his servant twenty pennies per body buried. Yet again a fleet had to set forth; for as long as Stortebeker and Godeke Michelson were living there was no peace possible. Under a Hamburg alderman, Simon of Utrecht, who commanded the fleet on board a mighty ship known as the *Coloured Cow*, they again set out. The name of this vessel is remarkable, and is the first instance we come across in Hanseatic history of a profane denomination for a ship. All the others are named after some saint or angel, under whose special protection it was supposed to sail. "The *Coloured Cow*, from Flanders, that tore through the ocean with its great horns," sings the folk-song, the "Stortebeker Lied," which a hundred and fifty years ago was still sung by the people. The Victual Brothers lay off Heligoland. Towards dark one evening in the year 1402, the Hamburg fleet approached them, and a daring fisherman came so near that he was able to pour molten lead upon some of their rudders, loosening them, and rendering the vessels unseaworthy. Next day the battle began. It raged three days and three nights, and only after a desperate resistance was Stortebeker conquered.

Some of the pirates fled, many were killed or thrown into the sea; their ships, richly laden with booty in the shape of linen, wax, cloth, &c., were seized, and Stortebeker with seventy comrades carried in triumph to Hamburg. The cell in which Stortebeker was confined was known as Stortebeker's hole as long as it existed. It was destroyed like so many of the antiquities of Hamburg in the great fire of 1842. Short work was of course made of his trial, and with his companions Stortebeker was condemned to death. When he heard his sentence it afflicted him much, and he offered the municipality in return for his life and freedom a chain of gold to be made from his hidden treasures, so long that they could span with it the whole cathedral and also all the town. This offer was, of course, indignantly rejected, and next day he was publicly executed, together with seventy comrades. In compliance with their dying petition they went to death dressed in their best, marching in stately procession, and preceded by fifes and drums.

After Stortebeker's death the Hamburgers searched his ships for the hidden treasures. Except a few goblets they could find nothing at first, until a carpenter broke the main-mast, which was discovered to be hollow and full of molten gold. With this fortune the merchants who had suffered at Stortebeker's hands were indemnified, the costs of the war paid, and out of the remainder a golden crown was made and placed on the spire of St. Nicholas Church.

Stortebeker was thus out of the way; but there still remained Godeke Michelson. So the Hamburgers with Simon of Utrecht and his *Coloured Cow*, once more set forth and once more returned victorious, bearing in their train Godeke Michelson, eighty robbers, and the under-chieftain Wigbold, of whom it is said that he had been a professor of philosophy at Rostock, and had exchanged his chair for the forecastle of a ship. These men also were all decapitated in the presence of the burghers and municipal council.

It was a heavy day's work for the executioner, and it is related that he waded up to his ankles in blood. After it was all ended an alderman asked him kindly if he were not much wearied. "Oh no," said the headsman, laughing grimly, "I never felt better in my life, and I have strength enough left to behead the whole lot of you councillors." For this treasonable speech he was at once dismissed from his post.

Various relics exist to this day to keep Stortebeker's memory fresh in Hamburg. Among them were a small whistle with which he gave the signal to his ships during a storm, an iron cannon nineteen feet long, his armour, and the executioner's sword.

But chief of all Hamburg preserved the so-called Stortebeker goblet, a silver bumper, from which tradition says he drank. "Whosoever comes to Hamburg and does not go to the Ship's Company, that he may drink from the goblet of Stortebeker and Godeke Michelson, and write his name in the book that lies beside it, has not been in Hamburg," says an old writer. This goblet is about a yard and a half high, and holds four bottles. A sea-fight is engraved on it, together with other incidents out of Stortebeker's life, and some rough rhymes. Once more modern criticism, destructive and intolerant of all picturesque legend, declares that the cup is of later date than Stortebeker's time, and can never have been his.

Soon after the death of the pirate chiefs, Hamburg sent an envoy as pilgrim to the shrine of San Jago of Compostella. Whether he was employed to bear thither the thanks of the city to the saint for their victory, or to return to Spain the relics of St. Vincent, history saith not. A medal was struck to commemorate the event. It bears Stortebeker's portrait and an appropriate inscription. Simon of Utrecht, the victorious captain of the fleet, who later won other battles for the Hansa, received high honours from Hamburg. When he died he was accorded honourable burial, and a gravestone to his memory was put outside St. Nicholas Church. Happily it survived the great fire. It shows the crest of Simon, a large three-masted vessel, with the figure of a beast at the helm; doubtless, the famous "coloured cow;" a swan draws this ship through the waves. Below is an inscription in Latin verse, recording the hero's feats against the pirates, and enjoining posterity to imitate the great deeds of their forbears, that the fame of the city may not be diminished.

IV.

THE FACTORY OF BERGEN.

We have seen how great was the Hansa's power in peace and in war; let us now cast a glance at the basis upon which the whole proud fabric rested. This is to be sought, beyond doubt, in its foreign commerce. How enormous the interest they had, especially in the Baltic trade, how great, indeed almost exclusive, was their empire in that sea, it is difficult to realize. And to retain this empire, to be masters of the mercantile relations between the eastern and western extremities of Europe, they considered no sacrifice too great. This was the keynote of their policy. Their purpose, simple enough in conception, was carried out with a disregard of other claims than their own, and often a violence which made them encounter resistance, and which in the end was largely the cause of their fall.

The political agitations and confusions which disturbed the Scandinavian kingdoms early in the fifteenth century were astutely utilized by the Hanseatics, who, having their settlements at Bergen and Scania, were able to keep out the Dutch and English, then just beginning to attempt a rivalry with them in the northern trade. The Dutch were easily disheartened. Not so the English; and we read of instances in which the Hanseatics and English acted towards one another with a savagery which proves that commercial rivalry can excite hearts as bitterly and furiously as political or religious fanaticism.

No matter at what cost, monopoly the Germans were resolved to have, and they succeeded in forcing the kings of Denmark to place an interdict upon English trading. This prohibition corresponded to another that they had extorted, according to which all merchandize coming from the extreme end of the Norwegian kingdom was obliged to pass through and halt at their station of Bergen. The purpose of the latter regulation was to concentrate all the productions of the country at a single point; thus offering to the Hanseatics the first refusal of goods, and a power of dominating the market.

Indeed nowhere did their imperious and self-seeking policy show itself in a less amiable light than in the dealings of the Hansa with the poor inhabitants of Norway's sterile coasts. The history of their factory at Bergen is from its earliest foundation the history of a relentless despotism, disfigured by violence and breach of faith in treaties. King Haguin had, in 1376, accorded to the German merchants the right to trade freely in all the burghs, villages, and harbours of his kingdom, but it seemed that they themselves preferred to restrict their business to the town of Bergen, which, it is true, combined uncommon advantages. It possessed an excellent harbour, the city was shielded by an amphitheatre of lofty mountains, and though, as regards climate, it could boast no advantages, more rainy days occurring there than at other points of the Norwegian coast, yet it had early been the staple of all Norwegian and Arctic products. Its geographical situation rendered it equally accessible for travellers from the north and south, while its harbour was so deep that even ships of considerable draught could anchor almost in front of the town's houses.

From the earliest times the inhabitants of Bergen had been traders. In 1393 they were grievously pillaged by the Victual Brothers; and ere they could recover from this misfortune, another pirate, Bartholauer Voet (1428), attacked them, just when the English were helping them to recover their commerce. It is pretty evident that his attack was countenanced, if not commanded, by the Hansa. At sight of his ships the inhabitants fled. The crew were thus enabled to land unhindered; they plundered everything, down to the bishop's palace and his library; and they despoiled the Norman vessels which had come there for the summer fishing. They then took their stolen goods to market, returning the following Easter for a second visit. This time the inhabitants were more on their guard, and made a gallant but vain defence. Once more the city was sacked, and the royal and episcopal palace and many private houses were burnt to ashes.

Shorn of its wealth, Bergen was now so weak that the conquerors were able to dictate their own terms. The city, which for five hundred years had been in exclusive possession of the Greenland passage had to renounce all maritime traffic. Further, the citizens saw themselves forced to pawn their land to the Hanseatics, in return for the mere necessaries of life, and as they could rarely redeem these pledges the whole city of Bergen gradually fell into the hands of these opulent traders.

Expelled from their old dwellings in ancient Bergen, which formed the part of the city known as the Bridge, the inhabitants planned to establish themselves on the harbour board that skirted the opposite side of the crescent. But the insatiable greed of the Hanseatics would not suffer them to stay there. The conquerors obtained this also for themselves, so that in the end the entire port was in their power.

Thus, and by means of an ever-increasing population of merchants, clerks, apprentices, sailors, workmen, they exercised a practical suzerainty over the town. Whenever cited to submit themselves to the local authorities they claimed the privilege of foreigners; they refused to pay city taxes, though they held the rights of citizens, while they paid custom duties at a reduction. They openly protected the enemies of the king, felled the forests, introduced themselves arbitrarily into the houses of strangers; in short, committed every offence with impunity. As in London and Novgorod, so in Bergen, the Hanseatic factory formed a state within the state.

The Hanseatics, in their arbitrary actions, repeatedly ran counter to the Hansa's command and how to keep order at Bergen became one of the most difficult problems at "Hansa days." It would seem as if the rude climate had exercised a deleterious influence over these naturally coarse-grained Germans.

As we have said, the whole harbour board was in their hands. The two sides were connected by the so-called Shoemaker's Alley, long the abode of strangers at Bergen, a quarter that became after a time the residence of all boors and doubtful characters, who shrank from no acts of violence, and defended the German monopoly after their own fashion, i.e., by means of fisticuffs and knives. Thus, as an example: the all-important fish market was so situated that the inhabitants of Bergen could reach it only by means of this street. Until the Germans had had the first pick of newly-arrived goods, the inmates of Shoemaker's Alley suffered no one to pass, and woe to those who ventured to disregard this prohibition. So completely broken was the might of these northern people—the descendants of the Normans, that most warlike race, the scourge of ancient Europe.

The side of the harbour known as the Bridge—the Bridge of the lice the natives called it in derision—was the actual factory of the Hansa. It consisted of so-called gardens, of which nine belonged to the community of St. Martin and thirteen to that of St. Mary. Each garden was isolated, and formed a separate factory, bearing its own crest and name, such as "The Cloak," the "Court of Bremen," &c. The common crest of the Bridge was odd enough, presenting half of the German imperial eagle, against a crowned cod-fish. Each garden was connected with the sea by a drawbridge, so that vessels could anchor in front. The ground-floor consisted of workshops and warehouses: in the first were the bedrooms of the resident merchants, above were the kitchens. Behind the house were mighty cellars, and above these again the "Schutting," a large windowless space used as a council chamber. Opening thence was the kitchen garden.

Every "garden" was inhabited by at least ten "families," each of whom had a husband as chief superintendent and magistrate, to keep order among the younger members and apprentices. As a rule the "family" came from the same Hansa town. The faults of the very young were punished by flogging, those of the apprentices by fines or imprisonment. In the summer the heterogeneous "families" dined alone, in the sad winter time they all met in the "Schutting," but ate at separate tables. At a fixed hour every one had to rise and go to bed.

Superintending the entire factory was a grand council, composed of two aldermen, eighteen members, and a secretary, who had to be a doctor of laws. When conflicts arose between the different members of a family, or between residents and travellers, the matter was referred to the aldermen for decision. Grave cases were sent up to the Hanseatic diet. The aldermen had further to watch over trade, taxes, and all that regarded the business transactions of the colony.

In its time of greatest prosperity the factory at Bergen counted about three thousand souls, all vowed to celibacy, which was imposed on them under most severe penalties. The fear was that union with the native women might lead to the divulging of Hanseatic secrets, or induce the men to settle permanently in this spot, and so become denaturalized. Members of the Hansa were strictly forbidden to spend a night outside the factory. Armed watchmen and savage dogs exercised a rigid guard.

These residents were usually agents for merchants in the Baltic cities. After ten years' sojourn, they were obliged to return to their native town to give place to new arrivals, who then had to go through the various gradations of rank, beginning as office boy, and ending, if luck favoured, as alderman. It was a sort of hierarchic organization, of which the rules were most rigidly enforced. Entrance dues for vessels, fines, and money penances defrayed the general expenses of the factory; each town paid for the board, wages, and arming of its representatives. Not all members of the Hansa, however, were permitted to trade with Bergen, the conditions being purposely made onerous and expensive.

In the same restrictive spirit, and to hinder a great influx of men to the factory, a series of probationary ordeals was planned, through which every new-comer had to pass. By rendering these tests difficult and repulsive they hoped to deter from Bergen the sons of opulent families, for whom the advantages to be gained there would be counterbalanced by the perils of initiation. These "games," as with grim humour they were termed, were entirely in keeping with the grotesque spirit of the age, and analogies are to be found, though less gross, in the religious orders and the institutions of chivalry. The mildest of them resembled in some respects the practices common to British sailors in crossing the line. It is scarcely strange, that in the frigid, rigid north, among a population naturally rough, far from home, friends, and the more refining influences of life, a prey to deadly *ennui*, imagination should have taken a fierce and coarse turn.

We cannot sully our pages by detailing the thirteen different "games" or modes of martyrdom that were in use at Bergen. Our more civilized age could not tolerate the recital. In those days they attracted a crowd of eager spectators, who applauded the more vociferously the more cruel and barbarous the tortures. The most popular were those practices known as the smoke, water, and flogging games; mad, cruel pranks, calculated to cause a freshman to lose health and reason. Truly Dantesque hell tortures were these initiations into Hansa mysteries. Merely to indicate their nature we will mention that for the smoke game the victim was pulled up the big chimney of the Schutting while there burnt beneath him the most filthy materials, sending up a nauseous stench and choking wreaths of smoke. While in this position he was asked a number of questions, to which he was forced, under yet more terrible penalties, to reply. If he survived this torture he was taken out into the yard and plied under the pump with six tons of water.

The "water" game that took place at Whitsuntide consisted in first treating the probationer to food, and then taking him out to sea in a boat. Here he was stripped, thrown into the ocean, ducked three times, made to swallow much sea-water, and thereafter mercilessly flogged by all the inmates of the boats. The third chief game was no less dangerous to life and limb. It took place a few days after, and was a rude perversion of the May games. The victims had first to go out into the woods to gather the branches with which later they were to be birched. Returned to the factory, rough horse-play pranks were practised upon them. Then followed an ample dinner, which was succeeded by mock combats, and ended in the victims being led into the so-called Paradise, where twenty-four disguised men whipped them till they drew blood, while outside this black hole another party made hellish music with pipes, drums, and triangles to deafen the screams of the tortured. The "game" was considered ended when the shrieks of the victims were sufficiently loud to overtone the pandemonic music.

When all the ordeals were ended a herald, who also occupied the *rôle* of fool, announced in a loud voice that the games were over, adding the fervent wish that the noble practice of ordeals might never be abandoned, and that for the honour and prosperity of the Hansa commerce and the Hanseatic factory they might ever be held in veneration.

Only those who survived and sustained these rites were admitted into the corporation at Bergen and could rise to the highest grades, with the prospect of assisting as spectators at the games in which before they had themselves played a part. Not till 1671 were these barbarous practices, which every year increased in ferocity, suppressed by order of Christian V. of Denmark, and only, of course, after the Hansa had sunk from its pristine power.

V.

THE HANSEATIC COMMERCE WITH DENMARK, SWEDEN, AND RUSSIA.

THOUGH the Government of Denmark was more enlightened than that of Norway, and though the Danes were jealously desirous of keeping their trade in their own hands, they, too, could not free themselves from the all-absorbing power of the Hanseatic League. In vain did they endeavour to raise up rivals to these traders; in vain did they even encourage pirates to attack them; in vain did they institute custom dues and taxes; each and all of these measures proved insufficient. The credit of the towns was unassailable. The Hanseatics knew how to vanquish all obstacles, and finally they found themselves in full possession of all their ancient privileges, as well as those which they had extorted in concluding peace with Waldemar.

The dissensions of the three northern kingdoms, which lasted for nearly fifty years, and which the Hanseatic League were by no means anxious to see settled (for, above all else, they feared the union of the three northern kingdoms under one head) were admirably utilized. The League played off one set of enemies against another, now aided this faction, now sided with that, never too openly expressed either sympathy or hostility, and yet always contrived so that any advantages accruing were theirs.

It was in those troubled times that Lübeck bought from the Danish king the town of Kiel and adjoining lands, while the queen pawned her jewels to the city in order to raise money for war purposes.

Denmark was of immense importance to the Hanseatic League, not only for the grain and cattle it produced, but because it was the key to the passages of the Belt and the Sound, the only maritime routes for passing from the Baltic to the North Sea. And, above all, the Sound was of first-class importance as dominating the coveted province of Scania, that mediæval Peru. This tongue of land, which juts out into the sea in form of a hook on the extreme south-west of Sweden, and shows to-day two miserable towns, Skânoe and Falsterbo, almost buried in driving sand, presented in the fourteenth and fifteenth centuries, from St. Jacob's to St. Michael's Day (July 25th to September 29th), a most animated spectacle. Nothing more strange is to be found in either hemisphere than was the tumultuous life of this arid province. Here each foot of ground was jealously disputed by fishermen and merchants.

Englishmen, Flemings, Danes, and peoples of tongues and customs the most diverse were found side by side. But the Hanseatics preponderated. They established themselves in a species of rude wooden barrack called by them Witten, where they at once instituted their peculiar rules and privileges, which gave them that united power which in the end enabled them to crush out all competition. For the device of the Hanseatics, though unexpressed, was "Monopoly," and during these centuries they carried it rigidly into effect. The word Witten still survives in the name of various fishing stations on the Baltic; for example, one not far remote from the old pagan city of Arkona, once the site of a temple, where the Christian Saxons bought the right to fish by paying tribute to the local god.

The main object of the trade in Scandinavia was herrings, but this brought many other industries in its train. Itinerant merchants offered cloth, linen, hardware, wine, beer, and many other articles to the natives, whose country boasted no handicrafts, as well as to the temporary residents. In short, the place became a market for the exchange of Western and Eastern products, natural and manufactured. Here could be seen the Lübeck cooks busy in extemporized kitchens that formed a sort of rude restaurant; here rough taverns in which German drinks were obtainable at easy prices; here German shoemakers plied their skill; above all, the coopers drove a lively trade, making and mending the barrels needed for the precious fish. The import of salt, too, was obviously of first-class importance, and this was entirely in the hands of the Germans. We might expect that during the busy period when thousands of men were hard at work fishing, salting, packing the herring, beer should have been drunk in large quantities, but the amount consumed almost passes belief. This also was entirely supplied by the Hanseatic cities. It was they, too, who shipped the indispensable fish and sent it to England, France, the Netherlands, the Baltic, nay, far into the centre of Germany, and even to Poland and Russia.

They had not in Scania, as at Bergen, a regularly organized factory, but the Witten stood under superintendence, while at adjacent Malmö they founded a permanent colony, under the jurisdiction of an alderman, who administered Lübeck law and watched over the Witten trade with jealous care. Here each town had its guild representative, often its house, and here annually a dignitary from Lübeck would pay a passing visit in order to adjust quarrels and investigate the state of trade.

The "Scandinavian travellers," as they were named, instituted a number of companies with rules of a religious, commercial, and worldly-sensuous character. Thus the "Pious Brotherhood of Malmö" buried every poor stranger with the same church pomp, costly palls, candles and masses, as they would one of their own members. No one was admitted into the brotherhood who was at feud with one of its associates. No one might enter the common room bearing arms. A member who introduced a guest was responsible for his good behaviour. In a word, the regulations were of a certain humane character, far different from those which obtained at Bergen. They were evidently copied from those of the guilds in the Hanseatic and other towns of the Middle Ages.

Until early in the sixteenth century the League retained in undiminished vigour its advantages in Scandinavia. To break their power it was necessary for the Dutch to discover a better mode of salting the fish. Then the fish itself came in smaller shoals to these coasts, and appeared instead near Scotland and Ireland, and, worst of all, modern Europe became Protestant, and fasting was hence no longer an obligatory fashion. Only a few sunken gravestones, still standing amid the desolation of this district, bear witness to the former importance of the site.

As for the rest of Sweden, the country, though not productive, was still of value to the Hanseatics, since they held the entire trade in their hands. As from Norway, they exported wood, iron, copper, skins, in a word, explored all its resources. In most of the maritime towns they exercised certain rights. Thus Stockholm itself was partly in their possession, the local administration being half chosen by them. In this wise they were able to bring pressure to bear upon the government. In short, they disposed of the whole commerce of Sweden, and it was not until the days of Gustavus Vasa that their might was rudely and completely shaken.

Indeed, in those middle centuries there seemed no limit to the Hanseatics' ambition and power. They early cast their eyes towards that immense territory in the far north, that Russian Empire which in those days was truly an unknown land. With quick traders' instinct they recognized that the country was worthy to be included in their vast monopoly. When they first established themselves in Russia is not known. Towards the end of the thirteenth century we find them in possession of a factory at Novgorod, on the river Volchor, a city which, with the province that surrounded it, was then an independent republic, for the Russia of those days was surrounded by various principalities mostly under Tartar rule. The natives were not strong enough to claim as their own a rich and populous city, whose liberties were protected by the Western Christians, and which had moreover been founded by aliens, namely, by one of those enterprising Norman chiefs, who in early times were, as we know, the terror of all states and countries.

It is thought that the Hanseatics had another similar establishment at Pleskow, a city on the Velika, and perhaps even a depôt at Moscow, but undoubtedly Novgorod was their most important station. Here merchants and artizans fixed their abode, and drew around them a rich commerce for the town. It was the staple for Arctic and Byzantine riches, riches which the more barbarian Russians did not understand how to utilize like our cunning traders. As early as the eleventh century we hear of a German trading settlement at Novgorod. In 1269 the local ruler accorded to the Hanseatics, "to the German settlement, the Goths, and all peoples of Latin tongue," special freedom in dealing with his province.

As usual, the Hanseatics created a monopoly and jealously excluded all strangers. Assigned in Novgorod to a special quarter of the town, they built a church of their own, dedicated to St. Peter, and grouped their guildhall, shops, stores, and dwelling-houses around it. The quarter soon became known as the Court of the Germans at Great Novgorod, or the Court of St. Peter. As at Bergen, it was built in such a manner that it could be defended, if need be, and at night it was closed and guarded by watchmen and fierce dogs.

There is happily preserved for us the Codex of this German colony on the Lake of Ilmen. It is called the Skra, an old German word which we encounter elsewhere in Hanseatic chronicles. This Skra furnishes a lively picture of the strange character of the Court of St. Peter. It appears that "the entire council, together with the common consent of the wisest of all the German cities," had decreed that the laws here laid down should be enforced on all who visited the court, "as it was done from the commencement." The non-resident merchants, who always travelled in large parties and accompanied by a priest, are spoken of as the "summer and winter travellers." They elected from out of their number the alderman of the Court of St. Peter. He became head of the settlement, received the income, fees, and taxes, and defrayed the general costs. The alderman of the dwelling court was the highest dignitary and, with the aid of the four wisest, adjudged all quarrels, personal or commercial. These aldermen had special privileges in the choice of residence, and the aldermen of the "winter travellers" were further allowed certain honours and comforts in the great common room. The land travellers had to yield to the seafarers in all matters of convenience and space. Their priest, too, was regarded as the chief ecclesiastic of St. Peter's Court, and to him alone was accorded free board and a salary out of the common funds. Any one who refused to appear in answer to a summons before the court was subjected to a heavy fine. The so-called "rooms" (i.e., dwellings) were common to all; except that the "winter travellers," secluded from all the world in midst of the long Arctic nights, were permitted special privileges. The "children's room," the abode of the younger clerks and apprentices, also enjoyed rather more freedom from strict rules than was accorded to their elders. A master might not dismiss his subordinate until he had brought him back to his country; he was also bound to care for him in sickness, and might not punish him arbitrarily, or on his own authority alone. As at Bergen, and at the Steelyard in London, the whole establishment partook of a monastic character, in which most stringent rules prevailed. And of these rules none was more strict than that which forbad social intercourse or partnership trading with natives.

A special brewery concocted the sweet mead or beer drunk by the thirsty brotherhood of St. Peter's; in St. Peter's cauldron was melted down all the wax brought in from afar; the wood for firing was felled in St. Peter's forests. A monotonous life it was, interrupted only in spring and autumn by the arrival of the summer and winter travellers with their rich wares. In the cosy warmth of the common room, over endless bowls of mead, these far-travelled men, snowed up here and unable to return till spring released them, would beguile the long winter evenings with anecdote and tales. In this wise the Scandinavian Sagas first penetrated into Middle and Southern Germany.

The rules made against the Russians were severe and offensive in the extreme. It is evident they were not trusted in the smallest degree. A Hanseatic enjoyed the first privilege in all respects. For example, if a native was bankrupt, the German merchant to whom he was in debt had the first right to be paid before Russian creditors, and the Germans could further insist that such a bankrupt should be banished the city with wife and child. By way of tax they themselves paid a piece of cloth to the ruler of the mainland between their Court and the sea, and a pair of gloves to the Russian officials.

For the rest their whole attitude was haughty and overbearing, and it is scarcely astonishing that quarrels and risings against them were of frequent occurrence. But they almost always kept or at least regained the upper hand. Their audacious motto was "Who can stand against God and the Great Novgorod?" No doubt many of their rigid measures were necessary to a small colony living amid a turbulent and rude population, differing from them in manners, language, and religion. The station was as difficult to hold as years ago was that of Canton for the English. Like the Chinese, the Russians hated the merchants, if for no other reason than because they were foreigners. In every possible manner they tried to cheat them, adulterating wax, furnishing bad furs, &c., &c. In consequence, the alderman of St. Peter's saw himself obliged continually to issue new warnings and rules to secure his traders from the Russian tricksters. So, for example, the dwellers of the Court of St. Peter were enjoined only to buy furs in well-lighted places, where it was easier to test their genuineness and excellence, further to accept no large consignments that had not been previously subjected to careful scrutiny. And notwithstanding the fact that their commerce in Russia was subjected to great danger, that they even had several times to close their court and withdraw, the Hanseatics clung tenaciously to their Russian monopoly, which was one of the chief sources of their wealth. They even watched to see that no non-Hanseatic learnt Russian, an indispensable acquirement for this trade. Nay, at one time they held the whole province of Livonia responsible for hindering such a proceeding. After a time, under penalty of one hundred marks, no Russian was allowed to live in Livonia. On pain of corporal punishment, they were enjoined to treat with Russians only for ready money, or more strictly for ready goods. Credit with these barbarians was not encouraged, for it was desirable in every way to simplify intercourse, and moreover then, as now, it was next to impossible to a foreigner to make good his credit claims before Muscovite justice.

The trade consisted in Russian products, furs, metals, honey, and, above all, wax, much sought after in those Catholic times, when the consumption of this article was wonderfully great. It would seem as though some obscure merit were attached to the burning or the gift of candles, the origin of which is probably heathen. What the Hanseatics brought to market was chiefly Flemish and English cloths and linen, as well as divers articles of luxury, eagerly sought after by the various princes and sovereigns and by the innumerable Boyars who ranked like petty princes.

In those large and small courts a barbaric and gorgeous display was common, and ostentatious rivalry existed between the princes. Probably this love of exterior pomp is explained by their neighbourhood to the East. The Hanseatics astutely utilized this Russian tendency, and spared no pains in bringing to market wares calculated to dazzle and please these grown children; children in this respect alone however, that they could be fascinated by finery and show. In other matters the Russians behaved like adults, and they kept a constant watch upon the Hanseatics, never neglecting any opportunities of annoying them or hindering their trade. Thus, if the League accused the Russians of want of good faith in commercial dealings, they returned the compliment, and complaints of linen goods as being too narrow, too coarse, or not according to sample, were frequent. Often these were justified, as often not. But on several occasions the Russians arrested Hanseatics, put them in irons, even on one occasion hanged a Hanseatic merchant from the door of the League's own factory. The Hanseatics met such insults by threatening to leave Novgorod; indeed, carried out this threat several times, but love of gain on the one hand, hunger after luxuries on the other, appeased the troubled spirits, and peace was re-established on the old footing. These treaties of reconciliation were sealed by the Germans with a key in a shield, the seal of St. Peter's Court. The Russians swore fidelity by kissing the crucifix.

But as such disturbances might always recur, and in order that the damage should not prove too heavy to members of the League, it was decreed by them in the fourteenth century that no merchant might send to or store at Novgorod merchandise exceeding in value the sum of a thousand marks. This shows that their position at Novgorod was rather that of a hostile encampment than that of a secure and permanent settlement.

Above all, the Hanseatics strictly forbade Russia to trade on the sea, and any Russian merchant ships that they encountered were captured and the captain and crew severely punished.

Early in the twelfth century the clever Lombards, already famous throughout Europe for their skill in all banking transactions, tried to gain a footing at Novgorod. It seems that their financial shrewdness was not always combined with the strictest honesty, and that hence they enjoyed an ill fame. Certainly the Hanseatics succeeded in 1405 in prohibiting "these dangerous men" from any residence in the Baltic cities, while in St. Peter's Court their presence was formally proscribed in 1346.

A serious interruption to the commerce of the League with Russia occurred in the middle of the fifteenth century, when the Prussian towns revolted against the oppressive supremacy of the chivalric order of the Teutonic Knights. Like all spiritual powers, when it is a question of the goods of this world, the Teutonic Knights fought ardently to regain their power, and this warfare long rendered the Baltic dangerous and impossible for trade purposes. Indeed, so long and so serious was this war that but for the fact that the League was in a sufficiently flourishing condition to be able to bear great losses, and also for the fact that the Russian trade was worth many sacrifices, the League might even then have been permanently crushed.

More serious was the next enemy who arose and who shook to its foundations the empire of Hanseatic commerce in Russia. This was the Czar Ivan II., known as the Terrible. He had conquered and chased from his domains the savage Tartar hordes that annually ravaged it; he was ambitious to unite the whole Muscovite kingdom under his sway. Like his successors to this day, he hated all that savoured of liberty and independence, and was resolved to exclude from his realms everything that approached a more advanced civilization and was irreconcilable with absolute rule.

He cast a jealous eye on Novgorod, with its political independence and its prosperity. Here, he said to himself, were rich spoils to be obtained; this power within his own domains must be broken. He tried, with success, to gain over to his side a portion of the population. These were, however, soon denounced as traitors to the community, and the great bell of Novgorod, regarded as the Palladium of popular liberty, was rung to call the city under arms. A violent struggle ensued, in which Ivan committed many of those acts of cruelty that have made his name notorious.

At last, after a gallant resistance, in which especially a woman, named Marsa, took a leading part, Novgorod fell into the hands of Ivan, who despoiled it of its liberty and riches, and sent its chief inhabitants into the centre of his empire and replaced them by his Muscovites; burnt, ravaged, pillaged, and sacked, so that at one blow the town lost its liberty, lustre, and prosperity. The great bell of freedom was carried to Moscow, where to this day it hangs, no longer inciting to revolt, but calling the people to prayer. As for the Hanseatics at Novgorod, they were taken prisoner and kept in cruel durance. Their merchandise was confiscated, and all their possessions, such as church ornaments, bells, silver vases, &c., were carried off in triumph to Moscow.

This blow came upon them like a thunderbolt, for all their privileges had just been reconfirmed by the Russian ruler. But to Ivan no sacred treaties were binding. Only after many years and long negotiations did the Hanseatics succeed in getting him at least to release their prisoners. When he did agree to this most had already died from the effects of privation. Of the confiscated goods he would not return a bale.

Thus ended the glory of the Hanseatic rule in Russia. It is true that under Ivan's son the cities once more endeavoured to open their court on the Volchor. But a twenty years' interruption of trade was not easily made good. They could not recover their monopoly, which had been usurped by Danes and Dutchmen. The last blow to all such efforts came from the English, who had discovered a passage to Russia by means of the White Sea and Archangel, and hence no longer needed Hanseatic mediation. In 1603 Czar Boris Gudenow wanted to reinstate the Hansa in its ancient privileges. It was too late. The dissensions that agitated Russia did not permit the League to derive any profit from his good intentions. Commerce had taken another direction, and kept it. When, some time after, a traveller passed through Novgorod, all he found to remind him of the German colony here were only the ruins of the stone church of St. Peter, a single storehouse, and one wooden shanty, which served as shelter for him and his servant. Of the former glory and prosperity there was no sign.

VI.

THE COMMERCE OF THE LEAGUE WITH THE NETHERLANDS AND SOUTHERN EUROPE.

AMONG the Western countries not even England attracted the attention of the League so powerfully as did the Netherlands, with their cosmopolitan market of Bruges, a market which, as early as the days of King Canute, was already of great importance. There was to be found every element needful to second their vast ambition and to foster their activity. In Flanders lived the most industrious nation in Europe, dwelling in opulent cities, having excellent harbours and markets, where all the necessaries of life, and all objects of luxury abounded. In these markets our traders could find all the articles most eagerly sought after by the inhabitants of more northern climes, while they, in their turn, could furnish the Flemings with the productions of the North, and especially with those which were necessary to a maritime people. Thus the League had cunningly got into their hands the whole monopoly of hemp, so needful for rope making. Indeed, it must ever be borne in mind that the Hansa had the monopoly in those days of the whole industry and of all the products of Northern and Eastern Europe. This active and profitable commerce was almost entirely carried on by means of the factory which the League had established at Bruges. It was here that its merchants supplied themselves in their turn with the manufactures of the industrious Flemings; with cloth, linen, and the costly tapestries admired to our day.

It was at Bruges, then, that the vast ramifications of Flemish and Hanseatic trade were united. Fifteen different foreign nations held established depôts in the city which was a very artery of commerce. Sixty-eight Flemish trade-guilds flourished in the town. It communicated with the sea by means of a canal and a not too distant harbour. Extensive privileges had been accorded to it by various native princes. The inhabitants were proud, rich, and independent. It was said of them by a contemporary that the merchant-aristocrats of Bruges "rode to tournament yesterday, bottled wine to-day, cut out garments to-morrow." A queen of France could not deny that the splendour and luxury of the courts were cast into the shade by the pomp and splendour of the maids and matrons of commercial Bruges. With these men commerce had already become a science, and various peoples who had till then the most elementary notions on the point came to the Netherlands to instruct themselves. It is surprising to read that, as early as 1310, they had instituted at Bruges an insurance office, and that the chief principles affecting exchange of values were already understood. These matters were novelties even to the Hanseatics, though they owed their prosperity and very existence to trade.

The League therefore found itself in a totally different position in the Netherlands from that which it occupied in poor or barbarous countries like Norway or Russia. Here was no question of submitting a whole people to their monopoly; it was rather a matter of obtaining gracious concessions and privileges. Hence the factory at Bruges in no way resembled those of Bergen and Novgorod, which were armed citadels placed in the midst of a more or less hostile people and constantly liable to warlike attacks. Here, on the other hand, civilization reigned and competition was active. The Hanseatic factory at Bruges partook more of the character of a general office and storehouse than that of any other factory of the League. But "the Residence of the German Merchants," as it was called, was organized in the main like that of its brethren. In its most prosperous days the factory consisted of about three hundred traders or agents, who executed the orders to buy and sell for those Hanseatic merchants who did not come to Bruges in person to carry on their trade. These resident merchants were not permitted to quit the factory until after a certain number of years' sojourn. During this time they were interdicted from associating with the natives. They lived in the Hanseatic building under the supervision of six aldermen and a council composed of eighteen members, and there were in force for them here as elsewhere rigid rules of life, among which the imposition of celibacy took a leading place. The factory was partitioned into several chief divisions called "districts," where the members from different cities abode in almost monastic seclusion. Less rude customs, however, prevailed than at Bergen. The Hanseatics being in the midst of a polished and luxury-loving people, acquired some of their more civilized habits. By way of Bruges comforts and refinements penetrated into German homes, and Flemish modes of thought and speech crept into German literature.

The factory at Bruges was in every respect of immense value to Germany and the Hansa. It grew into a sort of training college from which came forth the most able magistrates and administrators of the Hanseatic League.

The head of the factory was a president chosen by the Diet of the League. He was changed annually, usually at Whitsuntide, when the by-laws of the factory were read and the newly elected had to swear "to submit to its statutes, to see that these were observed without fraud as far as in him lay and according to his five senses."

As elsewhere expenses were paid by fines and customs dues. These latter some cities tried to elude at various times in a spirit of egotistic and most short-sighted policy. Chief among these was Cologne which was in consequence "unhansed" for some time. Indeed Cologne was always a more or less turbulent member of the League. The official meetings of the Hanseatic representatives at Bruges curiously enough did not take place in their own factory, but were held in the Reventer, that is to say, the refectory of the Carmelite convent. Their charters were deposited in the church sacristy, or more precisely in the so-called Noah's ark, this alliance between sacred and profane things being a common feature of those times.

As the might of the League increased at Bruges they insisted that every vessel sailing the seas must make an enforced halt at the port of Bruges, and thus give the traders a first chance of buying their wares or, in any case, of exacting from them a staple toll. Exception was made only in the case of ships sailing to England or to the Baltic seaboard. The possession of this privilege naturally proved a source of great wealth and power to the League, who grew proud and haughty as they increased in strength, and even ventured to oppose themselves to the Flemings, if they considered that these had in any way offended against "the majesty of the Hanseatic nation in the person of any of its members or officers." They would then threaten to transport their factory into some other city, and once actually carried out the threat. They suspended all trade with Flanders, blocked its ports, and refused to buy its goods. At the last the murmurs of the artizans thus thrown out of work, and the general distress among the people, forced the rulers to crave grace and to beg for the return of these masterful strangers, even according them new privileges, that is to say, new weapons of oppression. For the League, on these occasions of proud resentment, took the most menacing of tones and exacted a heavy satisfaction. Thus once, because one of its members had been, as it considered, gravely insulted, and others murdered, it demanded that a chapel should be built and masses founded to pray for the repose of the souls of those who had perished; and that a large indemnity should be paid to the relations of the dead and to the division of the League to which they belonged. And, further, in order to induce this division to return to Bruges, it was requisite that one hundred of the chief burghers should come in procession to the Carmelite convent and ask public pardon from the Hanseatics, and that sixteen of these should go in pilgrimage to Santiago de Compastello and four to the Holy Sepulchre at Jerusalem. Only after such expiation would the division allow itself to be re-established.

The dissensions and revolutions which, in the fourteenth century, convulsed Flanders and caused the sovereignty of the provinces to pass into the hands of the Dukes of Burgundy, did not, for a long time, touch the commerce of the Hanseatics. Their trade seemed able to cope with the subversive influences of tumults, seditions, and civil wars; their activity was not discouraged; their great credit enabled them to repair all losses, and even to draw profit from these very disturbing influences themselves. Each new ruler, guided by the same motives of interest, awarded the same favour to this association of strangers, who, in coming to their country, nourished its industries and profitably exchanged products. Even Charles the Bold—proud and warlike though he was, a declared foe to all liberty, attacking at that very time the Swiss people, who were striving to gain their national independence—openly protected the Hanseatic towns, and interested himself warmly in aiding them to overcome the English, with whom they had been at strife.

This good understanding, it is true, was impaired under Maximilian of Austria, his son-in-law and successor. This prince was a stranger to the Flemings, a German by birth, accustomed to exact blind obedience, the son of an emperor and his heir. On all these accounts he was distasteful to the Flemings, who rose up in revolt against him, and imprisoned him in the Castle of Bruges. It was on this occasion that there happened an event made famous in legend. Maximilian's Court jester, who loved his master, had formed a plan for his liberation. Horses, rope ladders—all were in readiness. The jester himself sprang into the canal that separated the castle from the mainland, in order to swim across and aid his sovereign. But it happened that his night raid alarmed the swans which were kept by the town on this canal. They raised a great noise, flapped their wings in anger, and threatened to kill the poor fellow, who was obliged to beat a hasty retreat, while his scheme, thus discovered, was rendered futile. For four months Maximilian was kept in confinement. No sooner was he liberated and master of the empire than he took his revenge. This audacity was punished severely, and ended in a loss to Flanders of its opulence and a great part of its industry. Above all, the town of Bruges had to submit to hard treatment, and ceased from that time forwards to be the most flourishing and important market of Europe.

The wily Hanseatics had, meanwhile, acted like the proverbial rats that abandon the sinking ship. Seeing the course that things were taking, they sought to establish themselves elsewhere, and Antwerp, long jealous of Bruges, obtained the reversion of its rival's trade: the fruits of which it enjoyed until the murderous hordes of Philip II., in their turn, crushed Antwerp as Maximilian had crushed Bruges.

No doubt, by means of the Flemish market, the League also treated with France, but our knowledge concerning this trade is very scanty. It seems certain that they had no regular factory in that country, though for a short time they held a depôt at Bordeaux. Probably their trade with France was chiefly indirect and by means of Flanders. The fact that for so long the greater part of the French seaboard was in the hands of the English may have had something to do with this matter. We know, however, that successive French kings accorded to them various privileges. Louis XI., on one occasion, speaks of them as a "Power," and proposed to make an alliance with them against England. Charles VIII. yet further enlarged the concessions granted by his father. It is even recorded that in case any difficulties arose because of obscurities of phrase in a contract made between the League and Frenchmen, these should always be interpreted to the advantage of the Hanseatics. They were further promised impartial justice, reduced custom dues, and a civil standing equal in all respects to that of the natives. The kingdom was open to them for trading purposes, and in case of a war breaking out between France and a foreign nation, the Hanseatics were allowed to continue their commercial connection with that nation without being regarded as violating the peace and friendship promised. France, on the other hand, reserved to itself the same privileges. But why France was willing to concede so much to these strangers does not appear. The commerce can in no case have been considerable. The manufactures of France in those days were few and limited. Their small navy did not require much wood, iron, or hemp. It is true they had their wines and their salt, and that in exchange they bought herrings and smoked fish, but there was no such lively and profitable intercourse as we encounter elsewhere. The land was still too poor, too distracted with wars and dissensions to be able to utilize its native riches. Besides this, her own direct commerce with the Mediterranean and Latin East, and the Crusaders and Italian traders, rendered her more independent of Hansa help.

Very scanty are the records that have come down to us concerning the trade of the League with Spain. This nation, incessantly occupied in wars with the Moors and in chivalrous exploits, neglected and disdained trade. They even went so far at times as to interdict it also to others. But all that has come down to us concerning the intercourse of the Hanseatics with this country is so vague, and borders so much on the fabulous, that it cannot be accepted as history. What does seem certain is that in 1383 King John of Castile forbade the Hanseatics to have any intercourse with his kingdom, that he confiscated eighty-four of their vessels, and that in 1441 the factory of Bruges received orders to practise reprisals upon the Spaniards and to close to them all the ports of the Netherlands. All details, however, are lacking. We only know, again, for certain that in 1472 the Spaniards raised the interdict against the League. No doubt they had suffered pecuniarily from the absence of these active traders. In 1551 Philip II. even went so far as to sign a treaty of commerce with the League, in which this prince favoured them as much as his predecessors tried to harm them. And this treaty, strange to say, was not quite a nullity even at the beginning of our own century. On the strength of certain clauses contained in it were founded various privileges enjoyed up to that date, in their commercial intercourse with Spain, by the cities that were then all that remained of the once mighty League—namely, Lübeck, Hamburg, and Bremen.

In Portugal the League was more fortunate than in Spain, and early established a factory at Lisbon. From this port they traded with the Mediterranean, and came in contact with the flourishing Italian commercial republics, as well as with the products of the Levant and India, for which Italy was the sole market. But the Italian trade was chiefly in the hands of the South German cities, such as Augsburg, Ulm, and Nüremberg, and the wares were transported by land. These cities formed a counter league among themselves, which, though in a measure affiliated to the Hansa, was never quite an integral part. Their sole object was the Levant and Italian trade. Already in the thirteenth century they had a depôt at Venice, the far-famed Fontego de' Tedeschi, which visitors to Venice behold to this day as one of the most lovely palaces abutting on the Grand Canal. This factory, however, was very differently constituted from that of other cities. The League never obtained a monopoly or special privileges in Italy. The Fontego at Venice was merely the warehouse or dwelling-house of the German traders, without any internal jurisdiction or president.

They were permitted to sojourn with their wares at stated times in Venice, received on their arrival the keys of the fifty-six rooms of the building, which on their departure they had to re-deliver to the Venetian authorities. In course of time the Germans, gaining refinement and acquiring a love of art from their Italian intercourse, spent large sums in decorating and adorning this palace, which, however, never passed into their real possession. Three Venetian citizens, under the title of Visdomini de' Tedeschi, and native secretaries, and a "fontegaro," always inhabited the building and kept strict watch over the traders, whose commerce was subjected to all manner of tedious restrictions. The house, as we have said, was only open to them at stated times of the year. They were only permitted to sell to and buy from Venetians; all wares exported or imported had to be weighed in the public balances, and only this weight was accepted as just. The Italian secretaries, one of whom always slept in the Fontego, kept strict account of all goods that came to hand or were sent away, and the control over these wares was in the power of the Visdomini. Nothing might be unladen in the warehouse without permission from one of these local officials. But in spite of all these restrictions, which the Germans would not have tolerated for a moment at Bergen or Bruges, their depôt at Venice was a favourite sojourn, and remained the centre of a pleasant, easy, and refined intercourse between Germany and Italy until the time of the Reformation. The influence of the Rialto made itself felt in Prague, Dresden, Frankfort, and the other South German cities, and has placed its imprint upon their literature and art. From Italy these cities brought the models to adorn their streets, markets, guildhalls, and churches. From Italy they brought the tales and fables that delighted listeners long before the days of printing, and awoke the native mediæval poetic art, so that the stories of Boccaccio became as familiar to the Germans as to the Italians themselves. In spite of all the restrictions they placed on their freedom, the foreigners were not unwelcome to the proud Venetian signoria. They even spoke of the German nation as their "cuorisino" (little heart), and in their sore need, during the time of the League of Cambray, formed by the Pope, the Emperor and the kings of France and Spain against the Republic of Venice (1508), they called upon their German friends for sympathy, and did not call in vain. The bond of a common interest, that of trade, bound together the proud rich city of the Lagoons and the less powerful, less wealthy, but by no means poor or insignificant, cities of Southern Germany.

VII.

THE STEELYARD IN LONDON.

Nowhere was the Hanseatic power so great as in England. Of none of its connections do we possess more ample records. As already stated, England was one of the first depôts of the "common German merchant," long before these combined under the generic name of Hanseatic. From early days the English kings had protected these rich foreigners, who helped them out of many a pecuniary difficulty. Indeed they accorded them such privileges and monopolies as could not fail to rouse the jealousy of their own people. We therefore find in the history of the Steelyard in London a mingled record of all passions and interests, hate and favours, honour and national prosperity, envy and violence, greed and poverty, pride and fear, in a word, a most motley record of which it is not easy to frame the contradictory elements into one harmonious picture.

During the long reign of Henry II., and under his sons, Richard Cœur de Lion and John, there was an active intercourse between Germany and England, encouraged by the marriage of Matilda, daughter of Henry II. with Duke Henry the Lion.

The rich merchants of Cologne were the earliest to obtain special favours. These were accorded by Richard Cœur de Lion, who, halting in that city to attend high mass in the cathedral after his release from Austrian imprisonment, received there such ample supplies towards the heavy ransom money required for his person, that, to show his gratitude, he gave to his "beloved burghers of Cologne" a letter of freedom, in which he released them from their annual rent of two shillings for their guildhall in London, and from all other taxes due to the king upon their persons or their merchandise. It was long ere King John, his successor, could make up his mind to renew these privileges, but his own difficulties with his turbulent barons, and the pressure which the merchants could bring to bear by their riches, at last overcame his hesitation. Edward I. and his followers further extended these prerogatives, for the Plantagenets found the Hanseatic

Rothschilds even more useful in aiding their war schemes than the skilful alchymists whom they had summoned to their Court, and who knew how to shape the Rose noble (the money of the period) out of artificial gold. Then, too, the Hanseatics were considerate creditors, who did not press unduly, and even overlooked a debt if some favour were extended in default of payment.

Edward the Third's crown and most costly jewels were long retained at Cologne in pawn for a heavy sum of money. The details concerning this transaction are preserved to this day in a correspondence deposited in the State Paper Office of London. It seems that when the time for redemption came the king had not the money. He was in special straits just then, for the celebrated commercial firm of the Bardi, at Florence, which constituted the very focus of the Italian money business, had failed, and the King of England appeared in their books as a debtor for the sum of one million golden gulden. The merchants of the Steelyard were not slow adroitly to turn the royal perplexity to their profit. They undertook to redeem the pawned jewels and offered the king loans of more money, although he already owed them much. Edward was in sore need, for the wars with France strained his resources to the utmost. He drew upon them for thirty thousand pounds, a sum worth fifteen times more then than to-day. Thus it came about that the great victories of the Black Prince at Crecy and Poitiers were gained in no small degree by the help of German capital. Needless to add that the Hanseatic merchants showed no diffidence in accepting for their factory important privileges in return for these services.

It was to a German merchant prince that the king let the tin mines belonging to the Black Prince in the Duchy of Cornwall. To the same firm he ceded a large number of farms situated in different shires for the space of a thousand years.

The Easterlings are spoken of in records as the allies of the English kings, and there seemed at last no limit to the royal favours.

That the people did not look upon them with the same friendly eye is easy to understand. The English, full of a just sentiment of what they could do by themselves, and of what they were hindered from doing by these foreign monopolists, bore their presence with extreme impatience. Feuds and riots were not infrequent, and no royal favours, no Hanseatic ships of war could save them from occasional brutal attacks at the hands of the mob. Thus during the Wat Tyler rebellion the people pursued the hated foreigners even into the sanctuary of the church, murdering mercilessly all those who could not pronounce the words "bread and cheese" with the pure English accent. But these rebellions were quelled by the royal commands, or extinguished themselves by the fact that the Hanseatics were also useful to the English people, oppressed by the feudal system and engaged in constant wars, whose trade industries were thus unable to develop quickly. Nor did such passing storms shake the power or the resistance of the Hanseatics. Bloody encounters, rude tumults were entirely in keeping with the license and roughness of those earlier ages, and were met by the League, more or less, in all their foreign stations.

With their usual astuteness they utilized wisely all periods of calm, and reckoned with the love of gain to help them in less peaceful moments. When the English made things uncomfortable for them at home, they revenged themselves upon them at Bruges or at Bergen, paralysing their commerce, and harassing their vessels, even forbidding them to enter the ports of Norway, Iceland, and Greenland. For verily in those days whosoever tried to outwit the Hansa was likely to prove the victim of his own plots. Circumstances aided the Germans, enabling them to make their power felt just when England had to betray weakness. The feeble and stormy period of Henry VI., often deposed and made prisoner, the Wars of the Roses, the long and continual hostilities waged with France, all favoured the League, and made the English submit to its demands rather than attract to themselves yet more enemies.

In no place, not even in Bergen, did the Hanseatics succeed in enjoying greater independence. Their factory was privileged, and while benefiting by English law, they were quite independent of it.

Everything, therefore, was favourable to their commerce, and they were hampered by no such restrictions as weighed, not only upon other foreigners, but upon the English themselves. To give a just idea of the degree of power to which their privileges and trade had raised the League, let us cite one example. It will serve in lieu of many, and it places in full light the almost incredible ascendency which a company of merchant cities, isolated and distant from each other, had gained over a great kingdom and a proud and valiant nation.

The English Government having been unable or unwilling to repress the frequent acts of piracy which its subjects practised against members of the League, these also took to piracy, and mutual recriminations ensued. The Lübeckers in particular revenged themselves fiercely. They also wrote a letter of complaint to the English king, "a letter full of pride and audacity," says Henry IV. It then happened that the Danes, at strife with the English for other causes, joined themselves to the Hanseatics, and united they harassed the English by sea and by land. These, in their turn, took possession of the Hanseatic depôt in London, and put in prison or killed all who lodged there. The League hearing this broke off commercial connection with England, closed their ports and the entrances of the Baltic, and seized English vessels on all seas and on all coasts. The Hanseatics even landed in England itself, and pitilessly ravaged many of the maritime provinces, hanging on the masts of their ships all the men they took prisoners. This war at last grew so ruinous for the English that they applied to the Duke of Burgundy, Charles the Bold, to mediate between them and their foes. A congress was assembled at Utrecht to put an end to this dire quarrel and to assure peace upon a solid basis. The mediator and his counsellors thought it but just to accord to the English a part of what they had desired so long, namely, liberty to trade in the Baltic and with the Hanseatic ports of Dantzig and Russia. This concession greatly favoured the commerce which their merchants were ambitious to carry on, or already carried on, notwithstanding all obstacles. But for their part the Hanseatics insisted on recovering all the privileges they had lost, and on recovering them with usury. In fact, by this treaty of Utrecht Edward IV. not only reconfirmed all their ancient monopolies, but accorded to them new and important favours, proving to what extent the English were still in the power of these foreigners. Such was the effect of the fear which the League inspired in the English; such, too, was the ignorance of their Government, which, being in possession of a power not less great and, had they desired, even greater than that of their rivals, allowed strangers to deprive them of the most useful of all independent rights, that of utilizing for their own profit the resources of their own labour and their own soil.

In reading this chapter of the annals of England, it is hard to believe that we are dealing with the nation whose ships now scour all the seas, whose tonnage exceeds that of all other countries combined, which is the greatest trader of the earth, and which trades not only freely, but also in that spirit of domination with which its ancestors reproached the Hanseatics, and which they endured with so much impatience.

This treaty of Utrecht served for a long while as basis for all subsequent treaties between the Hanseatics and the English, and well or ill observed, it survived until the reign of Edward VI.

The position held by the Hanseatics in England certainly has no counterpart in the international intercourse of the Middle Ages. The only exception, perhaps, is the position of Genoa, Venice, and Pisa in the Byzantine and Latin empires.

The chief depôt of the Hanseatics in England was in London, and was known first as the Guildhall of the Germans, then as the Easterlings' Hall, and finally, as its dimensions grew, as the Steelyard. It was situated in Thames Street, on the left bank of the river, close to Dowgate, just above London Bridge, in earlier times the only city gate that commanded the water. The whole length of this street leading to the post gate was lined with the wharves, warehouses, and dwelling-houses of the Germans. It is therefore easy to comprehend how they held, by their position alone, the key to the whole commerce of the City of London in days when goods were almost entirely transported by water-ways. As at Bergen, so here, they dominated the whole commercial situation.

There have been many disputes as to the origin of the name Steelyard. It has been now pretty well established that it took its rise from the fact that on this spot stood the great balance of the City of London, known as the Steelyard, on which all exported or imported merchandise had to be officially weighed. It was after the treaty of Utrecht in 1474 that the German factory first took this name, from the circumstance that its domain was then greatly enlarged. The whole place was defended by a high strong wall, fortress fashion, and there were few windows towards the front. This was as a protection from the frequent attacks of the London mob, and also as a defence against the robbers anxious to penetrate into a storehouse of riches. The chief building, still called their Guildhall, was a massive stone structure, of which, until 1851, some of the main walls still remained. The northern front, which looked towards Thames Street was especially imposing with its many stories, its high gabled roof, surmounted by the double eagle of the empire with its outspread wings. Three round portals, well protected and clamped with iron, were seen on its northern frontage. The centre one, far larger than the others, was rarely opened, and the two others were walled up. Above these three portals were to be read, in later days, the following characteristic inscriptions:

"HAEC DOMUS EST LAETA, SEMPER BONITATE REPLETA;
HIC PAX, HIC REQUIES, HIC GAUDIA SEMPER HONESTA."

"AURUM BLANDITIAE PATER EST NATUSQUE DOLORIS;
QUI CARET HOC MOERET, QUI TENET HOC METUIT."

"QUI BONIS PARERE RECUSAT, QUASI VITATO FUMO IN FLAMMAM INCIDIT."

The second of these couplets is attributed to Sir Thomas More, Chancellor of England, author of the "Utopia," and a good friend to the Hanseatics. This great hall was used for the meetings of the merchants and for their common dining-room. At one end was a low tower that served as depository for the documents and valuables belonging to the merchants or the factory. Close upon the river stood another strong building, the dwelling of the house master. Here was the capacious stone kitchen, in which ample preparations were made for the dinners of week-days and festivals. Between these two buildings ran the garden, in which the Germans had planted fruit trees and vines. On summer evenings they were wont to rest here after the business of the day, while the young people among them amused themselves with playing at ball or other recreations. It was a pleasant green spot with cool shady arbours, tables, and seats, and was frequented, not only by the Hanseatics themselves, but by the London citizens; for the League had the permission to sell their Rhenish wines in this spot. Threepence a bottle was the average price.

In "Pierce Penilesse, his application to the devil," we read, "Let us go to the Stilliard and drink rhenish wine;" and in one of Webster's plays a character says: "I come to entreat you to meet him this afternoon at the Rhenish warehouse in the Stillyard. Will you steal forth and taste of a Dutch brew and a keg of sturgeon?" This garden restaurant was also famous for its neat's tongues, salmon, and caviar. It would seem that the place was a favourite resort from the days of Prince Hal and Sir John Falstaff to those of Lord Herbert of Cherbury, the former the embodiment of boisterous enjoyment, the latter of chivalric and pedantic learning. A multifarious and varied company indeed that little garden harboured in its day, who met in "the Rhenish wine house" to close their bargains over their wine cups, for festive carouse or serious talk. There could be seen England's most honoured men; bishops, mayors, ministers, chancellors, naval and military heroes. Even Shakespeare's company of actors, London's merriest *gourmets*, are known to have turned in here. The spot did not lie far off the famous "Boar's Head" tavern, and Prince Hal's town residence in Cold Harbour Lane abutted upon the Steelyard. There, too, assembled the grave ambassadors of the Hanseatics, their delegates and merchants, their apprentices and agents; a motley crew indeed, who, until the days when the garden in Cosins Lane perished in the Great Fire of London (1666), constantly frequented the locality, and helped to enhance its wealth and importance. The memory of the place was kept up, till quite lately, by a large tavern, bearing the sign of the Steelyard, which still stood on the same spot, surmounted by a bunch of golden grapes, similar to those which we so frequently meet with in the narrow streets of old German towns.

No less busy, no less varied was the inner life of that small state within a state. A strange little world with its severe monastic discipline, its semi-religious character. In many rooms and halls, in warehouses and passages, were crowded a number of masters and men, assembled here from some sixty Hanseatic cities, busy superintending the stapled wares which arrived by river and were drawn up by means of the mighty crane that formed a notable feature in the water frontage of the factory. Some wares, too, arrived by way of the crooked streets. These entered the building through the small carefully guarded doorways. As time went on and there was not room enough for all the guests in the main building, adjoining houses were rented for the Hanseatics, but all were subject to the same rigid discipline, and were members of the same large household. In early days the London merchants had insisted that an Englishman should be head inspector of the Hanseatic warehouses, but from this they soon freed themselves, alleging that it was giving the sheepfold over into the keeping of the wolf. As elsewhere, the presidency was assigned to an alderman and twelve councillors. These were chosen from the different towns in rotation. As elsewhere, all residents had to remain unmarried during the period of this sojourn in the Steelyard. Not even the house-master was allowed to have a wife. In later years, a Cologne merchant who had decorated, improved, and enlarged the garden inn, and turned it into one of the most beautiful taverns in London, being a resident for life, was anxious to marry. But so sternly did the League hold by their decree of celibacy for their absent members, that they only agreed to make an exception in his case after fourteen members of the English Parliament had signed a round robin petition to the Hanseatic Diet to this effect. Those who trespassed against the by-laws of the house as to habits or morals were heavily fined. If refractory they were often imprisoned, and at times even the aid of the English constables would be called in. But this was not frequent. The Hanseatics preferred to manage their own affairs, and keep themselves distinct from the natives among whom they dwelt. In criminal cases the jury, as is still the custom in England under similar conditions, was composed half of Englishmen, half of Germans. At nine every evening the portals of the various dwelling-houses were closed, and the key given to one of the masters, who took turns to fill this office. Whoever played at dice in his room at the tavern, whoever entertained non-Hanseatics, whoever let a woman cross the precincts of the Steelyard paid a heavy sum, of which half went to the informant. Cleanliness was severely imposed both in person and in the use of the common sleeping and packing rooms. The fine for contravention in this respect was paid in wax, not in money. It was employed for the candles which the Hanseatics kept burning on their behalf in the church of All Hallows the More. Opprobrious language towards one another, blows or drawing of knives was fined by a hundred shillings paid into the common fund; a high sum truly if we consider that five pounds sterling was worth, in the fourteenth century, about four times its present value. They were even forbidden to fence or to play tennis with their English neighbours under out paying a penalty of twenty shillings.

Every merchant was bound to have in readiness in his room a full suit of armour, and all the needful weapons in case of an attack on the Steelyard, or on the Bishopsgate. For the City of London had ceded to the Hanseatics this gate, which they had to guard and keep in repair, relieving them instead of the annual tax towards the preservation of the town walls known as wall-money, of bridge money, and paving money. They also managed to obtain special privileges with regard to shipwrecked goods; the English being obliged to pay them damages provided that something living, if only a dog, or cat, or cock reached the shore alive from the shipwrecked vessel. This secured them greatly from the perils of wanton wreckage.

In London none of those gross manners and customs prevailed that we find at Bergen or Novgorod. The Hanseatics knew that in England they found themselves among a people fully their equals, and were careful not to offend them in any respect. Indeed they did all they could to conciliate them, and were liberal in presents. Thus the Lord Mayor of London received from them yearly a cask of the finest sturgeon, or two barrels of herring, or a hundredweight of Polish wax. An English alderman, annually chosen to adjust disputes between the natives and the foreigners, was presented each New Year's Day with fifteen golden nobles, wrapped up in a pair of gloves, by way of tender consideration for the feelings of the recipient. The Chief Inspector of Customs received about twenty pounds sterling, intended probably to make him indulgent in the exercise of his duties. And so forth, making as a whole a most goodly sum thus wisely spent in fees and in conciliating those in power and office. Every point relating to this as well as to the inner statutes of the factory was most carefully recorded in writing, and has, in large part, been preserved to us. It is a record of most quaint regulations, every one of which no doubt had its wise purpose and scope.

The Hanseatics purchased from the English the produce of their flocks and tillage, that is to say, wool, strong hides, corn, beer, and cheese. Wool was from the earliest date one of the chief and most important articles of their exportation from England. This was sent to Flanders and the Netherlands to be worked up. It was only later, as the English learnt to manufacture skilfully this costly produce, that the Hanseatics exported the finished goods in lieu of the raw material. The details concerning this wool trade show how many places in England were engaged in it, and how appropriately the Chancellor of England is seated upon a wool-sack as symbol of one of the main sources of England's ancient wealth. So valuable, indeed, was this wool trade that a special tax was placed upon the wool, a tax which Edward III. repeatedly farmed out to Cologne merchants for the space of several years in advance in return for ready cash.

Among the articles imported by the League we find pepper, potash, various kinds of wood adapted for building ships and making crossbows, iron and iron utensils, flax, linen, hemp, grease, fish, corn, and Rhenish wines. We even find that they imported French wines after the English had lost all their possessions in France with the exception of Calais. By their means, too, there came to England Italian and Oriental produce, such as choice spices, perfumes, medicines, metals, figs, almonds, dates, even gold dust, and jewels, with which they provided themselves at Bruges.

A very important branch of trade was that in salted cod-fish, or stock-fish as it was called, an article largely used on the Continent and in England too in the Middle Ages. With this the English were then accustomed to feed their troops when on service. Nor were even living creatures lacking among their cargoes, such as choice falcons from Norway or Livonia, for which the English nobility, who were then, as now, passionately addicted to sport, paid high prices.

Indeed, the Steelyard was one of the staple places for the export and import of all the principal necessaries of life before men had thought of the products of America.

Nor was London by any means their only depôt. It was the chief, but they also had factories in York, Hull, Bristol, Norwich, Ipswich, Yarmouth, Boston, and Lynn Regis. Some mention of them is found in Leland's "Itinerary." Under an invitation to the Hanseatics to trade with Scotland we find the name honoured in legend and song of William Wallace. In John Lydgate's poems we also meet with our Hanseatics. In relating the festivities that took place in London city on the occasion of the triumphal entry of Henry VI., who had been crowned king at Paris some months previously, the poet narrates how there rode in procession the Mayor of London clad in red velvet, accompanied by his aldermen and sheriffs dressed in scarlet and fur, followed by the burghers and guilds with their trade ensigns, and finally succeeded by a number of foreigners.

"And for to remember of other alyens,

> Fyrst Jenenyes (Genoese) though they were strangers,
> Florentynes and Venycyens,
> And Easterlings, glad in her maneres,
> Conveyed with sergeantes and other officeres,
> Estatly horsed, after the maier riding,
> Passed the subburbis to mete withe the kyng."

A love of pomp and outward show was indeed a characteristic of the Hanseatics in England who thus perchance wished to impress upon the natives a sense of their wealth. As times grew less turbulent and the German Guildhall less of a fortress, it was handsomely decorated with costly paintings and fine carving. Most notable were two large works by Holbein, who visited England at the invitation of King Henry VIII., desirous of emulating his rival Francis I. in protecting the fine arts. When the painter first came over he lived in one of the quaint houses that, before the Great Fire, stood on London Bridge, and some of his earliest works seem to have been two commissions for his countrymen, whose Steelyard was close by. They were destined to decorate the Great Hall, and were tempera pictures representing respectively the Triumph of Poverty and of Riches. When in the days of James I. the Steelyard ceased to exist as the collective home of the Hanseatics, the towns decided to present these pictures to the Prince of Wales, Henry, who was a lover of the arts like his younger brother, Charles I., into whose collection they passed on Henry's death. Unfortunately, they perished in the great fire that destroyed Whitehall. Federigo Zuccari, who saw them during his sojourn in London and appraised them as exceeding in beauty the works of Raphael, made careful drawings of them, and thanks to these and the engravings made after them we are in possession of at least an outline representation of Holbein's work. The pictures are conceived in the spirit of the age that loved such so-called triumphs in art and poetry. The figures, chiefly allegorical, were life size and in the richness of fantasy and learning that they display it is permissible to recognize the help and advice of Holbein's friend, the Chancellor, Sir Thomas More. In many cases the names of the personages represented are written beside the figures, after the quaint method of that time.

The Triumph of Riches shows a car of Plutus drawn by four white horses, driven by Fortune and followed by a motley crowd which includes Justice, Usury, Bona Fides, Sichæus, the rich husband of Queen Dido, Pythias (of whom Plutarch tells that he so loved gold that once when he returned hungry from abroad his wife placed gold before him instead of meats), and many figures, for the most part culled from the pages of Herodotus, Juvenal, and other classic authors. In the heads of Crœsus and Cleopatra it is said that Holbein painted likenesses of Henry VIII. and Anne Boleyn. In a corner of the picture is written the distich ascribed to Sir Thomas More which we have already met with above the central portal of the German Guildhall.

The Triumph of Poverty was purely allegorical, and appears to have been considered less attractive than the former work, whether on account of its treatment, or on account of its less pleasing theme does not appear. In this case the car is drawn by two oxen and two asses, designated as Negligence and Idleness, Greed and Sloth. This canvas, too, bore some Latin verses from More's pen, which, curiously enough, have not been incorporated in his collected works.

In all public ceremonies and processions the Hanseatics seem also to have taken a notable part; as we mentioned above on the occasion of Henry the Sixth's entry. We come across another detailed account when Queen Mary went in triumph through London the day before her coronation. At Fenchurch the Genoese had dressed up a lovely boy as a girl, who was carried before the Queen and greeted her. The Hanseatics had built up a hillock in the corner of Gracechurch, whence a fountain poured forth wine. On this hillock stood four children who likewise greeted the Queen. In front of the Steelyard they had placed two casks of wine, from which they poured drink to all who passed. This liberality cost them a thousand pounds, and heavy payments to cover such expenses are not infrequent in their account books.

In England, contrary to the usual custom, the Hanseatic League never had its own church. Perhaps this need was less felt in a land that professed the same creed than in Russia. The Germans frequented the parish church of All Hallows, contenting themselves with endowing a chapel, altars, special masses, and alms. They also presented the church with costly stained glass windows, in the decoration of which the German imperial eagle figured conspicuously, and with cunningly-carved stalls reserved for the use of the Steelyard authorities. As late as the year 1747 these seats were still in the possession of the master of the Steelyard and the other representatives of the guild. In front of these stalls there always burned five of the biggest tapers the church could boast. Indeed the Hanseatics were famous for their outward observances of piety, both while they were Catholics and after they, as well as the English, became Protestants. Of course the Catholic religion made more show. Saint Barbara was a saint whom they specially affected, and on her day (December 4th) they caused a most elaborate mass to be sung and afterwards treated the priest, their English alderman, and the royal doorkeeper of the Star Chamber to fruit and wine in the Cosin's Lane Garden. At Corpus Christi they joined the great procession of all the guilds and notabilities; and on midsummer night, and the eve of St. Peter and St. Paul, they illumined their Great Hall after the ancient Saxon fashion with Yule fires and torches. After the Great Fire of London the League presented All Hallows with a carved oak screen that ran the length of the whole church. It was the work of a Hamburg carver, and excites admiration to this day. In the centre it shows the large imperial eagle, as also the arms of Queen Anne; the main work consists of twisted columns and arches.

The Germans in England seem to have adopted the purer Protestant doctrines with great caution, if not tardily. At least we have it on record, that when in 1526 a commission, headed by Sir Thomas More in person, proceeded to make a domiciliary search of the Steelyard for writings of Luther, nothing was found but Old and New Testaments and German prayer books, while the whole body, both young and old, swore at St. Paul's Cross that there was not a heretic among them. Soon afterwards the Reformation was firmly established in England, as it already was in most of the cities belonging to the League, and from that time forward the Steelyard associates attended the English Protestant service in All Hallows Church.

Such were the life, the habits, and the nature, of the German community that made its English centre in the Steelyard, and which, so long as it was in harmony with the times, conferred many advantages not only upon themselves, but upon the people among whom they dwelt. For in thrifty activity the English in those days could not be compared with the Hanseatics, while in point of wealth no one could compete with these Germans, excepting only the Italian money-changers of Lombard Street, then, as still, a favourite locality of banking houses. But the Italians were exclusively occupied with financial transactions, while the Germans devoted themselves exclusively to mercantile affairs.

VIII.

THE ORGANIZATION OF THE HANSEATIC LEAGUE.

THE notices that have come down to us about the organization of our League are scanty, although we possess a vast number of minutes concerning their diets. It is doubtful whether there was even a fixed mode of governing and government, whether the whole was not rather in a state of flux controlled by the circumstances of the moment. That certain traditional modes of administration obtained, however, seems indisputable. It raises a smile to read that when some problem seemed insoluble, or some venture proved a failure, our naïve Hanseatics registered in their books, "of this matter let those think who come after us," thus throwing the burden upon the following generation.

There was no fixed place of meeting for the Hanseatic diets, but most frequently these were held at Lübeck, because it was situated almost in the centre of the various activities of the League. The assemblies were held in "the name of all the cities," and those who failed to send representatives were begged "not to take it amiss" if conclusions were arrived at without their sanction. "Every town shall consider the benefit of the others, so far as is in accordance with right and honour," runs one of their quaint formulæ. "Should strife arise between the cities, which God forbid, they shall settle their dispute according to the counsels of the neighbouring towns."

There was also no fixed time for these diets; they were assembled according to urgency or press of business, but usually they were annual, and met about Whitsuntide, as that feast falls in the fine weather, when travelling was easier for the delegates of the northern towns. At the close of each diet, the deputies present decided on the time and place of the next meeting, and Lübeck and other leading cities were charged with the care of making known to the cities unrepresented the decisions arrived at by the assembly. But default to send a deputy to the diet was not lightly overlooked. Some excuse had to be given, and the validity of the excuse was sharply criticized. Sometimes a town might be busy resisting its temporal or ecclesiastical lords, an internal revolution might have occupied all its energies, the roads might be unsafe, or it might have been visited by some public calamity like the Black Death. If the diet thought that these pleas were merely subterfuges to save the expense of sending a delegate, or to avoid explaining some infraction of the rules of the League of which the city in question was guilty, a heavy money fine was imposed, and in case of absence three times repeated it might even find itself "unhansed," deprived of all the pecuniary privileges belonging to members of this powerful association. By such rigid measures did the League hold its members together. Nor was this all. A deputy who did not arrive in time for the opening of the proceedings was fined a gold mark for each day of delay, a fine that was not remitted unless the causes for his default were found on scrutiny to be in every way sufficient.

On their arrival at the meeting place, the deputies were received in state by some member of the local municipal council, and were offered the wine of honour. The conferences began about seven or eight in the morning, and lasted till one or two in the afternoon. One of the burgomasters of Lübeck was usually made president. At the first meeting he would thank the members present for having come, and these would reply to him in courteous terms. Then when all their credentials had been examined, and the excuses of the absent sifted, the diet would proceed to the business in hand. This business was heavy and varied, covering the external and internal policy of the League, the needful moneys to be raised, the state of the various foreign factories. Even private quarrels between merchants were heard here in appeal. The diet decided on peace and war, sent despatches to foreign kings and princes; threatened, warned, exhorted, those who had failed to fulfil treaty obligations. Such was its power that it rarely failed to make its voice heard, and a threat indited by the city of Lübeck was not put quietly into the waste-paper basket by the northern courts. These missives were sealed with the seal of the city in which the diet was sitting at the time. Just as in their buildings, their guildhalls, and their towers, our forefathers knew how to express a quaint conceit, so also in a simple seal they understood how to express symbolically a summary of their activity. Thus the pious and wise Lübeck bore on its city seal a ship with high bulwarks, from whose single central mast waved a flag bearing the cross. An ancient pilot steers the vessel through the waves with his left hand while his right is raised in admonition. Opposite to him sits a youth busy with the ropes, who, with his uplifted right hand, seems to point to the help of heaven. This was to symbolize that prudence, energy, and pious confidence accompanied Lübeck in all its paths. The common Hanseatic seal was only used for foreign affairs. It represented the imperial double eagle with the inscription "*Signum civitatum maritimarum.*"

The decisions arrived at by the diet were all recorded in careful minutes, known as "recesses," of which an immense number have come down to us, escaping fire and other vicissitudes. They all testify to the thoroughly businesslike character that distinguished the League. Among other matters we often come across applications from cities to be admitted into the Hansa. Their candidature was generally addressed to Lübeck, and their claims and resources carefully scrutinized by the prudent League. As a rule the demand was conceded. The League was never sorry to see its strength grow, and its expenses diminish by being divided among a greater number of towns. Such admission, however, was made upon unequal conditions, according to the importance, the resources, and the situation of the city in question. This inequality had struck deep roots also in the very heart of the cities. The inhabitants were far removed from enjoying the same prerogatives, the Hansa was by no means a democratic association. The most important posts were reserved for a certain number of families know as patricians, who had distinguished themselves by services for the common weal, or who held power in the shape of wealth. An individual, however, could be "unhansed" as well as a city, if he had failed to observe some law of high commercial consequence, and it was even more difficult for an individual to be readmitted than a town.

From the inequalities in the position of different members of the League there arose conflicts of interest which were to prove "the little rift within the lute," that by and by should "make the music mute." For instance, the interest of the maritime towns was not always that of the inland ones. Schisms and divisions were apt, above all, to take place when there was a question of beginning a war, as this could never be done without general approbation. Each town was inclined to throw the burden on its associates. For as each was solely preoccupied with its personal interests, and only entered into the League with a view to the profits it could thus obtain, there was always in the minds of the delegates a tacit reserve to make as few sacrifices as possible, and as time went on they were even ready to abandon their allies, and let the League perish if they did not find themselves directly benefited by any sacrifice demanded by the common weal.

What held them together at all was, in a word, nothing more noble or ideal than personal advantage, the fear through exclusion of losing by exclusion, the great advantages that accrued from being a member of the League. No wonder that with an ambition so little exalted the Hansa was destined not to survive until our own day. For communities like individuals must strive after some lofty ideal if their existence is to be happy, and to have a sound enduring basis. The wonder is rather that seeing what motives animated its members, the defective character of the means at its disposal, such as the lack of a standing army, and the constant mutations in its form of government, it should have attained to such mighty results as we have roughly sketched in this, the second and culminating period of its existence.

PERIOD III.

THE DECLINE AND FALL OF THE HANSA.

INTRODUCTION.

FROM the law of change to which all human affairs are subject the mighty Hanseatic League was not exempt. Great though its power seemed to all outward appearance, and rich as were its members, still, for some time past, signs of decay and decline had made themselves manifest, here and there ominous rents and fissures, that threatened, if not an entire, yet a partial fall of the building.

The latter years of the fifteenth and the early years of the sixteenth centuries were a time of the greatest moment in the history of modern Europe. They mark the transition from the mediæval to the modern spirit, embracing two such potent factors in human development as the Reformation and the discovery of America. It is almost sad to think that the decrepitude of a powerful institution should have coincided with the transformation and rejuvenescence of Europe. Yet so it was. So it will ever be; we must march onward with our time, or be trodden down.

Many of the ideas of the Hansa had grown effete or were becoming gradually obsolete. Individuality in men, independence in nations were factors beginning to manifest themselves and to rebel against those notions of blind obedience and of selfish monopoly inculcated by the Hansa. The time was nearing when the old system of staple, of factories was to give place to the busy varied life of the Exchange.

The discovery that the earth was round, not flat, that Ulysses had no idle dream when he dreamed that there was another continent beyond the pillars of Hercules, was a matter of unspeakable moment to trade. When we recollect that almost to the same date belong the discovery of a maritime route to the East Indies, and the invention of printing, we cannot but recognize that a power, not willing to move with the times, but painfully, obstinately clinging to its own ideas and images, had to be left behind. The very causes for which the Hansa had been founded, insecurity of roads, want of international justice, and other barbarous and intolerant conditions, no longer existed. The League itself had developed from a liberator into an oppressor. It no longer fitted with the changing conditions; it too must change or perish. In vain did it point to ancient charters, evoke "inviolable treaties" acquired at the point of the sword or by might of wealth. It had to learn that of these treaties, as indeed of treaties in general, must be said that which is sadly, but too truly said of human promises, that they are "like pie-crust, made to be broken."

The spirit of revolution, or rather of change, was abroad. It made itself felt in manners, in institutions, in governments. The capture of Constantinople by the Turks contributed to the new development. By warning Europe of a new and menacing danger, it drew yet more closely together the different states which the Crusades had already put into relations with one another, and for which the feudal system formed a sort of common link. This same event turned the stream of sciences, letters, and arts towards Italy. On the other hand, the princes were finding out the means of diminishing the power of the feudal lords and nobles. The subjugation of the power of these vassals undermined little by little the feudal system, and allowed this worn-out institution to be replaced by institutions more in conformity with the needs of modern society.

Various states, that had been unable to develope their forces, owing to the abuse of the feudal system, moved swiftly forward, now that they were free from restraint, and, having succeeded in centralizing their power desired to give it a firm and equal step in the march onwards. Meanwhile the forces that existed in the hands of the rulers were active enough to assure the tranquillity of the people, but it was always possible to turn them from their destination; war might arise any moment out of the very institutions that ought to secure the maintenance of peace. The people, recognizing this and fearing lest ambitious rulers should form projects of aggrandizement and conquest, had recourse to that policy which the Italian republics had already initiated and in which Florence took the lead.

The democracy understood full well that it was for their good, and even essential to their very existence as a power in the state, that they should act upon the forces that determined the government, just as these re-acted upon them: that, in a word, they should mutually hold each other within the limits of the law and that general security could only arise from the equilibrium of the means of attack and defence. This new policy which demanded frequent communications between the parties interested, gave rise to the system of embassies, itself quite a new feature in international and political life, though it was really an extension of ideas and systems long ago pursued by the Hansa. In a word, the whole method of the world was changing, and it remained to be seen whether the Hansa could still keep ahead as it had hitherto done.

While other nations were looking about them all round the globe, the Hansa was, as ever, occupied in securing to itself the monopoly of the Baltic basin, in order that no other peoples should deprive them of the wealth of Scandinavia. And yet this "monopoly of the herring and the cod-fish," as it has been named, was steadily becoming less and less valuable. More than half of Europe was Protestant and no longer fasted; wax was no more required in quantities for Church ceremonials and the evidences of personal piety; the imitation of Italian and Spanish fashions in dress caused less demand for the furs of the North. The English were among the chief commercial rivals of the Hansa at this date, and after them the Dutch, those very Dutch whose cities had at one time formed part of the League, but who had seceded after the wars with Waldemar, finding it more profitable to keep friends with the Danes.

It is strange that this combination of merchants, generally so astute, should not have recognized whither the stream of things was tending.

Nor in its perplexities could it find any help from the emperor. The German Empire was suffering from the same ills as the League, and with equal steps was advancing towards its dissolution. Until now the Hansa had gone on its triumphal way in spite of all inner and outer political complications, indeed had rather profited than lost by these. This was now altered. It was now no longer a body animated by one will, one spirit. The disintegrating element of religious discord had entered among its members, they were mixed up with the bloody doctrinal wars, that followed the Reformation and ravaged Germany, and they were divided among themselves on this very point. At last, after the treaty of Augsburg (1555), which restored to Germany a more or less agitated peace of some fifty years, there followed the terrible, devastating Thirty Years' War, which gave the death blow to the League.

The Thirty Years' War left behind it only a heap of ruins. It had consequences so disastrous that from some of them Germany has not recovered even to this day. It caused her to lag in the onward march of progress, and for all her military strength at this present moment, she has not yet overtaken her neighbours and contemporaries in many important points of civilization, that are more unfailing sources of a nation's power than mere brute strength in arms or tactical skill in battle.

One of the first serious causes of decline in the Hanseatic power was due to the fact that as time went on and conditions of trade altered, the interests of the maritime and continental cities were no longer identical. The sea-board towns used to furnish to the inland the means of selling the produce of industries with profit in the countries east, north, and west of the Baltic. The Hanseatic ships and factories facilitated this distribution of goods. But when other nations, and, above all, the merchants of the Netherlands, and after them the English, Danes, and Swedes carried on a part of this commerce with their own ships, the inland cities no longer had the same interest in remaining united with the maritime. They even thought that their union with the League was more onerous than useful, and began to grow restive and would no longer pay their dues to the general fund, which consequently became much weakened and impoverished. Thus there were not only enemies from without, but enemies from within to contend against. "A house divided against itself cannot stand" is a saying of which our Hansa was very soon to learn the full truth.

But before the final collapse came the League was to know one more moment of proud prosperity, a moment which, had it been wisely and unselfishly used would have secured to the Hansa a prolonged dictatorship in Northern Europe.

After this rapid survey we will consider these events in detail and order.

I.

STORM CLOUDS.

THE centre of the Hansa's power had ever been the Baltic Ocean. On its shores the idea of the League had first taken shape: here it had grown and flourished, and here also it was to receive its death blow. As we have said, in the course of the fifteenth century the Dutch gradually came forward as serious competitors of the League. Their geographical position made them freer than the Hanseatics; enclosed in a sort of inland basin to which at any moment they might lose the key, their astuteness was not less keen than that of their rivals, and like their rivals they wisely made use of any quarrels or dissensions that might be abroad. They were not slow, therefore, to discern that the Scandinavian people and also the Scandinavian kings groaned under the heavy despotism exercised by these German merchants. They proposed themselves as substitutes for the Hansa, offering money and support to the kings and easier and better conditions of trade to the natives. These proposals were unofficially accepted. Neither rulers nor ruled as yet dared oppose themselves openly to the League, but they were not sorry to see its power reduced.

For awhile the Hansa were able to keep their rivals in check, worrying them by piracy on the one hand, and insisting on their ancient claims and trade rights on the other.

But Charles V. had ascended the throne; the greatest emperor that had ever governed in Germany since his namesake Charles the Great. He was ruler not only of Germany, but of Spain and the Netherlands, and to the latter people he was especially well disposed. He looked with no friendly eye upon the League, which made itself a power within his territory, and he was not sorry to see it weakened by competition. When the Sound, their Danish Hellespont, the gold mine of the League, continued to be jealously guarded by them, and its navigation denied to other nations, Charles V. declared quite openly that "he would rather miss three royal crowns, than that his Burgunders should be excluded from the Sound." This was a sort of challenge to the Hansa. Let us hear how other circumstances came about to enforce it from other quarters.

It may be remembered that since the days of Waldemar Atterdag, the League had always had a voice in the election of a ruler to one of the three northern kingdoms, and that it regarded with no friendly eye the attempts made at a union of those kingdoms under one common head.

In 1513 Christian II. had ascended the Danish throne. He was an unscrupulous and cruel ruler, known to posterity as the Nero of the North. Before ascending the throne of Denmark he had been governor of Norway, and in that capacity had conceived a bitter hatred against the overbearing foreigners, "those German cobblers," as he called them, who once even ventured to close against him the gates of his own town of Bergen. He had already favoured by all ways in his power the trade of non-Hanseatics, and tried to obtain some gentler treatment for the oppressed burghers of Bergen. Still so great was yet the fear of the Hansa, that when in 1513 Christian was crowned King of Denmark, he made no difficulties about renewing all Hanseatic treaties and privileges, and only stipulated that the harbours of Norway should also be accessible to the Netherlanders. In return he desired their assistance against Sweden, with which country he was at war.

For a time the League, and above all Lübeck, were rejoiced at this new king and his attitude towards them, but not many years had passed before they found out that they had to do with a more logical and altogether sterner man than any of his predecessors had been. Christian hated the Hansa, and rebelled against the subjection of the Sound, a Danish sea, to foreign control, and the absolute sway of the Hansa in his markets. Among many unwise words and deeds that live bound up with his memory, it was not the most unwise which he repeated after Sigbrit Willem, the mother of his beloved and lovely friend, Digveke (Little Dove), "that good friendship must be maintained with the Netherlands, and that Copenhagen must be made the staple place of the North."

Unfortunately for Christian, though he could repeat Sigbrit's sayings, and perhaps also in a measure recognize their wisdom, he had not the natural capacity to carry them into execution. This clever woman recognized that the aim of the king should be to reinstate the Scandinavian Union, to break the power of the aristocracy and the clergy, and to free his impoverished people from the fetters in which the Hansa had bound them for nine centuries. This was all right and well, but it needed to be carried into effect with tact and moderation. Christian did not possess these gifts; he made himself personally detested by his cruelty and his overbearing manner, he knew not that generosity which so gracefully becomes a victor. After conquering Sweden, he soiled his victory by causing the most illustrious personages of the kingdom to be executed, and still worse he stained his personal honour by violating the conditions of an armistice in causing Gustavus Ericson, of the house of Vasa, to be carried off captive to Denmark. It did not improve matters when Christian explained that he required him as a hostage. He caused Gustavus to be shut up in the strong fortress of Kalo in Jutland. Here the captive was put on his parole, and it is said suffered none of the rigours of custody. But the food put before him, salt junk, sour ale, black bread, and rancid herrings, cannot have comforted his enforced captivity in the material sense, while he confessed to having been maddened by the talk of the soldiers who guarded him, and who boasted that they would soon hold all Sweden, and jestingly parcelled out among themselves the wealth and beauty of the nation.

This young man so unjustly imprisoned was destined to become the avenger of his fatherland, and those of his fellow-countrymen who had perished upon the scaffold. He resolved to escape, hoping to reach Sweden in time to defend his country, or to take advantage of any favourable juncture that might arise.

It was in September, 1519, that, early one raw autumn morning, Gustavus managed to escape from the Castle of Kalo, disguised as a drover of oxen. He made his way to the city of Lübeck, and threw himself upon the protection of the burgomaster and council. Needless to say the town gave a generous welcome to the man who was foe of their foe—the King of Denmark. But it was not long ere his whereabouts became known, and Christian sent messengers to Lübeck, demanding in high-handed language that Gustavus should be handed over to him. He complained that Vasa had effected his escape contrary to his pledged word as a knight. Gustavus spoke in his own defence.

"I was captured," he said, "contrary to all justice and all plighted faith. It is notorious that I went to the king's fleet as a hostage. Let any one who can, point out the place where I was made prisoner in battle, or declare the crime for which I deserved chains. Call me not then a prisoner, but a man seized upon unjustly, over-reached, betrayed. I am now in a free city, and before a government renowned for justice and for defending the persecuted. Shall I then be altogether deceived in the confidence I have placed in them? or can breach of faith be reasonably objected to me by one who never himself kept faith or promise? or can it be wondered at that I should free myself from prison which I deserved by no fault, except that of trusting to the assurances of a king."

The shrewd burgesses who listened to Gustavus's defence were not misled by his rhetoric, but motives of policy told in his favour. They knew that if Christian were once undisturbed king of the three northern kingdoms, he would possess a power which, as he had already shown, he would not use to the advantage of the League. Here was a young nobleman of fearless character and high talent, a man who hated the king with hereditary hatred and personal animosity. Might he not become a thorn in his side and a clog upon his movements?

This was the view of the matter taken by the burgomaster of Lübeck and put forcibly before his colleagues. It was therefore agreed emphatically to refuse the king's demands, and, instead of giving up Gustavus, to furnish him rather with the means to return to his own country. "For who knows," said the worthy council, "what he may do when he gets there."

To this refusal to deliver up the hostage the King of Denmark replied, through his ambassadors, that he should make a house-to-house search for his prisoner. That was truly more than the proud city could stomach. They answered in the most haughty terms that they should never permit such an interference with their home rights and privileges, and in the presence of the Danish ambassadors reassured the fugitive of their protection and friendship.

When the news of this reply reached Christian, he regarded it as an act of great audacity. From this moment he became a yet more embittered enemy of the Hansa, whose chief city and spokesman he very properly recognized was Lübeck. He harassed them continually in fresh ways; he carried on a yet more envenomed war against the Swedes, of whom he knew the League to be the secret ally and the chief support.

At first success favoured his arms; he broke faith in all directions—plundered, ravaged, sacked. But at last he made the cup of wrath against him overflow by his cruel execution of ninety noble Swedes, in the autumn of 1520; vaunting the deed in insolent heartless words. He had shown them, he said, "how he roasted his Michaelmas goose." Further, in his wanton presumption he did not hesitate to give active expression to his hatred against Lübeck. When congratulated by his councillors that he could now rejoice in the possession of the three northern crowns, he replied: "So long as Lübeck is not in my power, I cannot be happy in my kingdoms."

Shortly after this, Christian set out for the Netherlands to visit his imperial brother-in-law at Ghent. The objects of his journey were various. He wanted to obtain the payment of his consort's marriage portion; to solicit the emperor's aid against his uncle, Frederick of Schleswig Holstein; and yet more to obtain his tacit, if not active assistance, against the Hansa towns on the Baltic, and especially against Lübeck.

It was on the occasion of this visit that Charles V., accompanied by Christian and Margaret of Austria, laid the foundation-stone of Antwerp Cathedral. After this ceremony they returned to Brussels, where Christian entertained his friends at a banquet. Among the guests was the great German painter, Albert Dürer, then visiting the Low Countries. He was then and there commissioned to paint the Danish king's portrait—a portrait that all contemporaries greatly admired as a faithful reproduction of Christian's manly beauty. The artist received thirty florins—a sum that seemed to him munificent, and called forth expressions of real gratitude.

Soon after, Christian presented a petition to the young and inexperienced Charles, in which he begged, as a gift from him, "a little town on the German side of his dominions, called Lübeck, so that when sometimes he passed over to Germany he might possess a place of his own in which to rest." Charles, enlightened by the burgomaster of Cologne to the effect that Lübeck was no "little town," but one of the four imperial cities, and a chief centre of the Hanseatic League, refused his brother-in-law's petition in decisive terms. Nor did Christian fare better with his other demands; Charles had been warned against him, and had been taught to see in him a possible heretic. It is even related that in his anger Christian tore from his neck the Order of the Golden Fleece, given to him by the emperor, and trod it under foot in disdain.

Christian returned home to find fresh difficulties awaiting him, for in his absence Gustavus Vasa had not been idle. This restless patriot had lingered but eight months in the hospitable German city. Young, full of enthusiasm and fire, he longed to be actively at work to aid his oppressed compatriots; and one morning, in the spring of 1520, after confessing his obligations and his gratitude to the Lübeckers, he stole over to the Swedish coast in a little fishing-smack, and landed in territory that was groaning under Christian's oppressions.

At first, Gustavus, who at once assumed the rôle of leader of revolt, could not make himself heard among the peasants. They replied to his instigations in their apathy of oppression with, "Salt and herrings will not fail us as long as we obey the king, but if we rise we are sure of ruin." But Gustavus was undaunted, though he knew a price was put upon his head. For months he scoured the country, travelling by by-paths, sleeping one night in the woods, another in the open fields;

assuming now this, now that disguise. Gradually he gathered a following around him, which grew in importance day by day. His influence increased above all after the tidings of the "Bloodbath," for so the terrible massacre came to be called, perpetrated by Christian upon the nobles of Stockholm, on the occasion when he offered them a banquet, apparently of peace, but which proved to them a feast of death.

Chief among Gustavus's allies were the people of Dalecarlia, among whom he went on his mission of revolt dressed in their native dress. This land of valleys is inhabited by a people who have many points of resemblance with the Scotch Highlanders; thinking themselves, as these do, of a superior caste and adhering even to this day to an exaggerated and antiquated mode of dress. Like the Highlanders, too, they are frugal; they are accustomed to drink only water, and often in case of necessity eat bread made of the inner rind of the birch tree, which grows so freely in their woods. It is said that one of the Danish commanders, learning this, exclaimed "A people who can live upon wood and drink water the devil himself could not conquer, much less any other. Let us go hence."

When the Danes heard of the army of peasants that was rising against them, they at first treated the news with great contempt. "If the skies rained peasants," they said, "we would fight them all." But they were soon to see that these peasants were not to be lightly despised. It was before Upsala that Gustavus's army, aided by troops sent to him from Lübeck made its first attack on the Danes. There was a heavy snowfall during the battle, in consequence of which the Danish cavalry and artillery proved of no avail, while the peasants with their irregular mode of warfare were less impeded by the elements. The victory was theirs, and the Danes had to confess that their boast was foolish, "For when God withdraws his hand from a warrior a poor peasant is as good as he."

From this moment success followed success and the prospects of the cause of Gustavus grew steadily brighter. His instructions to his followers were that "they must teach the tyrant that Swedes must be ruled by love, not ground down by cruelty."

In August, 1521, Gustavus was elected administrator of Sweden, and was virtually ruler of the land, though the whole was not yet in his possession. The time of shifts, disguises, and humiliations was now over. The scenes of these, however, the barns where Gustavus threshed, the different spots where he was in the greatest peril—are still pointed out with veneration by the descendants of those peasants who succoured him in his adversity, and boasted that they were the first to help him to a crown.

In this juncture Christian saw himself obliged to send out yet more ships and men against Gustavus. To meet the re-enforced enemy, Vasa turned to Lübeck in 1522 and begged of "his fathers, brothers, friends, and dear neighbours of that town," under promise of eternal gratitude, to help him against "the tyrant," saying he would in his turn and time "accord to them milder privileges and everything that could be to their profit." The burghers decided to accede to this request; ten strong ships were armed to aid Gustavus Vasa and sent out to meet the Danish fleet.

Meanwhile they did not neglect to use the weapons of diplomacy; weapons so often successfully employed by them during their career. They remembered that Duke Frederick of Schleswig Holstein was uncle to Christian II., and that the two had ever been at feud. It occurred to them that it would be well to gain the duke as their ally, promising him the Danish throne in event of their victory; of course in return for important privileges; the Hansa would have been untrue to themselves and their traditional policy had they for one moment left out of sight their own advantages.

This proposal met with assent, and the consequence was that a powerful enemy was thus raised up in the centre of the king's dominions. Christian, following the counsel of Sigbrit, planned another wholesale massacre of the nobles whom he believed favourable to Frederick's cause. The matter got known, and in consequence a council was held by them in which they drew up a deed, renouncing their allegiance to Christian and choosing Frederick in his place to fill the Danish throne.

A question arose as to who should convey the perilous document to the king. A certain monk of Jutland offered to bear the ill tidings. He met the king as he was proceeding to one of his castles. Assuming an open and cheerful countenance he managed to get himself asked to dinner by the king, and continued to amuse him and divert all suspicions till the king retired to rest. Then, placing the despatch in one of his gloves, he left it on the table, went quietly out and escaped by a boat which he had ordered to be in readiness. A page who found the despatch next morning carried it to the king.

Christian, who till then had blustered and disbelieved in real danger, grew alarmed when he read this unexpected paper. He wrote to those who subscribed it saying "that he submitted himself to the emperor and other disinterested princes as his judges. As to the massacre at Stockholm, he would atone for it; he would fill the country with churches and monasteries, and undergo any penance which the Pope might impose. The Council and States should have from him fresh securities, if only they would retract their step and turn from him this dishonour they had meditated." The nobles replied that they acknowledged no tribunal superior to their own; that the king had perjured himself so often that they could not trust him; that he had confessed himself guilty, that the deeds by which he had freed them from their allegiance were known to all the world, and that they had chosen the Duke of Holstein as his successor.

And indeed Frederick, Duke of Holstein, was proclaimed king of Denmark in January, 1523. The Hansa fleet by sea, the support of the clergy and nobles by land—that clergy and those nobles whom Christian had oppressed—conduced to this result.

A manifesto put forth by Lübeck made known to the Emperor of Germany and the Empire how "the city after long patience and repeated prayers, in consideration of her oaths and duties towards the Holy Roman Empire and remembering the inevitable damage done to body, honour, and goods, had taken up arms to prosecute the wanton insurer and aggressor of the Holy Roman Empire."

This manifesto was one of the little farces the Hanseatic League loved to play with their supposed liege lord and sovereign, the Emperor of Germany, each time they took independent action and showed by deeds how little they heeded his authority or wishes.

In vain Christian, after his deposition, tried to rally his subjects around him. Fearing probably that revenge would be taken upon his person for his cruel massacres in Sweden, he decided that discretion was the better part of valour. Choosing twenty of his best and fastest ships, he placed on board of them all the State papers, all the gold and silver that had been hoarded in the public buildings, and the State jewels. On April 13, 1523, he, his wife and three children together with Sigbrit, "the last packed away in a chest with the treasures," quaintly writes a contemporary chronicler, went on board the largest of the vessels, whereupon they all set sail for the Netherlands. It was nothing more or less than flight, and an acknowledgment that Gustavus Vasa and his ally the Hansa, through its representative Lübeck had conquered; that the League, though declining in might, was still able, as in the most glorious times of its history, to play with kings like dice, deposing and installing them.

Two years later the same city of Lübeck was called upon to arbitrate in a conflict between the two kings, which it thus had made, Frederick of Denmark and Gustavus of Sweden. As the price of its intervention and of the sacrifices it had made on their behalf, the city, in the name of the League, of course, asked great favours, favours which were accorded by treaty, and which were to be the last smiles of Fortune, about to become fickle to the union she had favoured so long.

Meanwhile, in June, 1523, Gustavus Vasa had been, by unanimous consent, elected King of Sweden. It is amusing to read that Stockholm, the last city to surrender to its new ruler, the last faithful to Christian, refused, even after it had capitulated, to deliver up the keys of the gates to Gustavus. The governor handed them over to two Lübeck councillors, present on the occasion, with the words, "We present to the imperial city of Lübeck the kingdom and the city, and not to that rogue, Gustavus Erikson, who stands there."

It must not be supposed, however, that Christian so quietly and easily abandoned his Danish crown to his uncle and rival. He made many attempts to enlist the various courts in his favour. Especially did he try to gain the help of his brother-in-law, the emperor, but the League was too clever and too strong for him. He did get together an army of mercenaries, but his means of paying them soon ran out, though to attain that end he pawned or sold all his treasures and the queen's jewels. At last, he had to fly in terror from his own soldiers who were enraged at his inability either to pay them their wages, or at least lead them to some town they could plunder.

Nevertheless, Christian was not daunted. He was a man not easily dismayed. He intrigued on every hand to regain his kingdom, and at last, fancying that the Lutheran doctrines he had embraced prejudiced the emperor against him, he formally renounced Protestantism and returned into the bosom of the Romish Church.

Christian had not erred in his calculations. This step induced Charles to be more favourable to him, and for a while he lent him his countenance, soon, however, to withdraw it. Still the brief favour sufficed to enable him to get together a strong army to attack Denmark. Frederick, alarmed, turned to Lübeck for aid, and did not turn in vain. Indeed, his ambassadors admitted that "Lübeckers had shown themselves in this time of need, not like mere neighbours, but like fathers to Denmark."

After many vicissitudes of fortune, Christian at last abandoned the idea of regaining his old rights by force of arms. He craved an interview with his uncle and a free passage to Copenhagen. This safe passage was accorded to him and its terms were couched in the most sacred and solemn words. The Hanseatic representatives enforced the promise on their own account. Not suspecting treachery, unwarned, Christian stepped on board the vessel that was to convey him to the Danish capital, and arrived in Copenhagen with the fond hope that Frederick would receive him like the prodigal son. Instead of allowing him to land at once, however, he was detained in the harbour for five days, under the pretext that Frederick was absent, and at last when permitted to set foot on dry land, he was invited to meet the king at Flensburg, and was told that the fleet had orders to carry him thither.

Then, and only then, the unfortunate man suspected that he had been betrayed. And so it was. Frederick and his councillors pronounced the safe conduct null and void; Christian was taken prisoner, and amid fierce ejaculations of rage and despair, was locked up in the "Blue Tower" of the Castle of Sonderburg. Here for fifteen years in company with his favourite dwarf, Christian had to suffer painful confinement that only ended with his death. His confinement was unjust, no doubt, but it was richly merited.

Unmourned by his relations, or the aristocracy he had oppressed, Christian's memory lived among the peasants and lower classes, of whom he had been the supposed friend, a friendship that no doubt had no higher aim than his own ends, but which never had occasion to show its true character. His name, consequently, became a watchword among the people, and inspired those who soon after were to be the leaders in great convulsions in the Scandinavian provinces. But this is outside the course of my history.

II.

KING FREDERICK AND KING GUSTAVUS VASA.

In speaking of Christian's continued aggressions and his death, we have somewhat anticipated the course of our story. We left our League in the proud consciousness of having made two kings and expelled a third. It was but natural that they should now look for some reward in the gratitude of Frederick and Gustavus. They thought that the moment had come to regain their ascendency in the Scandinavian north. But they were to learn the old, old lesson once again: "Put not thy trust in princes."

Frederick was the first to show his colours. It was true that he had sworn to the Hansa not only restitution, but extension of all their ancient rights and privileges, but when they demanded as a first pledge of friendly feeling, that the Baltic should be absolutely closed to the Netherlanders, and that indeed no one might trade in that sea but themselves, Frederick met them with an inexorable refusal. We should be wrong if we regarded this refusal as a mere display of ingratitude on the king's part. He saw that the claim was detrimental to the interests of his own subjects, whom, after all, he was bound to consider first.

But he went much further. He dissolved the German Society that traded at Copenhagen and insisted that all Hanseatics should be subjected to the same laws as his own subjects. Further, he took under his protection the inhabitants of Bornholm, which island was under the rule of Lübeck, having been given up to that city by reason of forfeiture. For the natives groaned under the Hansa's rule, and declared "they would rather be under the Turks, than under the German, Christian, imperial city."

In vain did Lübeck protest to Frederick; in vain did she remind him of his promises, point to his treaties, and recall his written and spoken words. She had to ask herself bitterly what she had gained in return for the great sacrifices she had made to change the ruler of Denmark. The uncle had become the nephew, that was all, and worse than the nephew, because less impetuous and passionate, and, therefore, more determined and dangerous. Added to this, they fell out about religious matters. Frederick encouraged the new faith, while the Queen of Hansa, stubbornly conservative in all matters, remained until the spring of 1531 an adherent of the old religion.

In 1553 Frederick died. An interregnum of more than a year followed, during which the hopes of Lübeck to re-establish her authority in the north revived; and were fed and fanned by the Burgomaster Jürgen Wullenweber. It was to prove the last flickering of the Hansa's glory.

But before we speak of the agitated period of Wullenweber's ambitious plans, let us see how, on his part, Gustavus Vasa showed his gratitude to the town to which he owed so much.

Gustavus Vasa had even less consideration than Frederick. During his residence in Lübeck he had learned to appreciate the material results that sprang from trade, and was secretly resolved that his own subjects and not these strangers should benefit by the country's resources. At first he, like Frederick, accorded the Hansa munificent charters. Indeed, he could not do less than assent to all their demands; he was deeply their debtor for money advanced during his wars, for material as well as moral assistance. He had no gold or silver to offer them, but he could accord them the exclusive use of those gold mines, the Baltic and the Sound. The Hansa should have the trading monopoly "for ever and ever," so ran the words of the charter.

But as soon as Gustavus felt the crown firmly planted on his head, and had in part paid off his debt, he applied himself to securing the commercial independence of his country and to making the League understand the meaning of the words "for ever," when they occur in a promise. He resolutely set his face against the Hanseatic claims for monopoly. "Gustavus was an angel at first," piteously writes the Lübeck official chronicler; "Alas, that he should so soon have become a devil."

In open assembly, 1526, the king did not hesitate to speak the following words of unmistakable clearness: "We must," he said, "withdraw from the strangers their unrestricted liberty; we must open the Swedish harbours to all ships." Next year even more definite words were spoken in the assembly. It was decided "to curtail the Hanseatic privileges without further delay, as seriously prejudicial to the kingdom."

There was one way by which Lübeck could retain in leading strings the "vassals," as she proudly called them, who had grown over her head. This was by means of their still unpaid debts. But Gustavus worked unremittingly towards attaining this end. His country, which was poor, had been yet further impoverished by wars, but still he succeeded, by means of heavy taxation, in raising supplies. He taxed everything that he could think of. It is said even hazel-nuts were subjected to this burden. Nay he even persuaded various towns and communes to melt down their church bells in order to expunge the national debt. By these trenchant means he succeeded in reducing it to a small amount by the year 1532, and then threatened the Hansa with yet more repressive measures, if they ventured to persist in claiming their ancient privileges.

No wonder that the ill-humour of the Lübeckers grew from day to day, and that they used to say to each other, "This is our thanks for having made an ox driver a king."

But Gustavus never swerved from his fixed resolve to make an end of Hanseatic privileges and monopolies as far as concerned his kingdom. By the time of his death in 1560 the power of the League was broken in Sweden beyond all hope or possibility of revival.

III.

WULLENWEBER.

AMONG the various disintegrating influences at work upon the League we have already named the Reformation. The new doctrines were destined at first to bring little blessing to the land in which they took their birth, and more especially to the Hansa was the purer creed to prove a source of dissension, resulting in eventual dissolution. Among other causes this was due to the fact that the cities did not all or at the same time embrace Protestantism. Thus a schism arose in their very midst: the Protestant cities eyeing the Catholic with distrust, and vice versâ. Moreover, these changes of view and system led to great disunion in the various towns themselves, often temporarily weakening the authority of the municipality and causing the city to be too much pre-occupied to attend to the common affairs and the welfare of the entire League. The movement also took different forms in different centres. In some it came about quite easily, and found the ground all ready prepared; in others, it entered with strife and bloodshed, or with fanatical excesses and absurdities, as for example in Bremen, and Münster, where the over-excited sect of the Anabaptists held sway.

It was especially in the North, that the trade in indulgences, consequent on a Papal need for ready money, found the most rigid opponents. The clear-headed burghers resented this demand as an insolent defiance of their common sense, and many who had already been half unconsciously influenced by the stream of tendency towards a reformed faith, manifested in the persons of Wickliffe and Huss, felt that this outrageous and unblushing traffic was too much for their credulity. The travelling merchants bought Luther's pamphlets, and carried them to their various homes. The wandering apprentices learnt the stirring psalms of the "Wittenberg nightingale." A new spiritual day was dawning, above all for the lower classes, who, ignorant of Latin, the language of the Catholic creed, were unable to follow or comprehend the services of the church they attended.

It was in consequence of this awakening, and the wider and nobler mode of thinking, and the educating force which it implied, that hand-in-hand with the religious movement there became manifest also a political stirring. The character of this was democratic, and it is not hard to understand why it was so. The people who had groaned under the oppression of the clergy and of the aristocracy, who almost invariably were their allies, began to assert their rights. They could now read the Scriptures in the vulgar tongue, and thence could learn that the blind submission demanded by the priests was by no means an integral part of Christianity. They remembered how the cities had been founded on democratic principles; they drew to light old privileges and charters; and by their memory and their ardour they made things far from comfortable for the burgomasters and patricians who held the government of the towns. Especially was their power felt by the arrogant and dissolute clergy, whose property they confiscated and devoted to public purposes, and whose churches and monasteries they converted into almshouses and schools.

It is necessary to realize the absolute moral corruption of the priests, monks, and nuns, in order to comprehend the anger of the populace, and to excuse the excesses into which they were led by their righteous zeal. Nor must it be forgotten that the people had groaned under the Vehmic Tribunal, which persecuted heretics, and that they had beheld Christians burn their fellow-Christians for the glory of God.

Already, early in the century, Dr. Johann Bugenhagen had been elected Bishop of the Lutheran Hanseatic cities, and their need for such an office gives us an indication of their numbers and importance. Bugenhagen was a man specially suited to work out the reform of doctrines and to set in order church affairs, and this work he performed for the whole of Northern Germany and Denmark. The new movement gathered strength. It advanced like a mighty ocean with resistless power. Only Lübeck, of all the northern cities, remained untouched by the storms beating around it. True to its stubbornly conservative character it continued longer than the rest faithful to the Roman hierarchy. But even Lübeck had to yield. The pressure to which it gave way came from the people. For some time past these had craved teachers of "the purer word" as the new creed was at first called. At first the demands were refused on imperial authority, but after a while concessions were made. It was needful to conciliate the inhabitants, for the funds of the city were low, thanks to the wars for Frederick and Gustavus, and it was foreseen that new taxes would be submitted to with a bad grace. Indeed, when in 1529 the rulers appealed to the guilds to support them in imposing new taxes they were answered by a delegation of forty-eight persons who replied to the municipal demands in bold terms, of which the upshot was that they would treat of "no money questions until the municipality should permit the introduction of the evangelical teaching" and the sacrament be administered in both forms. This language was unmistakably clear, and the city rulers seeing the townspeople were in earnest, yielded to all their demands. Thus in 1531 Lübeck openly acknowledged the Lutheran creed. The democracy had spoken and triumphed. They had made their power felt; they were conscious of their success, and they did not mean easily to abandon their newly acquired position of importance. The leader and spokesman of this demonstration was Jürgen Wullenweber, the man whose ambition and energy were to give to the Hansa yet one more proud moment of triumph; one more, and the last.

The origin and the life of Jürgen Wullenweber are to this day wrapped in some mystery. It suited the various party factions to represent him respectively as an idol and a scoundrel. Even the records that survive concerning him in Lübeck are few. But modern research has unearthed much, and proved incontestably that Wullenweber, even if personally ambitious, was a true and disinterested patriot. Time has thrown round his figure a sort of mystical halo. He has been made the hero of many German romances, and the protagonist of various German plays.

Of his family little is known except that they came from Hamburg, and were no doubt at first wool weavers, as the name implies. Jürgen's name does not appear in any Lübeck register until the year 1530, when he was chosen a member of the Burgher Committee. He is there described as a merchant.

This man had been the chosen spokesman of the democratic party on the occasion when they defied the city rulers. Soon after he was elected into the municipal council, and it was not long before it was generally felt that new blood stirred within that body. In 1533 King Frederick of Denmark died. During the interregnum that followed the Danes entered into a defensive alliance with the Swedes against their common oppressors, the Hansa. The Scandinavian nations wished to emancipate themselves from the League's tutelage. Wullenweber at a glance recognized the full gravity of the situation. He thought now or never the time had come to reassert, if need be by force of arms, the Hansa's might; now or never was the moment to punish for their ingratitude and faithlessness the two kings Lübeck had created. He called together a council, meeting in the guildhall, March 16, 1533, and with eloquent, ardent words, he laid before the assembly the whole political situation, its gravity, and its possibilities. He showed how the entire Hanseatic trade was endangered by the commerce of the Netherlands in the Baltic. He urged the bold scheme that Lübeck should take forcible possession of the Sound, and thus hold in its own hands the key to that sea.

It was a scheme which had often crossed the minds of the Lübeck councillors, but which since the days of Waldemar Atterdag they had never tried to carry into effect, recognizing probably that the might of the League was not great enough to retain such a point of vantage, even if their physical force sufficed to gain it.

Wullenweber's eloquence and self-confidence, however, carried the day. The next thing was to consider the matter of funds. Jürgen reminded his hearers of the silver and gold ornaments and church decoration confiscated by the State in consequence of the Reformation. These he said could be melted down. As before, he was listened to and obeyed. He spared nothing in his zeal, even the colossal chandelier of St. Mary's Church had to go into the melting pot to make cannons. So much for the funds. It was now needful to find the men. This was no arduous task. Lübeck was a favourite resort for the mercenaries who in those times roamed the world in search of adventure and pay. Among these men were Max Meyer, a native of Hamburg, destined to become the *condottiere* of the League in its last war.

The figure of Max Meyer is a most romantic one. His parents can never have credited what the fairies sang around the boy's cradle, that he would become a friend of the great king of England, Henry VIII., and have his portrait painted by the most eminent artist of his day, Holbein. He was born in the humblest circumstances, and brought up as a blacksmith. Two great iron conduits, the work of his hand, are shown in Hamburg to this day. He was a tall, strong, fine looking man, with lively eyes and large hands, and whoever beheld him at his smithy, swinging his large hammer upon the anvil, could not help fancying that he beheld some old Norse Viking, who was moulding his own sword, so bold and enterprising did he look. And, indeed, a desire for adventures stirred in his blood. He knew no rest beside his smithy fire. He felt he must go into the world. Already, as an apprentice, he had fought in some of the northern disturbances, had served as ensign under Christian II. Throwing aside his hammer, he once more ranged the world in search of danger and distinction. Coming to Lübeck, in the course of his travels, he was engaged by that city to lead the 800 men whom she was sending to the emperor as aid against the Turks. A year after he returned to his native city, glorious and victorious, rich in booty and honours. Hamburg received him as though he were a great and powerful lord, and he impressed all his friends and relations by his magnificence. When he rode away to return to Lübeck, dressed in a full cuirass, with nodding plumes upon his helmet, a local chronicler wrote that "he was so good to look upon, that, although he was a blacksmith, yet he was such a fine, clever fellow, he could pass anywhere for a nobleman." He left Hamburg in triumph, trumpeters heading the procession, in which there were forty men in full armour, and two great waggon-loads of booty. The foremost men of the city conducted him to the gates.

Arrived at Lübeck, Max Meyer entered it in the same proud manner in which he had left Hamburg, greatly impressing the townspeople by his wealth and splendour. Among those who saw his entry and beheld him with a favourable eye was the rich widow of the Burgomaster Lunte. She lost her heart entirely to the handsome blacksmith, and at last she married him, sorely against the wish and will of her family. Thus Max Meyer became a person of importance in Lübeck, thanks to his marriage and his wife's connections, and, consequently, he was thrown into close relations with Wullenweber. The latter was not slow to recognize that he was dealing with no common person, and that here might be the instrumental hand to aid his schemes. And, indeed, Max Meyer soon became Wullenweber's close ally.

It was while Lübeck was thus at war with the Netherlands that Max Meyer, as commander of the city's war-ships, approached the English coasts, hearing that some twenty-four Dutch merchant vessels were sailing in these waters. He hoped to capture them and to obtain rich booty. In this attempt, however, he failed; but he took, instead, some Spanish ships laden with English goods. This was a breach of the peace, since the Hansa was not at war with England; but, regardless of this act, Meyer, perhaps because in want of provisions, actually sailed into an English harbour and anchored his vessel. King Henry, who had heard of his presence, and knew him to be a Lübeck captain carrying on hostilities against the Netherlands, received him with great honour. The English king had his own private reasons for wishing to stand well with the Hansa. He knew they were Protestants, and that they were not too well disposed to the Emperor Charles, from whom he also had become estranged, now that he had grown weary of his Imperial Highness's aunt, the elderly Catherine of Aragon. As the Pope would not listen to the scruples of his tender conscience about having taken to wife his brother's widow, from whom he sought a divorce on that account—according to his own showing—he hoped, not wrongly, that the Protestants would take less stubborn and unscriptural views of the indissolubility of the marriage contract, and he therefore sought to conciliate all Protestant powers.

But the England of those days, like the England of ours, was a law-abiding country, and three days after King Henry had received Meyer with great feasts and honours at Court, the royal guest was arrested as a pirate. It was pleaded that he ought to suffer the common penalty of piracy, that is to say, death. In these straits the merchants of the Steelyard came forward to aid their representative, offering to stand surety for him. They succeeded in averting the sentence of death by restoring the value of the goods seized; they could not succeed in relieving him from the imprisonment which his breach of international faith had incurred. Max Meyer had to go to prison, whence he was released at last only by the intervention of the municipality of Lübeck, though not until he had almost served his time.

Justice satisfied, Max Meyer returned to King Henry's Court, and was once more made a welcome guest. Whether he was empowered by the city to act as plenipotentiary, or whether, in the first instance, he acted on his own account, does not appear. But what is certain is that he made a number of proposals to King Henry, to which the latter lent a willing ear, that Meyer was knighted by his royal host, and received from him a golden chain in token of the honour in which he held him, and that Henry further promised him a yearly income of three hundred and a half golden crowns. The terms were that the English king should advance a considerable sum to Lübeck towards her war expenses—a sum which the city promised to refund and to double, out of the first profits derived from the conquered Danish kingdom.

Henry's object in this alliance was chiefly to harass and annoy his Catholic compeers, and to have a rich Protestant ally in the complications that were thickening round him. There was not much result from the friendship on either side; but for the moment, the news that the King of England was their friend and supporter, gave renewed courage to the democratic party in Lübeck. It also gave them ready cash wherewith to carry on the war with the Netherlands and their friends the Danes. For war it must be. This Wullenweber openly advocated, after various vain attempts to induce the Danish king to grant the Hansa's requests. Wullenweber himself had on two occasions been sent by Lübeck as their ambassador to Copenhagen, and had returned home furious at the want of success that met his negotiations. Why should not the Hansa, he pleaded, once more play the rôle of king-maker? Gustavus Vasa had proved a failure and a disappointment to the League, had broken every promise he had made to them. Let a new king be put in his place. Those who had helped the Swedish king into power with a hundred marks, should help him out of power with five hundred marks, he boasted; adding that before the next carnival he should make a masquerade before King Gustavus that he would not despise. For Denmark too he had his plan; and this was no other than to reinstate Christian II., once the enemy of the League. Christian had always opposed the aristocracy and the clergy, and had proclaimed himself the friend of the people. Reinstated by the Hansa, he would owe them gratitude, so reckoned Wullenweber, and being popular with the lower classes in Denmark the League might reckon upon their support. To aid him in this enterprise the dictator turned to the Count of Oldenburg, a relation of the dethroned king, an intrepid and intelligent Lutheran known as the Alcibiades of the North.

Christopher of Oldenburg, at that time thirty years of age, handsome in face and stature, was one of those princelings of Germany, of which the race is not quite extinct, whose title was their sole fortune and who, in former days, were willing to sell their services to any king who needed their aid, and in more modern times are utilized to marry the redundant princesses of royal parentage, for whom no match can be found among the reduced number of reigning houses. These bold *condottieri*, whether in search of adventure, of booty, or of a marriage portion and ease, had little but their wits to rely upon. Christopher of Oldenburg, for example, possessed as his whole patrimony an old convent. He had attracted around him, however, a band of devoted troops, free lances, willing to follow wherever he led: men without fatherland, faith, or ideal, the scum of all lands, whose desire was bloodshed and booty, and whose sole religion was obedience to their chosen captain. Christopher of Oldenburg was not an ordinary chief. With the military courage of a *condottiere* he combined a bright intellect and a mind of real elevation. He was well educated and well read. A copy of Homer accompanied him in all his adventures; his passionate desire was to be a hero of romance. This was the kind of instrument Wullenweber required; the man who could realize, appreciate, and help to carry out his bold designs. And these were, in a word, to put the Hansa in possession of the Sound. Possessing this advantage, with two obedient monarchs upon the respective thrones of Denmark and Sweden, and enjoining the moral and material support of the English king, the League would once more be as in the days of its greatest glory.

So reasoned Wullenweber, and not without reason. But he was too ambitious, or, at any rate, too bold. He had not reckoned with the apathy and the economic egotism that dictated the policy of the sister towns. He was to play a dangerous game. He staked his all and he lost.

Wullenweber's original plan was to attack Denmark, while carrying on at the same time the war with the Netherlands. This proposal, which besides being audacious, meant a great outlay of money, alarmed the other cities, and, above all, the town of Hamburg. Owing to her endeavours, a brilliant congress was assembled within her walls during the month of March, 1534, when it was proposed to examine carefully the various points of grievance at issue between the Hansa and her opponents. There were present delegates from the various Baltic cities, imperial councillors, Netherland grandees, and Danish nobles. But none of them exceeded in outward splendour the representatives of Lübeck, Jürgen Wullenweber and Max Meyer, as they rode into the city of Hamburg, dressed in full armour preceded by the chief of Lübeck's militia, by trumpeters and drummers, and followed by sixty armed riders. The timid Hamburgers glanced at all this military display with some terror, feeling assured that such a proud bearing meant that the town that sent forth these men would not easily yield its claims. Already, before the first assembly of the delegates, Wullenweber had been regarded with an evil eye by many of the other Hanseatic envoys. They could not grasp the ultimate ends he had in view for the benefit of the League. They thought he was inciting to needless expense and disturbance. They did not understand, still less did they sympathize with, the democratic wave which had swept over Lübeck, and which had brought two such men as Wullenweber and Max Meyer to the front. Local chroniclers, speaking of this meeting of plenipotentiaries, call the Hamburgers "the peace loving," and accuse the Lübeckers of being "the instigators of the woful wars."

On March 2, 1534, the Congress was opened by the Burgomaster of Hamburg in the grand council chamber of the local guildhall, an historical room, unfortunately destroyed in the great fire that devastated Hamburg in 1842. In an eloquent speech the local magnate described the miseries entailed by the war in which the Lübeckers had engaged against the Dutch, and urged that peace should be concluded in the interest of the common Hanseatic merchants. The burgomaster was followed by an imperial councillor, who said the same things in yet stronger terms. Wullenweber was visibly angered. His anger was increased when the Dutch envoy rose to his feet and claimed that it should be laid down as a principle "that the sea and all other waters should be free to the shipping of whosoever listed," adding that "if the Lübeckers suffered damage in consequence, they should find comfort in God's will and in the mutability of all earthly things."

This was too much for Wullenweber's temper to bear. He declared with violence that if the speeches continued in this tone and spirit he and his colleagues should leave the assembly, and this, in fact, they shortly afterwards did. Not only did he leave the assembly, but the city also, after he found that all the demands of Lübeck fell on deaf ears. But before he left he made a powerful speech in the guildhall, wherein he asserted and maintained that all he had done had been done solely for the general benefit of the League. He even accused the other Hanseatic delegates of being Dutch in sympathy, "a thing," he added, "which they and the Dutch would repent of as long as he lived."

He was asked to explain his projects. He sketched a plan almost identical in spirit with the Navigation Act of Cromwell; it might indeed almost be regarded as its prototype. When taunted regarding the egotism of this proposal, when told that the sole purpose that inspired it was to prevent the vessels of other powers from deriving a profit out of carriage of goods, Wullenweber retorted as angrily as Cromwell might have done, and with the same contempt for the petty spirits that could see no higher object, nor any larger or wider aims than purely personal and financial ones. To Wullenweber's mind there was at stake not only vulgar profit, but the control and supervision of the Baltic trade, the maintenance of the Hanseatic colonies, indeed of all commercial navigation; in a word, of everything that had made the Hansa what it was.

The colonial policy pursued by the Hansa, which had been one of its sources of strength, became a cause of weakness, and ultimately led to its fall. It was based in all essentials upon the same principles as those pursued later by other nations with regard to their foreign non-European colonies, and which led in time to the loss of these same colonies. The chief points were these: that the direct intercourse and traffic with the Eastern settlements and their commercial domain were reserved exclusively to Hanseatic vessels, and that transport by land was forbidden, because in that case it was not so easy to keep watch upon business, and to be assured that no Hanseatic laws were transgressed. Foreign flags were excluded from all Eastern ports and non-Hanseatic merchants not admitted to their markets. All traffic from the Eastern cities to non-Hanseatic places, and all traffic with these places were to go by way of Lübeck. This is the sum of the Lübeck Staple Act, which had a little sunk into abeyance during the late disorders and which Wullenweber desired to see fully reinforced. Again, to refer to England's dictator, with whom Wullenweber had some points of resemblance, this Lübeck staple was neither more nor less than the

British staple, prescribed by Cromwell's Navigation Act, when it excluded foreign flags from American harbours, and interdicted the Americans from sending ships to any other European harbour than those of the mother-land. Two hundred years separated these two Tribunes of the People from each other, and yet, in some respects, their ideals and ideas were identical. But to return to the course of our narrative, which has been interrupted in order to make clearer the aims the Lübeck burgomaster had in view.

Wullenweber grew daily more angered at the tone adopted in the Congress, not only from his opponents, but by those from whom he had a right to look for support.

On March 12th, accompanied by Max Meyer, and the same military train with which he had entered, he left Hamburg, shaking the dust of the city off his feet in anger. He was soon followed by the delegates of the other Baltic cities. The congress had come to an untimely end, and nothing had been settled.

Wullenweber's object in returning so precipitately was twofold. He desired to know the wishes of the city under the changed circumstances, and he wished to complain of the colleagues who had failed to support him. This precipitous return greatly alarmed the citizens, all the more because during Wullenweber's absence the aristocratic party had tried to lodge various complaints against the absent burgomaster, and to stir up the people to revolt and discontent. They had even ventured to insinuate that he was guilty of "stealing and treason." Indeed, the tumult in the city was so great and seemed so threatening, that many timid spirits began to think that discretion was the better part of valour, and that it would be well to absent themselves awhile.

Into this state of affairs Wullenweber, by his unexpected return, dropped like a bombshell. He saw that energetic steps were needful here. He did not hesitate for a moment to take them. A meeting of the Forty-six was held, who were charged to invite the burghers to a general assembly in St. Mary's Church. More than a thousand persons replied to the summons. Wullenweber mounted the pulpit. In ardent words he expressed his patriotic intentions, and related in detail the reasons for his abrupt departure from Hamburg. He also complained most bitterly of the conduct of those who should have supported him. Next day he addressed a similar meeting in the guildhall, and spoke, if possible, in stronger terms, openly accusing his opponents of envy, and saying he was well aware that some among them even intended to attack him at night in his house, and to make him prisoner.

The upshot of his two speeches was that the democratic party once more gained the upper hand; that it was agreed that Wullenweber should act entirely according to his own discretion in the matter with the Netherlanders; that three of the municipal councillors inimical to him should be removed from their place; and that various burghers, whom he designated as "of Swedish or Netherlandish sympathy," should either be banished or imprisoned.

With his power thus increased, Wullenweber returned to Hamburg, and the congress was reopened. Since, however, he could gain no support from the other Hanseatic cities for his policy of continuing the war with the Netherlands, he at last consented to accept a truce of four years; a truce which he recognized would leave his hands free for the execution of his other plans.

Nor did he hesitate for a moment to put them into action. Riders and foot messengers were engaged in all directions; the "peace ships" were put into war condition; emissaries were sent to the sister towns to explain fully the purpose of the new attack upon the Scandinavian North, and to ask what assistance they proposed to render in money, ships, and men.

Wullenweber's plan was really a stroke of genius, and by no means so foolhardy or foolish as his enemies have since tried to prove it. It was: to form around the whole Baltic basin a sort of German confederation, and had it succeeded, or rather had it not been impeded by the petty vacillating policy of the other cities, it would have marked a re-birth of the Hansa, and there would have been no power in the North that could have opposed it.

In May, 1534, hostilities began with Denmark, and Sweden was also threatened with armed intervention, in case the broken promises to the Hansa were still left unfulfilled. To the people, the counter promise was made that they should have nothing to fear from the Hansa's armies, "if they did not second the arrogance of their king."

To this Gustavus replied by demanding help from his brother rulers, saying "that it was intolerable that the Lübeckers should put up for auction the three good old northern realms, just as if they were their market wares."

In a short time the whole North was in flames. At first extraordinary success crowned the attacks of the Hansa's fleet and armies, and by Midsummer, 1534, almost the entire Danish kingdom was in the hands of the Lübeckers. Then fortune somewhat turned, and Lübeck had to see an army surround its very walls, much to the consternation of the inmates. This danger was however happily averted, thanks to clever negotiations and force of arms; but meanwhile things had grown yet more complicated and intricate in the Scandinavian question. Party faction and religious jealousies prevented corporate action. There was a moment when things looked so black that even Wullenweber was daunted, and the confession escaped him that "if he were not in the middle of all this muddle, he should take good care to keep outside it."

In the midst of these difficulties dawned the year 1535, one of the most fatal in the life of the German States; a year destined to unravel and settle for ever the northern confusions.

Such a spectacle as the Baltic presented at this period it had not shown for many a long day. In the Sound, in all the Danish seas, in all the narrow waterways that separated the islands from one another, were seen waving from the tall masts of the Hanseatic "peace ships," the flag of the League, and in the harbours of Lübeck, Rostock, and Stralsund, more ships were put upon a war footing. There was likewise seen the white-and-black banner of the Prussian flotilla, sent to aid the imprisoned Danish king, while the flags of Denmark and Sweden fluttered from their respective vessels.

Nor was the spectacle on land less animated than that on the sea. Troops, mercenaries of every land and language crowded the shore of the mainland. It was evident that the encounter would be severe, the resistance great. The first check came to the Hansa in the shape of the capture of Max Meyer, owing to the false information given to him by the Danish commandant of Scania. Christian III. was proclaimed king of Denmark, and Gustavus Vasa lent the new king his most active aid. Things did not look well for the League, but Wullenweber, though he grew serious and thoughtful as he learnt the news, was not discouraged. He continued to confide "in divine help."

A vast number of intrigues were now set on foot, whose purpose was to alienate or conciliate, as the case might be, the various Catholic and Protestant kings and princes; thus giving to the entire quarrel a party character. Lübeck counted on the assistance of Henry of England, and offered the king in return for substantial subsidies the entire kingdom of Denmark as his booty.

Meanwhile Max Meyer was fretting at his enforced imprisonment and absence from the scene of action. In March, by means of a subtle, but not specially honest, subterfuge, he managed to escape from the castle that held him, and thanks to his fertility of resource, and to his popularity, he soon found himself surrounded by quite a little army, and resolved to carry on the war in his own manner, and according to his own ideas. It is said that he offered the throne of Denmark to Francis I. of France, an offer which that monarch refused. Nor did he forget his old friend, bluff King Hal of England, who, in his turn, seems not to have forgotten him. Though Henry nominally rejected the proposals made to him by Max Meyer, it is certain he continued to give him substantial and moral support, so that, owing to English help, Max Meyer was able to hold out in the seaboard castle of Vardberg, in which he had ensconced himself, until his tragic end. The gateway over its lintel, bore, till the time of its destruction, the arms of the Tudor, a delicate compliment from Max Meyer to Henry, implying that the castle was in very truth the king's.

The first great encounter of the armies took place by sea in the month of June. In number and excellence of ships the Hansa had the advantage. The Lübeckers were still the best shipbuilders of the northern world, and many of the Danish and Swedish vessels sent against them were nothing more than herring-boats and fishing smacks roughly put on a war footing. If victory depended on strength and numbers alone, it seemed assured to the Hansa. Unhappily, among the many secret methods employed by the aristocratic party to break the power of the democratic faction, there existed bribery and corruption of the ship captains. The usual Hanseatic concord was absent.

Indeed, herein is to be found in a great measure the explanation of the ill success of the Hansa. When Jürgen Wullenweber dreamed that he would revive the days and glories of Waldemar Atterdag he forgot that the burgomasters of those days when they set out for battle were followed by an army consisting of the burghers themselves, that, for example, in the struggle for Scania in 1368, no less than sixteen hundred citizens gave up their lives to gain a victory for the League. With the increase of wealth had grown up, as is usual, an increase of luxury and idleness. Citizens of rich Hanseatic towns contented themselves with keeping watch in turns at the city gates, with defending their own city walls, with interfering in street brawls and keeping order in the town. But when it came to active fighting, to going abroad to battle, they preferred to hire the mercenaries with which Germany was overrun, thanks to the disturbed state of the land arising out of the continual wars of Charles V. Hence arose the class known as Landsknechte; hence it came about that in those days German often fought against German, and that all true patriotic sentiments were extinguished. The rich Queen of the Hansa, Lübeck, had of course met with no difficulty in finding numbers willing to serve under her flag and to accept her pay, but these men, as is but too natural, did not fight with that enthusiasm and ardour which men display when the cause is their own. Jürgen Wullenweber was of the old Hanseatic type, but the mould that had formed him was broken. His contemporaries were not up to the level of his noble and patriotic ambition. Had he been ably seconded the whole history of Northern Germany might have been transformed.

As we have said, the fleets met in hostile encounter in the month of June. After some heavy fighting the heavens themselves interposed in the strife. A great storm arose, driving the vessels of the foes asunder. Two days later the decisive combat was fought on land. The place of encounter was Assens, on the island of Fünen, a spot where human sacrifices used to be offered to the great Norse god Odin. This battle of Assens ended in the complete discomfiture of the burgher army, and there followed immediately afterwards another meeting by sea, when the Hansa had to suffer the shame of seeing some of its vessels flee before the enemy, while others capitulated in cowardly fashion.

The consequences of these battles made themselves felt instantly. What Wullenweber had said the previous year when he was yet the victor was now realized, "that it was easier to conquer Denmark than to keep it." For not only Fünen, but Zealand and Scania fell off from the burgomaster's party after the defeat at Assens, and did homage to Christian III. as their king and ruler. Only Copenhagen, Malmöe, and a few small towns refused this allegiance, and still offered an armed resistance. But it was not to be of long duration.

Meanwhile the close of Wullenweber's proud career approached. It is characteristic of the whole course of German history, that the fall of Wullenweber, and the ultimate fall of the Hansa, were due not so much to external as to internal enemies. Petty jealousies, "particularism," to use their own phrase, that is to say, practising a church-steeple policy rather than a wide and liberal one, has ever been a danger to Germany. It defeated the efforts of Wullenweber, as it did those of the patriots of 1848, and of many more before and since.

In July the Hanseatic Diet was called together to consider the state of the League's affairs; and on this occasion a number of the cities, and chief among them the inland ones, found a much desired occasion to vent the wrath and envy which they had long nourished against Lübeck and its democratic dictator. A number of attacks, some of them of the most despicably petty character, were made against Wullenweber. The Lübeckers were told that they had permitted "irregular disorders," and that it was they who disturbed the general concord of the common Hansa. Most bitter of all were the charges launched by Cologne, the town that had long been jealous of the power of her northern sister. Forgetful of the whole course of Hanseatic history, she ventured to say that it would seem strange to the emperor and other princely potentates, that a town like Lübeck should meddle with such great matters as the deposition and installation of kings.

To this taunt Lübeck replied with dignity, pointing out that she had no wish either to change the faith of the kings or to murder them (as Cologne had previously suggested), but that according to treaty she had the right to act as she had done, and that she had acted, not for the sake of exhibiting her own power, but because of the natural, intimate, and needful relationship that existed between Denmark and the Baltic towns. Since olden days no king might be elected in Denmark without the knowledge of Lübeck, and on this they had ever acted.

The men of Cologne were not abashed by this reference to history. They replied that it might be so, and that the Lübeckers had the right they would not deny; but they repeated, it made a strange impression upon kings and princes that the men of Lübeck should make and unmake kings.

Alas! how were the mighty fallen! What a degradation of sentiment in the Hansa when the cause of one was no longer the cause of all!

Some days later, in reply to a similar attack, the Lübeckers replied, in the old bold spirit that characterized the Hansa in its best times, "In one thing they had made a mistake, and that was when they helped two such worthless men as the kings of Denmark and Sweden to power, and had further made them great, in return for which they were now ill repaid."

Cologne then tried to shift its recriminations on to the religious ground. Glancing at the excesses committed in Münster by the

Anabaptists, she ventured to question the benefits that had accrued to Lübeck and other Hanse cities from the Reformation, concluding with the shameless words, "In our city we hang, behead, or drown all heretics, and find ourselves very comfortable in consequence."

To most of these attacks Wullenweber as representative of Lübeck had to reply in person. He knew too well that many of them were aimed directly at himself. He strove hard to keep his hot temper in check and to reply with moderation and dignity.

The attitude of these Diet meetings, however, was but to prove the prologue to the intrigues which were to eject Wullenweber and his party from power, and to break not only the hegemony of Lübeck, but that of the whole Hansa—a consummation the opponents certainly did not intend. "Those whom the gods wish to destroy they first strike with blindness," says the Latin proverb, and its truth was once more made manifest by the attitude of the Hanseatic towns among themselves. They who had ever been so strong and so united, now no longer held together in brotherly concord, and weakness and disruption were the result.

The instrument that was to spring the chief mine on Wullenweber and his party was found in the person of Nicholas Brömse. This man was one of the leading personages of the Municipal Council of Lübeck in the early days of the sixteenth century, and was burgomaster of the town in the days when Gustavus Vasa arrived there as a fugitive. Indeed, he is said to have been one of the most zealous friends and protectors of the young Vasa. When the Reformation dissensions began to stir in the city, Brömse was among the most pronounced opponents of the purer creed, and repeatedly, by his personal interference, retarded its introduction. Indeed once, after it was officially introduced, he succeeded, in virtue of his personal influence with Charles V., in getting the Lutheran creed forbidden in the town. In so doing, however, he somewhat exceeded his limits; his action aroused suspicion in the council and hatred among the citizens; and finally, in 1532, he had to resign his post and fly secretly from Lübeck to escape the wrath of his enemies. He made his way to the imperial Court, at that time located in Brussels, and there he gained the ear and favour of Charles. Thence he watched with anxious curiosity the course which events were taking in his native town. He was biding his time to revenge himself upon the city that had ejected him, and upon the burgomaster who had supplanted him in popular favour.

When Nicholas Brömse learnt how the Hanseatic Diet had censured the action of Jürgen Wullenweber, he thought that the time for which he had long waited had come. He employed all his personal influence with the emperor to induce him to take a decisive step against the city of Lübeck, and with good result. For there issued from the imperial council chamber, June 7, 1535, a decree, stating that unless within six weeks and three days from the receipt of this document the town of Lübeck had abolished all democratic innovations and reinstated in the government Nicholas Brömse and other councillors banished together with him, the town would be declared under the imperial ban.

With Jesuitical astuteness not a word was breathed regarding Church reforms, but it was fully understood that a blow was aimed at the Lutheran creed quite as much as at Jürgen Wullenweber and the democratic party.

A Hanseatic Diet was sitting at Lübeck when this decree arrived. A committee was at once chosen to discuss the acceptance of the imperial mandate. It decided that obedience must be tendered to the dictates of the imperial council. In consequence the democratic party resigned power, and Wullenweber, who understood well that the whole was chiefly aimed at him, saw that there remained nothing for him to do but follow his party.

After delivering before the Diet a speech of great dignity marked by unusual moderation, in which he said if it were the will of God and were adjudged for the common weal that he should retire, he should certainly not refuse, he laid down in August, 1535, the office he had filled with such zeal and patriotic ambition.

It is characteristic of popular gratitude that when he returned from the guildhall, after completing the deed of renunciation, he was followed by a crowd that hissed and hooted him. This people of shopkeepers turned upon the man who was their true friend because the wars had impoverished them, had slackened their trade, and had brought distress within their walls. They did not recognize, or they forgot, that they themselves had encouraged the outbreak of these hostilities, and had applauded and sustained the man who proposed them; and that had he been better supported, his plans would have resulted in their pecuniary benefit.

It is evident that his fellow-rulers among the Lübeck Council knew that Wullenweber had been wronged, since they offered to bestow on him for six years the governorship of a neighbouring dependency. This he refused, but before he finally quitted office he took good care that the welfare and existence of the new creed should not be endangered by the return of the zealous Papist, Brömse, and also that an amnesty should be accorded to all political offenders.

Shortly afterwards Brömse entered the city in stately procession, preceded by a hundred and fifty horsemen. He proceeded at once to St. Mary's Church and took possession of the burgomaster's chair, whence he listened to the minutes decided upon by the Hanseatic Diet. The decree by no means pleased his Catholic soul that whatever else was reinstated, the new religion should be left intact; but he held his peace and trusted to time, as he had already done, with good result, while he waited at the Court of the Emperor Charles. In this one respect, however, he was to be disappointed. Lübeck never again changed its creed, or bowed its head to the Papal party.

But where now was the man to find peace who but recently had held as ruler both sides of the Sound, who had dared to fling the gauntlet to two monarchs, and who had been dictator throughout all Scandinavia? Notwithstanding many negotiations, peace had not yet been concluded between Lübeck and Denmark. Copenhagen was still held by the Hansa's allies. It is easy to understand that the temptation presented itself to Wullenweber to make common cause with them, and to try in yet another form to gain success for the League. But whether this was really his plan or not we have now no means of deciding. The latter years of Wullenweber's life are wrapped in much mystery, owing to intentional falsification of facts on the part of his enemies. Thus much is certain, that in the autumn of 1535 he set forth on a journey northwards, making for the province of Halland on the Cattegat, where lay the castle held by Max Meyer. Probably he wished to confer with his trusty colleague. His friends tried to dissuade him from his intention, reminding him that his road led him through the territory of the Archbishop of Bremen, one of his most violent opponents. It was impossible, however, to control or guide this headstrong and fearless man. Ambition and self-confidence made him fall into the trap which his enemies had laid for him.

Nicholas Brömse and his followers, hearing of this journey, at once sent messengers to the ecclesiastical prince, and by heavy bribes bought him over to their side. In consequence, scarcely had Wullenweber touched the archbishop's domains than he was seized and imprisoned, regardless of the letter of safe conduct he bore about him. He was carried off to Rothenburg, one of the archbishop's castles, and for some weeks the world knew nothing of his whereabouts, until his foes had matured their plans against him.

Wullenweber's brother, Joachim, at that time one of the Council of Hamburg, was the first to be uneasy regarding Jürgen's fate, and he succeeded in ascertaining the fact of his imprisonment and the perpetrator of the deed. He addressed a letter to the archbishop, demanding an explanation of this breach of faith. The audacious prelate replied, that "Since it was notorious how designedly and presumptuously Jürgen had acted against the will of God, of the emperor, and of the spiritual rulers of Lübeck, and how he had spent a night in his, the archbishop's domains without his permission, his will or a safe conduct, he, as the emperor's relative and as prince of the empire, had held himself in duty bound towards his Church to take the man prisoner. Further reasons for this step would be made known in course of time."

Armed with this insolent reply Joachim Wullenweber turned to King Henry VIII. of England in his sore strait, and implored him to befriend the man who had ever befriended him. To this request Henry lent a ready ear and he pleaded, but in vain, for his "faithful and honoured friend," with the Council of Hamburg and Bremen, and at last with the archbishop himself.

But Brömse and his party were not the men to release their prey when once it had fallen into their hands. They were determined to have their revenge. They hated Wullenweber; Brömse, in particular, hated him so much that it was possible for a contemporary chronicler to declare that he even tore Wullenweber's flesh off his bones with his own teeth. This no doubt is a baseless charge. Nicholas Brömse, the patrician, with the delicate coquettish features of a woman, with the lily white hands that were noted among his contemporaries, is not likely to have done such a thing. He might be false and cruel, but he could not have been actively bestial and ferocious.

What is certain is that Wullenweber's enemies were determined to destroy him. So great and powerful a man could not be simply put aside; he had to be sacrificed. A truly fiendish scheme of incrimination was opened against him; so painful and unfair that it awoke pity even in the breasts of his contemporaries. Among them, Maria, at that time regent of the Netherlands, was so deeply moved by the burgomaster's fate, that she felt herself called upon to demand that the prisoner should at least be brought before an imperial governor, in order that his case might have a more impartial consideration. But Wullenweber's foes would not listen to any mild or merciful counsels. Their chief endeavour was to spread abroad a belief that the dictator had acted in concert and sympathy with the Anabaptists, at that moment the bogey with which to scare both Catholics and Protestants.

The exact means employed to break Wullenweber's strong spirit during the first months of his imprisonment are not known. There is no doubt, however, that he was subjected to torture, and that upon the rack he was made to acquiesce in statements, many of them quite false, and others distorted to serve the purpose of his tormentors. Among the so-called confessions were said to be an admission of his Anabaptist leanings, an intimation that he had proposed to murder and kill as many nobles as possible, that he had abstracted for his own private ends public and church property, and other statements, so manifestly out of keeping with his previously known character and general bearing, that it is amazing to think how his contemporaries, even those most opposed to him, could for a moment have given them credit.

Hero though Wullenweber was in the moral sense he was no hero at bearing physical pain, and, indeed, the two qualities by no means go together, nor does nervous shrinking from pain necessarily imply moral weakness. The contrary is often the case. The man of finely strung nerves, to whom bodily pain is on this account less supportable than to his more coarse-grained brother, is, for that very reason, capable of a refinement of sentiment and action equally unknown to the other. The beef-built man is apt to be beef-witted.

It is quite certain that all the admissions undoubtedly made by Wullenweber were wrung from him under excruciating tortures. Indeed, in the hour of his death, and in two letters to his brother Joachim, he affirmed that "the jailer of Bremen, together with his mortal enemies, had forced him into the admission of political and moral sins." He says he was racked again and again, and on one occasion had to swear that he would not answer in any other sense than that demanded of him. If he failed in obedience to this command he should be torn to little pieces on the wheel, but, so God help him, he knew nothing whatever of Anabaptists or these other charges. He implores his brother to make known all this to his friends at Lübeck, and to beg that some honourable men would search his account books, and see whether it be true that he had abstracted State moneys. The brother himself might come and hang him higher than any thief yet hung, if he could prove that he, Jürgen, had stolen anything from the Lübeckers. Finally, he warns the zealous Lutherans that the purpose of all that he had to suffer, all that was now being done, was to restore the old state of things, and that he feared that his foes would effect this in Lübeck of all other places.

Meantime, King Henry of England repeatedly demanded of the Archbishop of Bremen that his "beloved and trusty servant, Jürgen Wullenweber," should be treated with more clemency. Receiving no reply from the archbishop, the king turned to the city of Hamburg for aid to release the imprisoned burgomaster. He said he had need of his "innocent servant" for most important purposes, and pointed out that it was for the weal, not only of his own kingdom, but also, and even more, for that of the German nation, that Jürgen should be freed. Baffled on all sides, the king demanded at last, that at least the reasons for this confinement should be made publicly known.

These reasons could not be given, based as they were on motives of the lowest kind, that would not bear the light of day and of judicial investigation. The inquiries, however, caused the archbishop and his wire-pullers at Lübeck to think it well to remove Wullenweber from his prison at Rothenburg to some other more distant place. In consequence, he was passed on in the spring of 1536 to the custody of the archbishop's brother, Duke Henry of Brunswick, a bigoted Catholic and zealous persecutor of heretics. He confined Wullenweber in his castle of Steinbrück, a strong fortress situated between the towns of Brunswick and Hildesheim. The dark dungeon with its walls ten feet in thickness, with its small door but a foot and a half in breadth, are shown to this day. Quite recently this inscription has been put up inside it—"Here Jürgen Wullenweber lay and suffered. 1536-1537."

Yes, suffered indeed. For a year and a half this unfortunate man suffered mental and physical tortures in this hole. On one occasion he was racked in the presence of Nicholas Brömse and other burghers from Lübeck, and in order that he might recant nothing he had previously been made to say, he was racked twice before this public torture came about, and threatened with instant death did his answers vary. The duke was present on all occasions, it being a special pleasure to him to witness the sufferings of heretics. At the end, when the questions and replies were read aloud in the presence of the Lübeckers and the lacerated man, the duke turned on him harshly, asking, "Jürgen what do you say to all this?" "I have said, yes," replied the broken man, in low tones.

A letter written to his brother a few days after this event is heart-rending in its accents of despair and sorrow that he had been made to incriminate others by enforced false testimony. He begs his brother to do his best to make this good; he says he knows that he himself will lose his life, though he had two kings of England to friend, but he wished to save those who had stood by him and aided him. Brömse and the others who persecute him, know well that all the accusations are false, but it suits their purpose to put them forward. "Vouchsafe me credit; if I am a thief, may you yourself help me on to the gallows; if I am a traitor, on to the wheel; if I am an Anabaptist, into the fire."

Thus Wullenweber's confinement dragged on, and public sympathy for his fate increased. Seeing this, his persecutors thought it desirable to make an end. They announced that "the honest country" should judge Wullenweber. They carried out this proposal in the most despicable and treacherous manner. On a Monday morning September 24, 1537, a large gathering of peasants was assembled in an open space in the neighbourhood of Wolfenbüttel. From their midst were chosen twelve farmers who had not the smallest knowledge of State affairs, and barely comprehended the question at stake against the accused. Then the charges made against Wullenweber and to which he had acquiesced under torture were read before them. Called upon to reply, Wullenweber boldly, in a speech of great dignity, denied the charges, and declared himself willing to die to prove his innocence. That he should die was unanimously resolved; indeed, the verdict was a foregone conclusion. As they were unable to resolve upon the method it was voted that the hangman should decide on Wullenweber's punishment. Master Hans, called on by the judge, said that he "deemed it right and fitting that Wullenweber should be led forth and quartered and his body be torn on four wheels, and that he should be judged thus between heaven and earth, that he might act in this wise no more, and that others should remember how he had been dealt by."

But even after this Wullenweber's enemies were not appeased. They read out three more articles of accusation against him, articles which the advocate said he could not hear because of the noise made by the crowd. Jürgen replied. It was true he had confessed this while in prison, but under great pain, and in order to save his body and soul. But in order that his soul might not lie before the stern judgment seat of God, he herewith exculpated those whom he had inculpated while in prison, and begged his gracious lord (Duke Henry was close by) not to stain his hands with innocent blood and to bring therewith his (Wullenweber's) soul to lasting damnation. He then requested, as a last favour, to be permitted to speak a word or two with the emissaries from Lübeck. Most unwillingly the two men came into the presence of their late chief. "Jürgen, what do you want?" said one of them, in harsh tones that roused all the pent-up ire of Wullenweber's soul. In presence of the miserable instruments of his oppressors he broke, for the first time, his silence of two years' standing.

"This," he said in loud, clear tones: "this is what you have striven after so long, even four years ago when you wanted to surprise and carry me off by night in my house, which God Almighty did not permit. Now after all you have succeeded, that I admit before God. But I also tell you before the whole world, that the last articles are false, and that what I said in prison, I said under torture and to save my life."

He wanted to add yet more, but the Lübeckers were afraid lest a tumult in his favour should arise among the people. One of them urged Master Hans, the hangman, to hurry on the execution. But the hangman had a soul of mercy. He listened to Wullenweber's prayer, "I have but a short while left. Let me say two or three words more, then I will gladly die." And yet again he repeated, taking Almighty God to witness, that he had in no respect failed in his duty or his obligations to the town of Lübeck; that he was no thief, no traitor! Then as though he had done with his conscience, with the world, he sank upon his knee, and bent his head to receive his death-blow. Master Hans severed the noble head from its trunk with one sharp blow. The body was then quartered and torn to little pieces on the wheel.

So perished the last great Hanseatic hero and with him the Hansa's power. At that time, so great was the fear of his foes, so blindly prejudiced the masses, that no one ventured to speak a good word for the dead man. But that all did not think that he had suffered justly is made manifest by a few little trifles. Thus, for example, a worthy Hamburg burgher of the period notes in his private diary the fate that had befallen this great man. In the margin he painted a red flaming sword and underneath he wrote the words, "This he did not deserve." The same man writing a few days later and speaking of his execution and quartering, notes again in the margin, "Duke Henry merited this." Even the chancellor of Zelle, one day in his cups, ventured the utterance that "Wullenweber had died as a martyr to the gospel."

Yes, he had died as a martyr; a martyr to his town and to his faith, and the Hanseatic League was not to see the like of him again. He was no perfect hero of romance. Indeed his impetuosity and his excitable temperament, which caused him to be carried away by his enthusiasms, hindered him from developing one of those firm characters that excite eternal admiration and respect; he was lacking in moderation, and in foresight; but combined with his faults there were grand and noble elements, and take him "all in all," he was a man to honour and admire, a true patriot, a true friend to the people and their cause.

In the archives of Weimar are deposited and can be seen to this day, the acts of interrogation and indictment planned against Wullenweber by his enemies; curious documents, well worth the study of a student of humanity, as proving how even truth can be distorted to bad ends. In one of them Wullenweber's signature is scarcely decipherable; no wonder when we learn that he had just before been hung up for four hours by his thumbs!

Jürgen's friend and ally Max Meyer had not survived him. He too fell a victim to treachery and cruelty. Vardberg's walls were subjected to hot bombardment, from which sacks stuffed full of wool taken in booty could not preserve them. Then too the hired soldiery had grown restive, their wages being in arrear, owing to the delay with which supplies arrived from England. In the month of May, 1536, the castle was forced to surrender and open its gates to the enemy. Max Meyer was promised a safe pass, a promise that in accordance with the usages of the time was broken. The whilom blacksmith was delivered over into the hands of King Christian III., who caused him to be put in irons. He was then accused of all manner of offences, many of them, as in the case of Wullenweber, purely imaginary; was tortured, and made to confess to fictitious crime; and finally, given over to the keeping of the Danish governor from whose guardianship he had months before escaped by his happy ruse. On June 17, 1536, Max Meyer was beheaded at Helsingoer, and his body quartered and torn upon the wheel. So ended this handsome adventurer, and with his death, and that of his friend Jürgen Wullenweber, ended also an important and picturesque episode in Hanseatic history.

IV.

THE HANSA LOSES ITS COLONIES.

THE prominence which we have had to accord to the history of Lübeck in the preceding chapters would almost make it appear as though we were dealing with the adverse fortunes of only one town, of a town moreover that was fighting mainly for its private and special interests and that succumbed in the combat. But this conception would be wholly erroneous. In those days the German Empire had no maritime commerce save that carried on by the Hansa; this commerce had no protection save that afforded to it by the League. The League was only powerful so long as Lübeck with a firm hand and high spirit held together its various members and led and encouraged their more feeble and often vacillating steps. For there were few among the cities that heartily supported the Queen of the Hansa in these latter days. At the cost of great and real sacrifices she insisted that the prerogatives of the League should be maintained, and if in return she also asked for some privileges for herself, this can scarcely excite wonder. It is therefore obvious that the declining power of Lübeck necessarily brought with it an enfeeblement of the whole federation.

After the failure of Wullenweber's bold schemes and his ignominious death, after the enmity against Lübeck, and consequently against the League, that had been fanned to yet greater fury by late events, it is easy to understand that the relations of the Hansa to the Scandinavian kingdoms suffered an entire change. Denmark was the first to avail itself of the liberty it had regained. The country forthwith began to draw profit from its "gold mine" the Sound. Then Norway followed suit. The town of Bergen, above all, so long oppressed by the League, now took its revenge. Gradually as the inhabitants beheld the enfeeblement at home and abroad of their rivals they withdrew from them privilege after privilege until the time came that the natives of Bergen recovered both their commercial activity and their fortune.

The justice of history is less pressed for time than the justice of man, but it is yet surer and more inexorable.

This inevitable justice, which punishes the children for the sins of their fathers, fell upon the Hanseatics in full measure at Bergen. The time actually came when it fell to the people of Bergen to advance funds to impoverished or ruined Hanseatics, and, on the principle of returning a tooth for a tooth, an eye for an eye, insult for insult, they advanced these moneys under the same hard conditions that had been employed towards themselves. The dispossession of the Hanseatics was naturally a work of time, but in course of years it became complete. The last occasion when the four chief "games" were performed, which according to a reporter at the Hanseatic Diet were designed "to keep off rich folks' children from Bergen and secure the profits of the trade to poor young fellows," seems to have been about 1590.

It is true that up to the eighteenth century German merchants retained certain prerogatives in Norway, but they were no longer the Hanseatics of the League, they were merely the members of an association reduced to slender proportions, an association as impotent to sustain its dignity as to restore the rights of its predecessors.

Sweden was no less happy in its efforts after emancipation from Hanseatic tutelage. Gustavus Vasa laid the foundations for this exemption from tolls, monopolies, and harassing restrictions. He taught his subjects the great lesson how to trade to their own profit. After his position as ruler was once well assured he did not hesitate to speak in open court of the German merchants as "butchers," comparing his predecessors to "good milch kine," and adding that he should never forgive himself, but should be ashamed before God and man, did he sacrifice the well-being of his kingdom to the rapacity and selfishness of the Lübeckers. And he kept his word. So long as he lived he checkmated the League with all the resources at his command, and he left his desire to raise the commercial prosperity of his kingdom as a legacy to his son.

Nor was it enough that men had come to hate the Hansa with that fierce hatred which is felt towards those who, holding power in their hands disgust and oppress their inferiors by overbearing conduct. Even nature seemed to turn against them in that dark moment of their national life. In the years following the burgomaster's war, as Wullenweber's war grew to be called, the herrings which had already failed once or twice during the course of the fifteenth century, either entirely abandoned the Scanian coasts, or came in such small quantities as not to repay the cost of maintenance of the "Witten." There was yet worse in store. Not only did the herrings abandon the Hansa, but they favoured their rivals the Netherlanders, coming in great masses into their waters, and thus enriching them at the expense of their enemies; a circumstance that furnished the pious preacher Bonnus with the theme for a sermon, in which he pointed out, to his own satisfaction, how this was the direct punishment inflicted by Almighty God, for the war so wantonly entered upon by the Hansa.

A fresh blow of great force came to the League in the year 1553. The English, so long forcibly kept outside the navigation of the Baltic, had suddenly opened out for themselves a road to the mouth of the Northern Dwina by means of the Arctic Ocean, thus discovering the White Sea, and offering a new route to merchants trading with Russia.

The discoverer of this new ocean route was Sir Richard Chancellor, who, together with Sir Hugh Willoughby, had been commissioned by an association of London merchants, to undertake the search of a road to China by way of the icy sea. They set forth in three stately vessels, the *Bona Esperanza*, the *Bona Confidentia*, and the *Edward Bonaventura.* For four months the ships kept close together, but in the region of the North Cape the *Edward Bonaventura*, which Chancellor commanded, was separated, owing to ice and storms, from its comrades—never more to rejoin them.

Sir Hugh penetrated with his ships as far as the harbour of Artschina in Northern Lapland, whence he could not continue his journey, owing to the intense cold and the lack of means of sustenance. In this desolate spot, he and his whole crew perished. Long after, fishermen found their bodies. Beside Willoughby's corpse lay his journal, which closed with the desponding words: "Then sent we three men south-east three days' journey, who returned without finding of people or any similitude of habitation." The diary, which has been lately printed, is a touching record of patient endurance and heroic enterprise.

Meantime the more fortunate Sir Richard had penetrated to the spot where Archangel is now situated, and where then stood a monastery dedicated to St. Nicholas. After resting here, he made his way to Moscow, where Czar Ivan held his Court. Here he was received in the most friendly manner, remained some months, and was finally dismissed with a royal letter to the young King Edward VI., in which Ivan expressed his great wish that their two countries should henceforth approach each other in more intimate relationship. Nor were these desires of the Czar's fruitless.

After Sir Richard Chancellor's return, and on hearing his report concerning the terms under which the Czar would allow the English to trade in and with his country, a number of London merchants formed themselves into a commercial corporation under the title of "The London and Muscovite Company." This company once more despatched Chancellor to treat with the Czar, and the result was that by the year 1555, mutual trading relations between Russia and England were established.

Now if an earthquake had shaken the whole of Northern Europe, it could not have produced a greater commotion in the entire Baltic North than did this Russo-Anglican alliance, "The London and Muscovite Company." The good understanding between England and Russia was at once recognized as a danger of first-class importance to all the merchants along the Sound and the Baltic. They saw their entire commerce in imminent danger. What did it now avail them that the Sound had been closed for centuries against the English ships, if the London merchants could carry their goods to Russia by another route? Above all, the Hanseatic League recognized the danger that menaced both them and their colony of Livonia, the colony of which the city of Bremen was wont to boast that it had been the godmother. What would happen, they asked themselves, with good reason, if Czar Ivan, already their enemy at Novgorod, should also take unto himself Livonia, if he should open its harbours to his new friends, and thus obtain for himself the mastery of the Baltic?

In order to fully appreciate these fears, we must remember that the province anciently called Livonia embraced all the departments now known as Esthonia, Courland, and Livonia; in a word, the whole Baltic coast of the Russian continent. This district was entirely governed by the Germans. Three hundred years back a priest named Meinhard had founded the first Christian Church at the mouth of the Dwina, and from that time forward Germany had not ceased to send the flower of its aristocracy, the *élite* of its burghers, its monks and its priests, its merchants and citizens, its *landsknechte* and mercenaries to these northern coasts to spread the Christian faith, and to found a German colony.

Colonists of all kinds rapidly established themselves in Livonia, and while the industry of the merchants raised prosperous cities and safe harbours along the river and the seaboard, the nobles dotted the land with their castles and strongholds, and the clergy with their churches and convents. It was a special characteristic of this greater Germany that it faithfully retained and reproduced the outward features of the mother-land. With German speech, German law and German customs had become naturalized.

On the gates of the citadels the knights beheld the same coats of arms that greeted their eyes at home. In the towns were seen the same architectural features, the same tightly-packed gabled houses, with their quaint projecting storeys, and their yawning cellars, for the storage of goods; the cocklofts, with their heavy, pendant cranes, that distinguished the northern cities and made them all resemble, more or less, those toy towns of our childhood that come from Nürnberg, and are so deftly packed into their box that, once removed, no unskilled fingers can replace them.

The monks and the priests, on their part, formed in Livonia their accustomed cells, their silent cloisters, the glory and weird wonder of the Gothic cathedral, with its tall, pointed spires and steeples, its coloured glass windows, through which the northern sunlight broke in soft rays, staining the floors of God's house with glory.

In a word, everything here reproduced mediæval Germany. Of the natives of the land there was little trace, though some of these still lingered in the country and ventured secretly to pay worship to their old deposed gods in sacred thickets and on lonely heaths. To this day Livonia retains its German character; the German language still reigns supreme there, German customs prevail, German names survive. In the times we speak of it was entirely under Teutonic sway.

Was this rich, important colony to be lost to the mother-land and to the Hansa that had created it? No wonder the League was alarmed.

Nor was it alone in its fears. Sweden and all the West took fright. In imagination, they already beheld the East—in the shape of Russia and its barbarous dependencies—descending upon them with the weapons furnished to them by England. At the instigation of the King of Sweden and of the Livonians, who, in 1556, expressed their fears on this subject before the Hanseatic Diet, the League, desirous to dispel this European peril, warned the Emperor of Germany, the Kings of Denmark, England, and Poland, and the Duke of Prussia, not to facilitate Russia's projects of invasion by putting at her disposal either the munitions of war or the means that would help to civilize her, and thus render her yet more redoubtable.

To these requests England turned a deaf ear, for her commercial policy then, as now, was a trifle selfish and insular. Judging that the distance which separated her from Russia gave her entire security, she did not dream of disturbing a traffic which she found lucrative. Queen Mary, admonished by the King of Sweden to interdict to her subjects the new navigation to Archangel, contented herself by forbidding the shippers who traded with the White Sea the exportation of arms.

It was not long before the alarms expressed proved themselves to be anything but chimerical. Danger first showed itself in the shape of dissension. Livonia, seeing itself suddenly grown of enhanced importance to the League, took up certain pretentious airs towards its foster-mother. It broke through ancient contracts and statutes, among which was a stern interdict against trading on its own account with Russia. The next step was to put the Hanseatic League commercially upon the same footing as a stranger; and the Livonians were, consequently, able to turn against them some of their own laws—for example, that which declared that guest should not trade with guest.

Meanwhile Russia, which had now completely thrown off the Tartar yoke and was beginning to feel its strength, cast more and more greedy eyes towards Livonia, with its rich cities and wide seaboard.

Under pretext of bringing about a fusion of the Greek and Latin branches of the Catholic Church, the Czar Ivan had sent successive embassies to Germany, who there recruited for him workmen, artists, learned men, and officers, all of whom were to aid in putting the newly-welded Russian Empire upon a civilized basis. While there, these men had learnt the fact that Livonia, which stood under the government of the Teutonic knights, had been divided by internal dissensions since the death of the Grand Master, Water von Plattenberg, who, early in the sixteenth century, had saved the province from falling a prey to the Russian desire for conquest.

Ivan, hearing this, felt the moment was favourable. He saw that the German Empire looked on indifferently at what was passing in the extreme corner of its possessions—the German Empire always had the knack of being indifferent at the wrong and critical moment—he perceived that the Hansa League was ill-disposed at that instant to her stubborn and disobedient daughter; while Sweden and Denmark glanced with all too loving eyes at the German colony on the Baltic Sea. He felt now or never was the time for action. Moreover, Livonia had but one friend, and that a nominal one, Poland, which masked designs anything but friendly under the cover of an amicable alliance; it had but one man on whom it could count—the present Grand Master of the Teutonic knights, Gotthard Kettler. But this man, though of dauntless courage and a true patriot, was condemned to rule over the once bold company of Knights at a moment when too long-continued peace and prosperity had sunk them into sloth, indifference, and vicious practices.

Under the pretext that a certain toll had not been paid him, Ivan quite unexpectedly sent into Livonia a herd of barbarous soldiers, under the leadership of the erstwhile Khan of Kasan. The money not being forthcoming, this army took possession of Narwa, a port just about to enter into the League. Thence they overspread all the province, burning, razing, sacking, robbing, and violating.

They met with little resistance. The enervated nobles—"usually so ready for a scuffle," says an old chronicler—fell like flies before them, and the strongest burghs were quietly delivered over into their hands. Dorpat, one of the strongest, opened its gates to the invader without the smallest opposition, the citizens having been seized with panic at their approach. Here there fell into their hands rich treasure, stored in the fort, affording them the sinews of war. Reval, also besieged, turned to the King of Denmark for aid against its foes. He sent back the Livonian ambassadors laden with a thousand sides of bacon and other victuals to stay their hunger, but more effective aid he could not or would not afford.

In short Livonia was being rapidly broken up and divided among the various greedy nationalities that surrounded her—the two Slavonic, Russia and Poland, on the one hand; the two Scandinavian, Sweden and Denmark, on the other.

In these sore straits the Grand Master of the Teutonic knights, Gotthard Kettler, made "the sad plaint of the Christian Brothers on the Baltic," heard at the Imperial Diet. The Emperor Ferdinand, to whom the Grand Master made personal appeal for speedy help, promised his assistance, and did send a letter to the Czar, begging him to desist from his persecution of the Livonians; but the letter was so lukewarm in its wording, and it was so evident from its tenour that the Emperor had no intention of following it up by action, that the Czar did not hesitate to send a very haughty and defiant reply. In this letter he proved that it was not difficult to find excuses for his conduct. The Germans, for instance, had oppressed his subjects; had taken from them their churches, and converted them into storehouses for their goods; had forbidden to his people free-trade in their markets. Some of these complaints were doubtless not quite groundless, for we know with what a high hand the Hansa was wont to treat the inhabitants of a land they had taken under their protection.

Livonia now turned to the League for aid; but the League had been offended by the late independent deeds of its colonies, and was not inclined to bestir itself much. The Hanseatics did not perceive the folly of their action at the time; they did not observe that in thus yielding to personal feeling they were losing their finest, richest dependency. It seemed as though with Wullenweber all Hanseatic ambition, clear-sightedness, and enterprise had sunk into its grave. An able scheme which would have rescued the entire colony for the Hansa, at a cost of some 200,000 dollars, was allowed to gather dust, unregarded and unconsidered, in the archives of Lübeck.

The weakness of Germany, the supineness of the League, the cold calculations of the King of Poland, all combined to deprive the hapless land of support. It became a prey, on the one side, to the barbaric vigour of Ivan IV., and, on the other, to the machinations of Sigismund Augustus, king of Poland. By the year 1561 the colony of Livonia was lost to Germany and to the Teutonic knights, and was divided among the various nationalities that surrounded it, Sweden coming in for no inconsiderable portion. Thus fell Livonia, the Russo-Baltic province to which in those days was assigned the rôle accorded to the Ottoman Empire by a certain class of statesmen in our own time, namely, that of a rampart of civilization against barbarism.

As we look back upon the course of history and the state of opinion in those times, it seems almost incredible that this fall should have been permitted, that neither the Hansa nor Germany should have stretched out a hand to help the oppressed colony. Incredible, because at that time the whole German and Scandinavian Baltic coast resounded with the cry of alarm that the Muscovite was seeking to make himself master of the Baltic. It is true that this result, equally bitter for Germany and for all Northern Europe, was only accomplished in the days of Peter the Great; but the foundations of this Russian Empire over the inland sea were laid in those times, and Germany had largely itself to blame for the disasters that happened in consequence.

The immediate result of the loss of Livonia was that Lübeck became involved in its last war—a war that was to leave it exhausted. These hostilities lasted seven years, from 1563 to 1570, and were instigated by a desire on the part of Lübeck that the Hansa, though it had lost Livonia, should not lose all profits accruing from trade with the Russian continent. The quarrel began by Eric XIV., Gustavus Vasa's successor, professing that he would reinstate the Hansa in all her privileges in his kingdom; but demanding in return from the League far more than it had ever possessed in Sweden, namely, a factory and special privileges in every town of the League.

When this was not granted he suddenly chose to take umbrage at the fact that Lübeck had never ceased to trade with Narwa, although he had, as he alleged, repeatedly told the Lübeckers that by so doing they strengthened the hands of the Muscovite, the common enemy. He complained of this to the Emperor Ferdinand, who, on his part however, was satisfied with the reasons for their actions put forward by the Lübeckers. Eric who, on his side, was by no means satisfied, now demanded in the most emphatic terms that the Hansa should cease all navigation to Narwa or to Russia, in order that the Muscovite might not be strengthened by the importation of arms. He contended that the channels of Finland were not the open sea, but belonged to his dominions, and that he had a right to hold sway over them, and to capture or harass any vessels he found in their waters.

It is strange indeed to find Lübeck replying to this, that the open, rude Baltic had been recognized by nature herself as a free sea; Lübeck which had ever contended that this sea was an inland lake and should be so treated, that only those should trade in its waters to whom she, its mistress, graciously accorded permission. The conclusion of the dispute was that Lübeck made an alliance with the Danish king, Frederick II., in which it was resolved to carry on war against Sweden. The sister towns, apathetic and most unwilling to fight, did not fail, however, to obey the Danish king's mandate that they should at once cease from all trade and intercourse with Sweden.

On June 9, 1563, the Queen of the Hansa issued her declaration of war against Eric XIV. of Sweden. The king, to whom the document was addressed, referred it with contempt to the magistrates of Stockholm, saying that "kings must write to kings, but burghers and peasants should treat with their peers."

But though Eric was so contemptuous, these burghers, whom he professed to despise, were to cause him some uncomfortable moments. Not inglorious for Lübeck was this last seven years' war waged by her, and its results might have been of some consequence had she been supported by the whole League. But this was far from being the case. Still she won several important victories, and on one occasion captured the Swedish admiral's vessel. In the midst of the hostilities Eric was deposed, and here again would have been the Hansa's opportunity had it known how to profit by it.

But in vain did Lübeck counsel union and implore the other Baltic cities to make common cause and crush the common enemy. They only replied complaining of the expenses entailed by this thoughtless war, and by alleging that more advantage might be obtained by diplomacy. In the end Lübeck had to bend to the common sentiment.

Imperial diplomacy was put into motion, resulting in a congress held at Stettin, in December, 1570, in which a reconciliation was brought about between Denmark, Lübeck, and King John of Sweden; and of which the conditions were, that the Hansa might trade with certain Russian cities; "so long as the emperor permitted it;" Sweden was also bound over to pay some of the outstanding debts which Gustavus Vasa had contracted with Lübeck.

King John assented, but no sooner did he feel himself firmly seated on his throne than he too forgot all his treaty promises, and once more demanded that all Hanseatic commerce with Russia should cease. He defiantly styled himself "Lord of the Baltic," assigning as his claim to this title the fact that to the Swedish crown had passed the heritage of the Hansa, both on the seas and in the Livonian colonies.

An Imperial Diet assembled at Speyer shortly afterwards and discussed these new complications, and professed great anxiety for the welfare of those deluded subjects of the empire, the Hanseatics. It also made sympathetic reference to the fate of Livonia, and made no secret of its embarrassment and annoyance at seeing now the Muscovite, now the Pole, now the Swede in possession of the Baltic.

But the anxiety and the sympathy did not go beyond words. The Hansa was weary; the empire was impotent to aid. It is true that Sweden had offered to restore to the Germans all the portion of Livonia she had taken for herself in return for the costs of war, but even this proposal was allowed to drop. When, by 1579, the Swedes perceived that the empire made no effort to regain its lost possession, they quietly assumed that none would ever be made, and their assumption did not prove erroneous.

Curiously enough, at the diet held at Frankfort, in the autumn of 1570, presided over by the Emperor Maximilian who was ever well inclined to the Hansa, and repeatedly urged them to unity, there was also present the infamous Duke of Alva, the Catholic butcher, who murdered human beings to the glory and honour of God. It was he who urged that by all possible means the exportation of armour and fire-arms should be hindered, lest the Muscovite, in possession of a European army, should one day bring sorrow not only to the Netherlands, but to all Christendom.

The German merchant world was to blame, in the first instance, for the loss of the prosperous colony; and that this was perfectly understood by outsiders is proved by the rough utterance of a Tartar Khan who had been imprisoned together with a Livonian. Spitting into the face of the latter, the barbarian said, "It serves you German dogs quite right that you have lost your province; you first put into the hands of the

Muscovite the rod with which he whipped us, now he has turned it against yourselves and whipped you with it."

But the League's troubles were not at an end with the loss of Livonia and their Russian trade. They were to learn by bitter experience, what individuals too have to learn, that mankind cannot resist the temptation to kick the man or nation that is down.

Bitter ingratitude was first to be shown them by their ally, Denmark, in return for all the heavy sacrifices they had made on her behalf. Lübeck was treated with overbearing contempt, while the neutral cities were punished, as perhaps they more justly deserved, for their cowardly policy. Thus Rostock, which had furnished the Swedish admiral with food supplies in 1566, was forbidden to trade thenceforth with Scania; Hamburg, whose ships had been captured engaged in the same unpatriotic business, had to pay a hundred thousand dollars to regain them; and Danzig, too, was fined the same sum by the King of Denmark for a like offence.

But the keenest humiliation was yet in store for Lübeck herself, in King Frederick's behaviour concerning the Island of Bornholm, so long the Hansa queen's special possession. First a Lübeck governor was formally ejected by the Danes, then the inhabitants of the island, encouraged in insubordination by seeing how the authorities at Copenhagen dealt with their masters, refused to pay their dues, finally one of the towns even forcibly ejected some Lübeck traders. It was ominous that King Frederick opposed all mention of Bornholm during the treaties for peace. Suddenly, on the 7th of September, 1575, he informed the city of Lübeck, "that as the fifty years' possession, accorded to them by his grandfather, would have expired on the 19th of the month, he intended to retake possession of the island." On the city's replying that the peace of Hamburg had extended their right of possession which they held for unpaid Danish debts, King Frederick was not ashamed to reply to the council of Lübeck, that they should reasonably consider that this treaty was invalid since his father, who had made it, was not at that time crowned, and neither he nor his councillors had been consulted in the matter. Frederick did not for a moment consider that the Hansa had in all respects acknowledged the "uncrowned king," and had helped him into his kingdom.

Lübeck felt too weak, too exhausted, seriously to resist the king's claims. It sent an embassy to Copenhagen, begging for the extension of the possession, held by them as a pledge, for another forty, thirty, twenty, fifteen, eight, seven, six, five, or at least one year. Thus low had the Queen of the Hansa sunk, thus was she broken, that she could beg so abjectly. She begged in vain. King Frederick was deaf to entreaties; he saw his rival's weakness, and he profited by it. Had they not had enough return for helping Frederick I. to power by holding the island fifty years? Lübeck was forced to yield; the only concession that was made to her was, that Frederick graciously permitted her to convey one hundred tuns of Rhenish wine free of duty through the Sound for the space of ten years, to supply the town cellar of the capital. In the summer of 1576 Bornholm was formally delivered over to the Danes, and the Hansa lost yet another source of wealth.

For a while the League still strove to carry on some trade with Russia, at first by Reval, then by Narwa, but in 1587 the latter town was finally taken by the Swedes. By good fortune Lübeck and its friends found in the Czar, Feodor Ivanowitch, a prince inclined to deal favourably with them. Indeed, so well disposed was he, that in the year 1586 he reduced the existing custom dues by half in their favour, and placed at their entire disposal once more the factories Novgorod and Plestrow. But in recovering the possession of their establishments, the Hansa were far from recovering their monopoly, which time and events had undermined for ever. Annoyances without end awaited them from the Swedes and the Poles, whose territories they had to cross to arrive at their settlements. They were made to pay heavy transit tolls; their goods were subjected to annoying, and often disastrous delays; their ships were often captured and ransacked by Swedish and Polish pirates, who were well aware that their devastations were regarded with no evil eye by the home authorities.

The last embassy sent by the old and veritable Hanseatic Confederation to the Muscovite Court, in January, 1603, only attained their ends very partially, notwithstanding the truly royal presents which they laid at the feet of the then reigning Czar, Boris Féodorowitch Gudenow. The chronicles tell that the presents consisted of valuable silver-gilt vessels, representing ostriches, eagles, pelicans, griffins, lions, also a Venus and a Fortuna. Presents were also added for the Czar's son, but by an unlucky oversight, the all-powerful Russian Chancellor had been forgotten in the matter of gifts; this want of thought lost the Hanseatic ambassadors his potent favour.

The ambassadors consisted of councillors from Lübeck and Stralsund, and there went with them besides a certain Zacharias Meyer, an old Lübeck merchant, who had lived for many years in Russia, and knew the language and habits of the people. The embassy met with little success.

The monarch whose geographical knowledge was not very extensive, and who confounded the names of the Hanseatic towns who sent him this embassy with those that had passed into the possession of Poland, his arch enemy, categorically refused to recognize the Hanseatic League as such, and would only allow the city of Lübeck to be spoken of, which it seems was less unfamiliar to him. Towards this city he showed himself well disposed, and very generous, and said it might establish factories and storehouses in various localities, according to traditional custom, and trade freely without vexatious custom dues as far as Moscow. In return he demanded only a money duty on the weight of the merchandise imported, no matter of what nature. In vain the ambassadors pleaded that the towns could not separate themselves. The Chancellor exclaimed with anger—

"Then we will separate them; the Czar does not know the other towns, and those which he knows are in the hands of princes who are his enemies."

And from this decision neither he nor his royal master could be moved. This entirely personal favour to Lübeck naturally changed the character borne hitherto by the Hanseatic commerce in Russia, and helped yet further to fan the fire of discontent already smouldering in the bosom of the League. All attempts made by the other cities to profit by the advantages conceded to Lübeck remained fruitless; and this city herself, though she seems to have preserved these custom privileges until the middle of the seventeenth century, does not seem, judging from appearances, to have obtained any durable or profitable result from them. There always remained the disturbing fact that either Swedish or Polish domains must be crossed, or a long détour made by way of the White Sea, where again obstacles of yet another kind awaited them.

In very truth the Hanseatic commerce with Russia was slowly dying. Some efforts were made to resuscitate it by the cities that remained united when Czar Michael Feodorowitch sat on the imperial throne. The Hansa's demands were actually supported by the Netherlands. But even goodwill on the Russian side was impotent to raise a commerce which had been practically strangled by the powerful grasp of Sweden. Gustavus Adolphus, it is true, annoyed at the new direction commerce was taking, and the consequent loss to his kingdom in transit dues, tried all in his power to revive the old movement upon the Baltic. In this spirit and with this desire, he concluded various treaties with Russia that obliged the Hanseatics to pass through his domains, and especially to touch at Reval, the Lübeckers, who held their depôt at Novgorod, naturally preferring to pass by way of Narwa. But Gustavus Adolphus and his successors, after all, did not depart from the previous policy of Sweden. He and they, like their predecessors, sought to make themselves masters of the entire Baltic commerce, and to impose their intervention upon the outside nations, whom they crippled with custom dues. Various promises of relaxation which were made to Lübeck by Sweden were ill kept. The hand of this country continued to weigh heavily upon all the Baltic coasts, until there arose on the scene the figure of Peter the Great, who in his turn reduced them to submission, and who made himself practically lord and master of the Baltic lands.

Thus ends the history of the Hanseatic commerce with Russia, which might be said to have ended already, under Czar Feodorowitch Gudenow, for it was no longer one League, but only an individual city that maintained communication with Russia in those latter days. The confederation of cities known as the Hanseatic League had ceased to march together, or to figure by name in the various treaties and negotiations made after the accession to power of this Czar.

V.

THE LEAGUE IN THE NETHERLANDS.

THE successive losses of factories and Hanseatic liberties in the kingdoms of the North and East, were of themselves a fatal shock to the prosperity of the League. It must be remembered that the great privileges attained by the League in times past in England, the Netherlands, France, and Spain, were all based on the monopoly acquired by them in trading in the products of Russia, Denmark, Sweden, and Norway. This monopoly, as we have seen in the last chapters, had been seriously threatened; factories had been forcibly closed, natives and strangers had competed with the Hanseatics; the League's prerogatives and charters had been trodden under foot and disregarded.

All the efforts made by the Hanseatics at the end of the fifteenth century and in the early years of the sixteenth to expel from the Baltic waters their various competitors, had ended in failure. It obviously followed that, with the loss of this monopoly, the privileges extorted on the strength of it would vanish also; and this was speedily the case, for under what pretence of preference could the League now invoke special favours at the hands of the Eastern nations?

These general causes of failure in the West were destined to be complicated in the case of the Netherlands with the adverse fate which befell the town of Bruges at the end of the second period of our story, and of which we have already spoken. The disaster which deprived the town of its commercial importance also contributed to ruin the Hanseatic factory established in that city. Then the Hanseatics themselves were not wholly blameless, seeing how at Bruges they repeatedly revolted against paying the tax enforced for storage of goods, a tax that was a regular condition in the statutes of the League, and which was exacted in all its foreign settlements; and, besides this, there are also other circumstances to be reckoned with, of a more general character. The closing of the factory of Bruges was one of many signs of the course of events. A new spirit was abroad affecting commerce and progress in all directions, a spirit against which, as we have said, the League resolutely set its face, and which it refused to recognize until it was too late.

After the invasion of the territory of Bruges in 1488 and the ten years' blockade of the harbour of Sluys, by the Emperor Frederick III., to avenge the confinement of his son, the city found her trade almost ruined. Two important branches were lost to her, by the Italians who brought their own silk stuffs to the rival market of Antwerp and by the Flemish cloth-workers who had settled in England and likewise sent their goods thither.

Under these circumstances the Hansa could scarcely hope for the continued prosperity of Bruges. The tumultuous activity that had hitherto reigned in the factory gave place to a death-like silence. The profit that was lost to the town fell chiefly to the lot of Amsterdam and Antwerp, but partly to the fairs held annually in various localities of the Netherlands, which benefited by this abandonment and which came gradually to attract to themselves all the business of the East.

It must not be supposed, however, that the Hanseatic Diet did not observe with dismay the visible and rapid decline of the prosperity of this once flourishing factory; but what could they do to hinder the general desertion of its merchants? Could they, reduced as they were in strength and influence, restore to the city of Bruges its character of general depôt for the West? Could they remove the obstruction of the Zivin, ordered by the emperor, which, by a canal had connected Bruges with the sea? Were they not themselves so weakened that their own members refused to pay the imposed dues, violated all the factory laws, and traded and made common cause with the natives?

In vain did various diets send ambassadors to Bruges to recall to the minds of the faithless traders the laws under which they were constituted and by which they were bound to abide. In vain did the alderman of the factory itself plead with the men living under his charge. The spirit of individualism and insubordination was abroad, and since the League could no longer ensure its old profits to its foreign members, these no longer found it to their own interests to obey its behests, many of which they rightly felt to be antiquated. Add to this, that the failure to pay the appointed taxes made negotiations often impossible for lack of means, and it will be seen how crippled and handicapped was the League in its relations with Bruges.

The Baltic towns, ever the most public-spirited and perhaps also the most commercially enlightened recognizing this state of affairs, had in 1530 combined on a fixed tariff, which they thought should be paid to the factory at Bruges for its maintenance. But the other cities would not listen to this, and the absence of concord, that of late had made itself felt and heard too often in the councils of the League, was manifest again on this occasion. Town after town stated through its deputies that it would not contribute to this general tax unless some special favour were granted to it, unless some special merchandise were allowed to pass free into the Netherland domains; the merchandise named being usually that in which the bulk of the town's trade consisted. If ever an association gave practical exemplification of the homely saying of "cutting off one's nose to spite one's face," the League was doing it at that moment.

As usual Cologne was one of the most restive and obstructive of all the towns. It actually proposed to pay a lump sum of a hundred guilders annually, and so be free from all custom duties of whatever kind. By the time the dispute was at last decided, and a sum fixed upon by all the towns together, the dominion of Bruges had hopelessly passed away from the Hansa, and the League was busy with the thought of removing its factory to Antwerp.

For they finally admitted that they must cut loose from the old moorings; that it was necessary to quit the ancient factory, where disunion and grave disorders had crept in. The merchants who had deserted had many of them become naturalized citizens of Amsterdam, or Antwerp, where they quietly continued their commercial relations with the confederated towns, without taking notice either of the confederation or of its factories. Under these changed circumstances what could be done? There were only two courses possible to the League: to afford free trade to the Netherlands, and so renounce its ancient methods, or to maintain the old system, and make an attempt to apply its principles in a new locality. The first course would have been the most rational, and the most in keeping with the spirit of the time. But the Hanseatics, as we have frequently had occasion to see in the course of our story, were not men easily to lose hold of prey, or to break spontaneously with a past that had been glorious and lucrative. They decided in favour of the second course, and at once set about seeking for the spot which would best secure their interests. Various places offered themselves for their choice, such as Bergen-op-Zoom, Middlebourg, Haarlem, all of which promised the Hansa considerable advantages, in order to attract it to themselves. It would, perhaps, have most inclined to Amsterdam, but it could not forget that this town had often fought in the ranks of its enemies, and had put forth in the Baltic a special activity very prejudicial to its monopoly. Antwerp was finally decided upon, for it was manifest already in 1513 that the great commercial movement of the epoch seemed inclined to tend towards that spot.

The story of the rise of the city into importance is most interesting. Formerly its houses had been all thatched with straw. Its inhabitants lived on the results of agricultural labour and fishing. Since the English merchant adventurers had patronized the town, wretched habitations had given place to fine solid houses; ease and wealth had taken up their abode among the burghers. As an instance of this, it may be mentioned that houses which fifty years previously let for forty to sixty dollars of annual rent, now fetched four to eight hundred dollars a year. The Hansa asked themselves, very naturally, were not some of those good things to fall to their share.

It was in 1545 that it was finally settled by the Hanseatic Diet that a depôt should be established at Antwerp, but the negotiations regarding it dragged on. It was, however, at once decided, that the factory should become, like the factories of the past, an obligatory intermediary of all the relations between the Hansa and strangers.

In 1561, the League was fortunate enough to obtain from King Philip of Spain the confirmation of the privileges which they had extorted in the fourteenth and fifteenth centuries from the Dukes of Brabant, and which permitted them to bring in their goods at a minimum rate, and accorded to them other valuable privileges. And besides this liberality on the part of the ruler of the land, the interested city also showed itself willing to further the weal of the League. The Hanseatics were offered by the town of Antwerp a spacious tract of land, free of rent, situated between two canals, on which they were to be allowed to erect a factory. Besides this, Antwerp offered to defray a third of the costs, laying down for this purpose the large sum of thirty thousand guilders. Annexed to the establishment, which was to be the free possession of the confederation, was an open public square, that formed a sort of exchange—free to all comers—where prices were to be settled, and sales and auctions held. A public balance, adapted to the weights in use among the Hanseatics, was to serve in the residence itself, for weighing the merchandise imported by them, while the public balance of the town was to serve for weighing their purchases. Other very favourable conditions with regard to the exportation of unsold goods, and of goods in storage and in transit were added. In return for all these favours, the Hanseatics had to promise not to abandon Antwerp, unless very real and serious causes, such as a war or a plague, should force them thence; and that Antwerp should enjoy in Hanseatic cities such commercial liberties as were accorded by the League to the most favoured nations.

On May 5, 1564, the foundation-stone of the splendid House of the Easterlings, at Antwerp, was laid, with great pomp and ceremony, in presence of the local burgomasters and the representatives of the League. In four years the stately edifice was finished, and formerly handed over to the aldermen of the Hansa, and such Hanseatics as were in Antwerp, who were regarded by the city as the representatives of the confederated towns.

The first Hanseatic Syndic General, Dr. Heinrich Sudermann, of Cologne, then put the finishing touch to the great work by sketching out for the factory a projected code of statutes for its internal management. It was laid before the Hansa Diet for revision, approved, and at once promulgated. This code enumerated the qualities requisite for admission to the enjoyment of Hanseatic privileges, determined the methods of nomination, as well as the duties of the various functionaries attached to the factory, and other details. The accounts were to be placed under the supreme supervision of Lübeck. Further, the merchants were to maintain the traditional monastic discipline, were to live under the same roof, and partake of their repasts in common in the great hall of the factory. A few of the rules recall the old hostile attitude always maintained by the League towards strangers. All disputes of Hanseatics among themselves were to be submitted to the jurisdiction of the factory.

In a word, in the outer magnificence of the factory building, as well as in the elaboration and rigour of the statutes, all the ancient traditional Hanseatic forms had been revived. Indeed, as regards the statutes, these attained at this epoch their greatest scientific perfection.

But perfect, correct, traditional, though the forms might be, they were no longer in accordance with the times; no longer the expression of the epoch that gave them birth. It was easy to foresee that the first adverse breath would dissipate them.

And so truly it proved. Indeed, certain complications showed themselves before the building was finished, and foreshadowed the nature of the troubles to be expected in the future. Money, as usual, was the touchstone of discord. Various cities refused to pay in the stipulated sums, others protested against the regulations proposed. Danzig even went so far as entirely to object to the new settlement as too distant from the centre of business, and contended that the pact of the League with the town of Antwerp had been concluded too hurriedly, and without due consultation.

In consequence of these difficulties, the factory, when completed, found itself crippled, and hampered by debts, from which it was never able to free itself. This was an unfortunate start, and was entirely due to the apathy and bad faith of the cities, among whom it became more and more evident that the old spirit of union was rapidly dying out.

Another difficulty was, that the traders began to object to living in common under one roof. The reasons in ancient times for this regulation, such as the defective conditions of public security, no longer existed in these more civilized times. Merchants did not care to submit to the often tiresome and petty restrictions on personal liberty involved by the monastic rules that existed in the factory.

In vain the Syndic of the League put forward for the consideration of these unruly members, that the concentration of all the Hanseatics in one factory building made the defence of their privileges more easy, while their dispersion in the various towns and villages facilitated exactions by the natives and the raising of taxes. In vain he pointed to the example of England, where the Hanseatics, thanks to their unity of action and of existence, had kept their prerogatives intact during three centuries, while, on the contrary, in the Netherlands the spirit of isolation had produced in course of time an augmentation of at least treble their original dues. In vain he demonstrated that partnerships made with foreigners were onerous for the Hanseatics themselves, and drew down upon them the too great probability of conflicts with the rulers of the Netherlands, who thus would find their interests betrayed.

Expostulations, appeals to the statutes, and menaces, proved powerless to change the state of things, or the direction in which affairs were tending. There was no longer a strong support to be obtained from the League as a body, in return for obedience; its threats were no longer followed up by deeds, it had grown too feeble to quell resistance, especially such resistance as was made by towns strong in themselves—as, for example, Danzig and Cologne.

The jurisdiction of the factory was no longer respected as supreme by its own members. It frequently happened, even in the early days of the settlement, that Hanseatics residing at Antwerp brought their differences before the local tribunals instead of before their own court. It is related, that one day one of the Hanseatic aldermen, anxious to repress this mode of violating rules, reprimanded a citizen of Cologne, one Mathern Schoff, on this account. The accused fell upon the official dignitary and belaboured him with his fists. The matter created a scandal and was brought before the High Court of Brabant. This court took part with the rebellious Hanseatic, with the result that the authorities of the factory were forbidden, under the most heavy penalties, to take any action against him. They were even threatened with the loss of all their privileges.

Such incidents, and a number of others like them, presaged a catastrophe at a time not too far distant. But circumstances unconnected with the factory rendered its position still more difficult and precarious and hastened its fate.

Chief among these external causes was the war between England and Spain; the war whose chief incident was the destruction of the great Spanish Armada by the force of the elements, which ranged themselves on the side of the English Queen. This war, which made the navigation of the seas unsafe, was of course a most serious interruption to trade. Nor did the destruction of the Armada bring peace to the Hansa. Besides this there had broken forth in the Netherlands the great revolt in the cause of freedom against the ecclesiastical and civil despotism of Philip II., which was permanently to change the whole state of that corner of Europe, and which for the time being absolutely extinguished all trade by sea or land. Glorious as these events proved for the cause of liberty and of freedom of thought, they were disastrous to the League. Each of the militant nations interdicted it from all relation with the other, and security for commerce was of course quite at an end.

Now it must be borne in mind that the revolt of the Netherlands began while the Hanseatics were still building their new residence at Antwerp. The League was no longer, as in old days, strong enough to make its neutrality respected, and the consequence was, it had to yield to the demands of whichever party was at the moment the strongest. Thus the Prince of Orange manifested from 1571 onwards a desire that they should interrupt their communications with Spain. As a result, when Antwerp was taken, and pillaged by the Spaniards, November 4, 1576, the Hanseatics were forced to see themselves treated not as neutrals, but as friends of the rebels. Their papers were seized and their goods confiscated; even their charter was seized and the price of ransom fixed at the high rate of twenty thousand guilders. Further, if we may deduce inferences from the minutes of the Hanseatic Diet of the same year, 1576, it would seem as though King Philip II., and the Prince of Orange each in their turn placed a tax of 10, 20, and even 40 per cent. upon the merchandise imported by the Hanseatics into the Low Countries.

The League, in this desperate situation pleaded for help now from one leader, now from another, but could obtain no efficient relief or support from any side. At last in April, 1577, the Spanish governor of the Netherlands offered conditions to a Hanseatic embassy which under the circumstances seemed sufficiently advantageous. It was proposed that to indemnify them for the losses suffered during the pillage of Antwerp, the Hanseatics should for twenty years be completely exempt from all taxes imposed in Holland or Brabant, and from half the taxes established for Zealand. Besides this the heads of the factory were once more to be recognized as alone competent to pronounce judgment in civil suits between Hanseatics residing in the Low Countries. On their part, however, the Hanseatics would have to submit to the necessities of warfare. Further, full latitude was conceded to them in the matter of re-exportation of their goods, unless imperious need opposed this, in which case they should receive current prices for their merchandise.

That these promises were ill kept, and that the factory, scarcely born, was rapidly nearing its end, is proved by the complaints addressed in 1581 and 1582, to the city of Lübeck by its representatives residing at the factory of Antwerp. They pointed out how money was absolutely wanting in the establishment; that the Hanseatics, resident and non-resident, did not pay the contributions promised; that the Spaniards harassed them, and rendered their indebted position yet more difficult; that they had no means of enforcing payment, and that if any one city, or private person did pay, it was out of pity. Then followed complaints of certain cities, especially of Cologne, which sent merchandise to foreign agents. The document further states that the rooms, cellars, and storehouses of the factory were quite empty; that the imposition or rather the faithful payment of some of the various taxes had to be taken into serious consideration; and that as the canal duties in Zealand were always rising in price, contrary to treaty, it seemed to the petitioners advisable that reprisals should be made on the natives of that territory, residing in or treating with Germany. Finally, they announced to the city that they were about to charge an able secretary with the permanent duties of looking after the affairs of the factory, if such a plan were pleasing to the town of Lübeck, and if the factory was to continue its existence. This last phrase is significant.

Lübeck, in its reply, offered to the factory of Antwerp mere empty phrases of consolation, promising in a lukewarm manner to see that the outstanding Hanseatic dues were paid, in order that a beginning might at least be made. But it opposed the advice given by its representatives at Antwerp, to practise reprisals towards the Netherlanders, because in that case they would seek for themselves other routes and the Hanseatic port would remain abandoned and neglected.

One of the Hansa's earliest and most able historians, commenting on this reply from the city of Lübeck makes the following very just remarks: "Nothing betokens more clearly the end of the Hanseatics' commercial dominion than this last passage in Lübeck's reply to its petitioners. Formerly the League would have interrupted all intercourse with the country that so misbehaved, and would thus have punished it, would have avenged the very smallest infraction of its privileges. Now it did not even dare have recourse to this measure for fear of completely sacrificing a commerce the pursuit of which had become possible independent of the Hanseatics."

A little later than the documents referred to above, an Antwerp Hanseatic alderman wrote that he saw no hope for their body, and that the debts were of such a nature, so numerous, so onerous, that within twenty-four hours the representatives of the factory might be arrested, and the factory itself put up for sale. This piece of news did arouse the apathy of the cities. Indeed it created such alarm that even Cologne showed itself disposed to pay the stipulated taxes faithfully and regularly, within the course of the ensuing years. Unfortunately however at the point to which the Hansa had come, this tax which was levied on goods proved fatal to the Hanseatic commerce, already crippled by other custom dues, while it assured an ever-increasing advantage to their two commercial rivals, the English and Dutch. It was in consequence of these heavy duties, too, that many a Hansa citizen renounced of his own free will the liberties that had come to cost so dear.

The Hansa Diet could see no remedy save in their old traditional measures. These import duties they insisted must be paid by the towns, and to insure this they established payment stations in divers localities of the Low Countries, such as Dortrecht and Amsterdam. But all these efforts failed to bring about the needful result, and the chief alderman at Antwerp was menaced with imprisonment. Indeed, it is said he was actually confined for some while.

In sore straits, the Hansa resolved to confide the administration of its Antwerp factory to a manager and a secretary chosen from the town of Cologne, who in critical moments should seek advice of the towns of Lübeck and Bremen.

Unfortunately the best administration in the world—and that of Cologne was perhaps not the best—could not restore life to an establishment irrevocably doomed. The few promises made, the few guarantees given, whether by the United Provinces or by the Spanish Netherlands, were not kept. Two Hansa embassies which passed through Antwerp early in the seventeenth century—the one bound for England, the other for Spain—halted at the factory to inspect it. Their official report sent to the Diet was, that this factory was completely fallen into disrepute and decay, and that in the general ruin every one thought only of himself, and the general interest was not considered. They added, that places formerly bustling with commercial life had been converted into barns for the threshing of corn.

A faint new hope was excited by the armistice which in 1609 was concluded between Spain and the Low Countries; and Bremen was charged with the administration of the factory in the place of Cologne. But this was a mere passing delusion which was to vanish before the reality; for in 1624 the Spanish soldiers took up their headquarters in the factory, and never quitted it until after the lapse of nearly thirty years, by that time having made its hundred and seventy rooms entirely uninhabitable.

A very pardonable, and indeed in this case very laudable, *amour propre* made the town of Lübeck too late desirous to restore this factory, which recalled the greatness, as well as the decadence, of the Hanseatic League. But the Queen of the Hansa, the most patriotic, the most energetic of all the cities, was not supported by her confederates in this costly enterprise. She therefore saw herself forced to abandon the establishment to its fate.

Still, before that date, indeed immediately after the pillage of Antwerp, the trade of the Hanseatic League with the Low Countries had ceased to be a commerce placed upon a regulated footing and ruled by prescribed laws, laws emanating from the factory and punctually and faithfully obeyed by the members. A faint activity and revival occurred in the seventeenth century when the Dutch and Hanseatics made a mutual trade pact. But this proved of little profit to the latter, as far at least as their traffic in the Low Countries was concerned; for, like impatient heirs, the citizens of the United Provinces endeavoured to enfeeble their rivals, to whose succession they looked forward.

VI.

THE END OF THE HANSA'S DOMINION IN ENGLAND.

THE Hansa had been more fortunate in England than in the Low Countries. Up to the middle of the sixteenth century nothing had occurred that had sensibly modified its old relationship with the English nation. Nor had the factory diminished in power or the commerce in importance. It is true that at various times, now the kings themselves, now the people, had grown restive under the heavy monopoly of the Hansa League; but, to the kings especially, the League with its riches, its command of ready money and of ships, was of great use, and all attempts at restriction of privilege ended in failure.

But as Russia became consolidated after she had thrown off the Tartar yoke, so England also gained in strength after she had once renounced the foolish desire of making herself mistress of France, and after the long civil war of the Roses was ended, and a new and peaceful reign inaugurated.

Henry VII. left the Hansa privileges intact. The same was the case under Henry VIII., who even confirmed and extended them. The patron of Max Meyer, the friend of the democratic burgomaster Wullenweber, found it to his own interest to have the theological and political support of the maritime Baltic cities, and was regardless of the interests and deaf to the entreaties of his native merchants. It is true that this hot-tempered and capricious monarch several times threatened the League with a restriction of their rights. Once indeed his threats seemed so likely to take effect that the Hamburgers, in alarm, advised the Steelyard authorities to remove from the factory all silver vessels and all ready money. However, these threats were not serious; they were perhaps but a ruse to extract more pecuniary or moral assistance from his allies.

The successive checks, however, which the League was encountering in other foreign countries were not without their reactionary effect upon

England. Various discussions arose between Hanseatic and English merchants, and led to more or less violent squalls, which were certainly the prelude to the coming tempest.

The Hansa, for instance, complained that they had been suddenly forbidden to export English goods into foreign countries, that is to say, countries other than Germany proper. Above all, an attempt was made to prevent them from carrying English cloth into the Low Countries. This traffic the Merchant Adventurers, an association formed partly upon the pattern of the Hansa, wished to reserve to themselves alone.

The Hanseatics further revolted against the old-established custom that made them all responsible for infraction of privilege, and punished them for the wrong done by one or several of their cities against some individual Englishman.

On their side the English insisted with much bitterness that the German towns refused to render them justice within their dominions; that they had even laid violent hands upon such of their compatriots as were occupied in fishing in Ireland; and that they had, in the days of Christian II., harassed their navigation in the Baltic.

During the hostilities between Francis I. and Henry VIII. the mutual recriminations diminished. The German Empire supported the English king, and the League had one more opportunity of playing the old game that had so often turned to its advantage. Solicited by both parties to lend its support, it played off one against the other; and insisting upon the neutrality of its members, traded freely and advantageously with both combatants.

It is quite certain that, notwithstanding some vexations and disputes, King Henry VIII. of England remained until his death the staunch friend of the Hansa, as well as of the Low German towns that formed part of the Smalkaldic League.

The reign of his young son and successor was to witness the first serious shock to the Hansa's power. This boy, who ascended the throne at the early age of ten years, confirmed all the Hanseatic privileges on his accession. Destined to give some rude blows to the confederation, he conformed in the first years of his reign to the ways of his ancestors. One incident is worth mentioning in order to illustrate the immense influence which the Hansa had gained in England. It was the rule, contracted years ago, that the name of the Hansa should figure in all treaties between England and France.

But after Edward had reigned a few years he lent willing ear to the requests of the Merchant Adventurers, all the more readily that their petitions were supported by Sir Thomas Gresham, the honoured founder of the London Exchange. This man made clear to the young king and his guardian, the Duke of Northumberland, that unless the Steelyard were destroyed, the price of exchange could not rise, because the fiscal privileges accorded to the Hansa weighed too heavily upon the English. Besides this, the men of the Steelyard were subjects of the emperor, whom the young Protestant king hated as a persecutor of his fellows in the purer faith.

Still the Hansa suspected no real danger from King Edward, and the less so, as they had completely acceded to his desire that they should abstain from all trade with Scotland. In April, 1551, a plot laid against the hated and envied strangers by the London burghers was discovered. In the course of the inquiry into the plot, it was needful to examine the Hansa's claims. Confiding in the goodwill of the king's councillors, the "New Hansa," as Sir Thomas Gresham called the Merchant Adventurers, poured forth a long catalogue of grievances against the League. It was stated that English merchants had been ill-treated in various Hansa cities, notably in Danzig and Stralsund; that the commerce of the English was hindered in all possible ways; and that serious loss was incurred by the royal treasury from the circumstance, suspected to be true, that the Hansa permitted persons foreign to their association to enjoy with them the benefit of their privileges.

In the list of complaints retailed before the king by the discontented burghers and merchants of London, and by the Merchant Adventurers who found themselves less favoured than these foreigners, an attempt was evident on the part of the English to place on one footing and to consider as equally prohibited, the fraudulent importation by the Germans of merchandise belonging to non-Hanseatics, and the importation by them of merchandise which belonged to them, but was not produced in their territory.

The fact was urged that, since the Hansa paid only the usual custom dues, even for the foreign products they imported, and for their exportation of English goods to lands outside the rule of the Hanseatic League, they were thus able to paralyse with the greatest facility all English competition in these different lands.

Certainly nothing better justifies the murmurs of the islanders against the foreigners than a comparison of their various commercial transactions. From these it appears that the English themselves, in 1551, exported 1,100 pieces of native cloth as compared with 44,000 pieces exported by the Hansa League in the same year.

It is true that all these complaints were not new. But this time they fell upon more fruitful soil. The government were perhaps all the more ready to give an attentive ear, as of late the national commerce had taken a very vigorous start, so that the royal treasury might hope for considerable receipts, even if the Crown should lose the duties paid to it by the members of the League.

In consequence the representative members of the Steelyard were cited before the Privy Council, which after a very brief examination of the claims brought forward by the Hansa, decided hastily (February 23, 1552) "that the Hansa, an illegal body, the names and origin of whose members were unknown, had by importation and adulteration of foreign goods forfeited the privileges accorded them by Edward VI."

The following day, also in Privy Council, the suppression of all the old Hanseatic privileges was decreed and the League placed on an equality with all other foreigners, none of whom had special favours granted them. This decision seemed to promise that at last the English would gain pre-eminence over their redoubtable rivals.

Meantime, the Hanseatic Diet, informed of this step on the part of the English Government, sent over an ambassador to treat with the king and Council. The result of his efforts was that, in July of the same year, the Hansa's privileges were re-established provisionally "as far as was reconcilable with the justice, fairness, and honour of the king"—so ran the clause.

Of all the negotiations a detailed and interesting account has been preserved to posterity in the Diary of the young King Edward, one of the most interesting documents for the knowledge of his short reign.

The concession granted to them made the members of the Steelyard think, and very rightly, that it would be well for them to put their own house in order, and of their own accord to initiate various reforms in their body, reforms much needed, for complaints against them had been loud and long. They secretly hoped to be in this wise restored to their former favoured position.

The disorders, however, in the body of the Steelyard were not, on the whole, those from which other foreign factories suffered. The taxes and other enforced contributions, both from residents and from the towns trading with England, were punctually paid, and the finances of the establishment were flourishing. The complaints, moreover, addressed to the Diet, that the members of the Steelyard loved luxury, wine, women, and gambling too well, and that they rebelled against their semi-monastic life, were not more frequent from England than elsewhere.

The difficulties were chiefly that trade regulations were not faithfully observed; that rules of the strictest nature, on which largely depended the Hansa's success, were circumvented and disregarded. For instance, no man who had not attained his majority was by statute allowed to become a member of the League and trade on his own account; nor was one who had not learnt English for at least six months. This latter precaution was the more requisite, as past experience had taught that, by ignorance of the native language, these men were apt to compromise the interests of the factory. Then there were other abuses that led to grave results, such as trading illicitly with natives and then absconding with their debts unpaid; the whole factory in such cases becoming responsible for the debts.

In 1553, therefore, the members of the Steelyard drew up a series of new statutes which they proposed to lay before the King of England for approval. If these minutes are well considered it will be seen that whatever else was dead or moribund, Hanseatic astuteness was not. The new laws, it is true, tended to abolish the abuses that had crept into the use of their privileges, but they did not make the least sacrifice of the liberties that the Hansa had acquired in the course of years.

King Edward, however, seemed little inclined to consider these statutes, or to revoke permanently his somewhat arbitrary decision—a decision undoubtedly just towards his subjects. Then happily for the Hanseatic League, though not for his country, he died in this same year, and the crown passed to his sister, the fanatical persecutor of Protestants, Bloody Queen Mary, as the popular mouth has named her.

The new sovereign speedily made it evident that she meant in all respects to pursue a different policy from that of her predecessor. The first to fall was the Duke of Northumberland, the pronounced enemy of the Hansa. Immediately after, the queen showed by various signs that she was graciously disposed towards these strangers, who had boldly greeted her proclamation as queen against her rival, Lady Jane Grey, by draughts of Rhenish wine liberally bestowed upon the populace at the gates of her capital. On the occasion of her triumphal entry into London they were foremost in welcoming her with pomp and splendour, as we have already mentioned in a former chapter.

Scarcely was the queen firmly seated on her throne, than the Syndic General of the Hansa, Dr. Sudermann, waited upon her, attended by councillors from some of the chief Hansa cities. The result of their representations was that one of the first acts of the new queen's reign was to annul the royal statute of Edward VI. that so grievously threatened the League. This almost unexpected good result was, it is whispered, not due merely to Queen Mary's reactionary policy, but also to the corrupting influence of Hanseatic gold, judiciously distributed.

Our League thus recovered its entire liberties and rights in the matter of export and import, notwithstanding the opposition of Parliament, of the Lord Mayor of London, and of the citizens. It is therefore not astonishing that they were willing to show themselves liberal on the occasion of King Philip's entry as husband of the English queen; and that in order to maintain the favour of this couple, various cities, especially Lübeck, showed themselves far from friendly to Protestant refugees who sought protection in their precincts.

A valuable memorandum, drawn up by the Syndic Sudermann and happily preserved to our times, gives a vivid picture of what was implied by the Hanseatic privileges in England.

Taking merely into account one article of their commerce, English cloth, it appears from this report that from the month of January to the month of November, 1554, the Hansa had exported from England 36,000 pieces of cloth, as against 1,100 exported by the English themselves, a third dyed and two-thirds in the rough; that they only paid for the right of exit threepence each piece, while other foreigners paid five shillings and ninepence; that they could use their own servants for packing and expediting merchandise, and so were relieved of various custom dues; that had they not possessed these privileges they would have had to buy this cloth on the Antwerp market, paying about £1 sterling more for the same; that they further gained £1 on each undyed piece, which they alone were allowed to export in this state, and which they resold after having had it dyed. If it be further considered that in reality they paid less than threepence a piece in the pound as custom duties, because the price of goods, fixed in ancient statutes, had gone up, while the Hansa still paid at the old figure; if, in short, this and various other matters be taken into account, it is no wonder that Syndic Sudermann could prove that on English cloth alone the Hansa earned, above that made by other foreigners who traded in this branch, a sum of about £61,000 sterling.

Small wonder, therefore, that the trade was as much coveted as it was prosperous, and that the mayor and municipal council of London did not cease from laying their complaints before the queen. They literally pestered her with petitions and demands on this subject.

For some months the Hansa succeeded in averting the storm from their heads, but finally the leading members of the Steelyard found themselves suddenly cited to appear before the Queen's Privy Council, and had to listen to a long catalogue of grievances drawn up by their accusers.

The sum total of these grievances was, that the Hansa did not contribute sufficiently to the resources of the English Crown; that it was prejudicial to the English navy, because it refused to employ any vessels but its own; that it harmed the very quality of English cloth, for the makers, seeing the Hansa would be sure to buy, presented them often with inferior qualities. An amusing complaint is the following: Whereas, say the memorialists, the Hanseatics are all bachelors, they greatly injure English trade at Antwerp, because the increased leisure this state gives them, allows of their trading more extensively and actively. Further, they once more brought forward the time-honoured objection that the Hansa would permit of no reciprocity, and while nominally allowing the English to settle in their towns, crippled their trade by heavy taxation and vexatious regulations.

That these assertions were not without foundation, not even the Hansa could deny. They could but point to ancient charters to justify them in a measure. The result of this last formal complaint was, however, that the Privy Council decided that henceforth the Hansa should abstain from importing English cloth into the Netherlands, and that the quantity of undyed goods they might export be reduced by two-thirds. They further added that any infraction of these orders would result in entire suppression of all privileges.

The Hansa, who did not easily own themselves beaten, and who desired at all costs to hinder their rivals from supplanting them, sent various embassies in the course of the next few years to the Court of England. They also once more attempted the agency of bribery and corruption by means of Hansa gold, to attain their ends. In vain. Embassies, seductions, led to no result; not even a letter which King Philip of Spain was induced to indite to his wife, the Queen of England, on their behalf, could modify by one iota the decision taken by the Privy Council.

Despairing of a good result from these measures, the League resolved to have recourse to its ancient mode of exerting pressure upon obstinate peoples, by threatening to break off all intercourse with them. The measure was, however, likely to have brought destruction to them in England; that it did not was due to the circumstance that the towns were no longer, as in past days, blindly obedient to the orders issued by the Hanseatic Diet. The Hansa, issuing such an order, forgot that they were no longer the exclusive masters of the North and East.

Such was the state of things when Queen Mary died, and Elizabeth, the Virgin Queen, took into her firm and able hands the reins of the English government (1558). It is true that she gave a gracious reception to the Hanseatic embassy that waited on her in May, 1560; but between a gracious reception and a confirmation of the ancient privileges of the League the Hansa were to learn that there lay an abyss she would never bridge over.

That the Hansa's power was effectually broken in England ultimately was due to that queen and to her wise statesman, Lord Burleigh.

It was soon felt by the nation at large that, with the advent to power of Elizabeth, a new spirit was infused into English life and enterprise. After a hundred years of weakness, England awoke to renewed life and vigour, and with vigour awoke ambition.

The Merchant Adventurers, encouraged by Gresham, put forward their desires; and they, too, asked that the Hansa should be kept down. These desires were listened to by the patriotic sovereign. She reconfirmed all the new tariffs with which the Hansa had been charged by Edward VI., and she further made various demands which the Hansa were most unwilling to concede; for they implied a strict investigation of the affairs of their factory—an investigation that they had no wish to provoke.

In the following years an active correspondence took place between the English queen and the Hansa cities, which made it most emphatically manifest to the latter that they must renounce all their antiquated pretensions; but that, on the other hand, the English queen was willing to place them in the category of the most-favoured nation clause, so that they would still pay less than other foreigners.

The Steelyard authorities, being on the spot and better able, therefore, to estimate the bearings and value of Elizabeth's letters and threats, strongly advised the Hansa towns to conform to the queen's concessions and demands. They foresaw that worse things were in store were this not done. But the League—to whom the smallest and most equitable sacrifice always seemed an enormity—resolved, before yielding, to try as a last resource what could be effected by endeavouring to obtain the intervention of the emperor.

It is strange that, after the lapse of so many years, experience should not have taught the Hanseatics that from the German emperor no effective help could be obtained. In this case, as in many previous ones, the reigning sovereign contented himself by writing a letter of remonstrance—a letter so worded that it was easily manifest to the recipient that words would not be followed by deeds. Both the Hansa and the emperor involuntarily revealed that, even after the ancient special privileges were withdrawn, the League would still enjoy great favour in England.

The emperor's letter was presented to Elizabeth by the aldermen and councillors of the Steelyard. The queen's privy councillors, and especially the trusty William Cecil, Lord Burleigh, in reply, made it very clear to the deputation that they had nothing to hope for beyond the last concessions offered.

Burleigh was the special object of the Hansa's hate. This arose, perhaps, from the fact that he had, according to a contemporary reporter, insulted one of their ambassadors by accosting him "with almost indecent rough speech." But Burleigh's speech can scarcely deserve these epithets, if the complaints and remarks are founded on his saying, that it was a bad shepherd who desired to pasture the cattle of strangers more richly than his own flocks; nor could they complain that they were excluded, so long as they might trade as freely as the English, and more freely than the French, Flemings, Dutch, Scotch, and other nations.

The Hansa, blind, unwise, stuck to its old policy, and like Shylock demanded the very letter of its ancient bond. It is true that Elizabeth insisted, on her side, that her subjects should be favoured in the Hansa towns; that this reciprocity should be granted was already a clause in the Treaty of Utrecht, concluded, it will be remembered, in 1474, but it had never been carried into effect.

It must be admitted that, all things considered, Queen Elizabeth treated the Hanseatics with a good deal of consideration and long-suffering, and demanded from them no more than what she had a right to demand. When they refused the offer to be placed on an equal footing with the English the queen issued an order that their export of English cloth should in future not exceed five thousand pieces. Cologne tried to retaliate by putting on an import tax, but it was an isolated measure, and had no effect.

In a word, the victory remained in the end with the English Government, on the side of which fought, not only its own vigorous organization, but also the disunion among the Hansa towns, which grew more serious daily, and the grave disorders that existed in the Steelyard itself.

For some time past serious complaints had been heard against the alderman of the factory, Peter Eiffler, a man who filled this high post for several consecutive years. He was accused among other things, of having tampered with the funds of the establishment, of having administered the factory without the help, or advice of the council; and of having divided unfairly among the Hanseatic merchants, the five thousand pieces of cloth permitted to them for export. Further, he was reproached for having in 1563 made a journey, leaving the Steelyard and the care of the treasury to young men incapable of so high a trust, who had done great damage to the factory.

After all these accusations had been duly sifted, this unfaithful servant of the Hansa was of course deposed from his post of trust, but his dismissal brought no fresh order into the shattered condition of things. As is frequently the case in the face of a public calamity, public spirit was extinct. Each individual thought only of himself, and of what he could rescue from the impending general ruin. On the one hand, there was the selfishness of the individual towns; on the other, the selfishness of the foreign factories. The London Steelyard, seeing that the fabric of the League was tottering, tried to save its individual existence out of the general wreck. It thought to acquire an independent life, and act and trade on its own account. Hence when the League knocked at the doors of its strong-room, to obtain the funds that should prolong or, as they hoped, even dispel the death agonies of the other foreign factories, whether by bribing nobles and kings, or by sending embassies to foreign courts, the Steelyard was careful not to listen to these demands, thinking of the future, when it might need all funds for itself. It was thus that in 1567, the London factory, in reply to a reprimand sent it by Syndic Sudermann for delaying to pay a sum of over one thousand florins into the public fund, made known to the town of Lübeck that this delay must not be imputed to it as a fault, that the times were not favourable to saving, that the annual expenses of the Steelyard amounted to eight hundred pounds sterling, and that other sums no less high had to be expended by it, in maintaining the factories at Lynn and Boston. The memorandum went on to explain that, if the English establishments were not kept in good repair, they would become forfeit to the English Crown. Then, again, the Hansa taxes had grown so heavy that no one could bear them. If the Diet wished, the Steelyard would be quite ready annually to send its accounts to Lübeck for revision, in accordance with the ancient usage, which however did not seem very firmly established; but, on the other hand, they would prefer not to act thus, since they feared lest their account-books should fall into the hands of their enemies, who by inspecting them, would gain an undesirable insight into Hanseatic commerce, and might thus perchance despoil them of their last privileges. The memorandum winds up by saying, that the Steelyard would feel greatly obliged if the League would refrain in future from making demands for pecuniary help in times of public difficulty.

If this was not the language of insubordination, it is difficult to say what else would be. Whither had vanished the blind obedience which the League had ever exacted, and till now obtained from all its members, and which was the source of its greatness and strength?

Whether all that was stated by the Steelyard in this memorandum was true, it is difficult to decide. Substantially no doubt it was so, but in the reports of the Hansa Diets during these years, we come across frequent complaints of the prevarication practised by the aldermen of the London factory.

Perhaps we must not blame either the towns, or the factories too much for yielding to the all-powerful instinct of self-preservation. When the Hanseatic towns as a whole recognized that they were impotent to demolish the rising commerce of England, or to break the firm will of its lady sovereign, they were almost forced to desert a cause which was a losing one, and to work each for their own separate advantage.

Hamburg was the first among the confederate cities to recognize whither matters were tending, and to adjust its policy with a due regard to the new spirit of the age. It concluded a convention on its own account with England. Matters came about in this wise. The chief foreign trade of England was gradually passing into the hands of the Merchant Adventurers. Now to this company the Netherlands were closed, owing to the conflict raging between Elizabeth and King Philip of Spain. Hence these merchants had to seek elsewhere the depôt which they had found in the Low Countries for their English merchandise. Owing to its situation and its excellent harbour the town of Embden, which did not belong to the Hanseatic League, seemed to unite in itself all requisite conditions, and it was indeed towards this place that English commerce was directed. In consequence Embden, within a brief space, grew most prosperous.

This prosperity, however, speedily proved noxious to the city of Hamburg, till then one of the great staple towns for the traffic in English woollens. Seeing its gains passing thus into the hands of strangers, the city deliberated whether the situation could not be changed, and whether it would not be wiser, more lucrative, and altogether better, to open its own gates to the Merchant Adventurers, conceding to them a factory, various privileges, and great commercial liberties. Thus it would secure the double profits arising from their sojourn, and from the commerce that passed through.

In 1567, Hamburg put this project into execution, concluding a formal treaty with the Merchant Adventurers for the space of ten years. It was cautious at first not to name a longer term. The experiment was but tentative, as it assured those of its burghers, who, clinging to the old Hanseatic ideas, opposed the scheme.

That the project was also opposed by the Hansa Diet will be easily inferred. Bitter reproaches were addressed to Hamburg by the Diet held at Lübeck in 1572. They were told that they had been guilty of treason to the common cause. Their delegates replied with warmth, rejecting this reproach. They recalled to the memory of their hearers the treaty of Utrecht which stipulated reciprocity for England, and they endeavoured to prove that their townsmen had acted, not only in no spirit of narrow egoism, but in the interests of the entire League, since in consequence of their treaty with the Merchant Adventurers, the export of undyed cloths from England had been permitted in larger quantities, and that the German waters were freed from British pirates. Further they contended that every town had a right to think also of its own interests. Embden had received the Merchant Adventurers, and had extracted profit from them; why then should such profit be grudged to a town that was a portion of the Hansa?

The delegates were able to point also to the tangible fact, that in the short space of the first two years, the factory of the Merchant Adventurers had turned over in Hamburg, the sum of three and a half million of dollars.

This was all well and good for Hamburg, but beyond question the treaty still further disturbed the relations of the cities towards each other, and helped on the pending catastrophe. And the worst of all was that Elizabeth could not be induced to reconfer the old Hanseatic privileges, even after her subjects had been received by Hamburg.

Still, for the moment, nothing was changed with regard to the new position taken up by Hamburg, though the agitation on the subject within the League itself continued unabated. When the ten years of treaty were ended, and the Hansa was desirous of renewing the convention, then the storm broke forth with fresh fury. Appeal was even made by the Hanseatic League to the Emperor Maximilian II., who decreed solemnly that no town might treat with England without the consent of its allies.

Still the Queen of England did not at once break off all relations with the Hanseatic League. She temporized, not being willing to lose for her subjects the advantages gained at Hamburg which she hoped to see further extended. The Hansa, on its part, demanded that the queen should re-confirm its privileges; then it would accord a factory to the English. The queen replied that she wished first to see the factory accorded; then it would be time enough to speak of the privileges.

In this wise the negotiations did not progress. Each of the parties was rolling the stone of Sisyphus, as Elizabeth herself remarked. It was quite evident that at that moment the queen was resolved not to resort to extreme measures, and though she threatened, she did not carry out her threat of putting the Hanseatics on the same footing with other strangers. The moment had not yet come. It came later, when she could do without certain of her imports, such as raw materials for ship-building and for stores of war, among which latter gunpowder took a great place. Then, too, before the defeat of the Spanish Armada had occurred, England did not feel her maritime power great enough to venture a *coup de force*.

Meanwhile, each new meeting of the Hansa Diet put in a stronger light the radical difference between the policy pursued respectively by the towns of Lübeck and Hamburg. This difference may be said to form the tame epilogue to the great tragedy of Wullenweber's failure and death.

The Lübeckers wanted the old privileges, the whole privileges, nothing but the privileges. What cared they for the changed condition of the world's affairs? Syndic Sudermann's ideal was the restoration of the good old customs in the factories, the continuance of every measure that in the past had made the Hansa great. But Sudermann was no military hero, who could win back privileges at the point of the sword, or "hold down foreign nations under his thumb," as the secretary of the Steelyard expressed himself. He was a learned, well-nourished, well-paid Hanseatic Syndic, thorough, pedantic, earnest, long-winded. It is on record that one of his memoranda destined for the Imperial Diet was so long, that a hundred and fifty dollars had to be paid in the Imperial Chancery for having it transcribed—an enormous sum in those days of cheap labour—and that the imperial councillors roundly declared that they would not read it at all, if it were not shortened. He it was who on all occasions represented Lübeck as her spokesman, and the ideas he expressed were those of the city.

Hamburg, on the other hand, could not refrain at times from remarking that the kingdom of England, like other kingdoms, no longer presented the same aspect as two or three hundred years ago, and that hence account must be taken of modifications, and actions be regulated accordingly. Its delegates cited the case of Antwerp, pointing out that that town's prosperity dated from the days it had opened its gates to the English Merchant Adventurers. Till then the houses had been thatched with straw, and the inhabitants had subsisted on the profits accruing from agriculture and fishing. And now what commercial activity, what a busy life was to be seen in the marts of Antwerp, what wealth was found among all classes of its burghers! To cite one instance alone: dwellings that fifty years ago were taxed at a rental of forty to sixty dollars, now cost eight hundred dollars.

But Lübeck would not recede from its old standpoint, and would not relinquish its old conservative ideas. It seemed to have none of that elasticity of mind that can adapt itself to changed conditions, and profit by them. It could but plead repeatedly—how far it was in earnest it is hard to tell—that the government of the League might be taken from off its shoulders, for the burden had grown too heavy. As a substitute it proposed either Cologne or Bremen. It could not find words to express the sorrow which Hamburg and other cities had caused by relinquishing the general weal for their own private good. It said it would itself retire from the League, in which the old sentiments no longer lived, were it not held to its duty, or what it deemed its duty, by the force of old memories. It could not realize that its system was antiquated, its ideas played out. Like some old people, it could neither give way gracefully, nor assimilate intelligently the new thoughts that sway the younger and rising generation. Like the old, too, it overlooked the fact that the young must win, time being in their favour.

In a great Diet held in 1591 the following resolution was actually put forward, namely, "that each town present should declare whether it intended to remain Hanseatic." This question was indeed significant. It should be mentioned that during the sitting of this Diet Syndic Sudermann died—a man who deserved well of the League, even if his opinions were sometimes narrow and mistaken, and not up to the level of the current ideas. Like Wullenweber, he had reaped nothing but ingratitude in return for his ardent and patriotic labours.

It is remarkable that Cologne was the first of the cities to reply in the affirmative, that she wished to remain in the League, Cologne ever so insubordinate and stubborn. Bremen also acquiesced, provided twenty more cities sided with Cologne. They stated that they decided thus for the sake of their posterity, since, having once acted, they must go through with it at all costs.

While all these dissensions were going on in the heart of the League itself, England continued in its onward path, evincing that feverish activity of commercial enterprise that has ever distinguished it.

Elizabeth sent ambassadors in all directions, courted and bribed the German princelings, distributed her gold everywhere, and by means of her spies neglected no means of making herself feared or beloved, or both.

The League meanwhile had to look on with impotence, for it lacked resources to do otherwise. Day by day it was losing its influence. It is true that both the Hanseatic and the Imperial Diet tried to prevent the English from settling in Germany; but the towns that saw their profit in receiving them either openly or secretly disobeyed commands which neither party could enforce. As a sample of the replies given to the Diet by the Hanseatic cities may be cited the case of Stade, which, when called to account, answered "That Almighty God had put the English in their way, and thus sent them some means of subsistence, in order that the citizens might get a bit of bread, and keep off the pangs of hunger."

Thus year by year England's influence increased and that of the Hansa declined. Then occurred a further cruel blow to the League. In consequence of the strained relations between England and Spain, Hanseatic trade in that country and in Portugal had risen to some importance. The Hansa supplied those countries with grain, munitions of war, and shipbuilding materials. Queen Elizabeth naturally looked on all this trade with an evil eye, and regarded it as so much support accorded to her enemies. She did not fail to make the League acquainted with her displeasure, even threatening to treat its cargoes as contraband of war. The Hansa in its turn pleaded that it merely exercised the right of neutrals, and persisted in not abandoning a lucrative trade.

Then came the defeat of the invincible Armada which left to England the empire of the seas, and gave her a boldness and self-confidence which she has happily never since lost. Sixty Hanseatic vessels were encountered by Norris and Sir Francis Drake about to enter the mouth of the Tagus. They were laden with grain to provision the Spaniards. These were seized, and no subsequent negotiations ever succeeded in causing Elizabeth to release her hold either on the vessels or their cargo.

Needless to say, that this proved the last straw in the load of Hanseatic grievances against the queen.

Meanwhile the King of Spain, to compensate the League, and to win it to his side, offered to enter into a firm alliance with it. But they would not break with the Netherlands, now in full revolt against King Philip. There remained only the last and almost hopeless resort, to appeal once more to the empire.

On August 1, 1597, after fifteen years of nearly useless solicitation, and when it was quite too late to remedy matters, the Emperor Rudolph caused an imperial mandate to be issued at Prague, which enjoined the English to quit the Empire within the space of three months. This mandate was couched in proud and fierce terms against the English queen, and menaced with severe punishment those Germans who, on German soil, should put themselves into communication with the hated Merchant Adventurers of England.

Great was the joy of Lübeck and of several other towns at this order, and they kept strict watch that the imperial mandate should be obeyed. They hoped from it the most salutary effects in modifying the resolutions of Elizabeth.

They had reckoned without their host, or rather they had not duly judged the character of their opponents. Driven from Germany, the English found a refuge in the Dutch town of Middleburgh, whence they conducted a lucrative trade with the empire, awaiting some happy chance that would be sure to arise from the now ever active discord in the League, and that might reinstate them on the shores of the Elbe and the Rhine.

Elizabeth meanwhile, in 1598, driven to yet further exasperation by a Hanseatic attempt to hinder the export of grain to England and Holland, sent word to the merchants residing at the Steelyard that they must depart out of these premises and quit England within the space of fourteen days. The Mayor of London, attended by the Sheriffs, formally presented to the authorities of the Steelyard this decree, which authorized them to take possession of the building and all that pertained to it.

Ten days after this compulsory taking of possession the Germans filed out of the Steelyard in orderly procession. The authorities wrote to the Hanseatic Diet, stating that, after duly protesting against this forcible act, they "marched out of the gate, the alderman at the head, and we following him, sad in our souls, and the gate was closed behind us; nor should we have cared to have remained another night within the walls. God be pitiful."

Thus the last sacrifice was consummated, which had been long demanded by Sir Thomas Gresham and his friends, and which the now flourishing condition of English trade required. In order that the English merchant might thrive unchecked, he had to drive away from his midst his old masters, the Hansa, the men who had taught him how to trade, a lesson the pupil had learnt too well. Such was the mournful end of the German Guildhall on the banks of the Thames; an institution older than the Hanseatic League itself; the most honourable monument which Germany could point to abroad of her strength and enterprise. Yet it is, perhaps, rather the fact that it endured so long, than that it perished, that should surprise us. It is certainly wonderful, and much to the credit of the English, that musty parchments sealed with the seals of the Plantagenets, should have been honoured so late, honoured when England's commerce and navy could boast men such as Sir Thomas Gresham, Sir Francis Drake, and Sir Walter Raleigh.

Of course the Hanseatic League did not at once give up all for lost. They intrigued, they negotiated, they even flattered themselves with hopes of success. Then suddenly the news of Elizabeth's death broke up a congress held with this end in view. The Hanseatics at once cast glances full of hope at her successor. They trusted he might prove less inexorable. Experience had often shown them that with a change of ruler came a change of policy.

But they proved greatly mistaken. The reply received by the first embassy they addressed to James I. rudely shattered all their hopes. They resumed their intrigues at home, trying to stir up the emperor to hinder the export of wool from Germany, and to encourage the manufacture of woollen goods at home.

It was the great De Witt who wisely said that the one weak point in the German Hansa was that it was not backed by manufacturing interests. They were merely carriers and intermediaries, and this made itself felt in the days of their decline.

Negotiations, entreaties leading to nothing, and the Germans being impotent to hinder, the English soon found their way again into the empire with their persons and their goods, and once more Hamburg was the first to receive them formally and to conclude a treaty with them. This time neither the emperor nor the League protested. It is true the Steelyard in London was ultimately restored to the Germans, but the old privileges enjoyed with it were gone for ever. Nor was it, when restored, regarded any longer as the property of the Hanseatic League such as we have known it—a compact body, willing and able to defend its rights. It was rather the property of the Germans living in England, and this it remained. In 1853 the Steelyard property was sold to an English company for building purposes for the sum of £72,500, by the cities of Lübeck, Bremen, and Hamburg, the sole heirs of the once powerful Hanseatic League. The present Cannon Street Station stands on part of the site.

With the death of Elizabeth the history of the Hanseatic League as such practically comes to an end in England. Then followed, quickly afterwards, the Thirty Years' War, which gave the League a mortal blow, from which it never recovered.

Even before the last stroke fell, John Wheeler, a secretary of the association of Merchant Adventurers, had declared regarding the Hanseatic cities (1601), "Most of their teeth have fallen out, the rest sit but loosely in their head." His judgment was verified all too soon.

VII.

THE THIRTY YEARS' WAR KILLS THE LEAGUE.

John Wheeler's diagnosis of the condition of the League was too correct. It is true that an ostensibly official document enumerates fifty towns as forming part of the Hansa League in 1603, but we know that at the same time only fourteen had a seat and voice in the Diet and duly paid their fees. Indeed, the more we examine the internal condition of the League at this period the more we wonder, not that it fell asunder, but that it endured so long. It had become utterly disorganized and was decaying fast.

In 1606, the Emperor Rudolph II. evoked a feeling of alarm among all the towns by suddenly demanding to see their charters, and to know whence they derived their privileges and statutes. Thus the results of appealing to imperial aid, in the English complications, bore their inevitable and unpleasant fruit. The emperor's ulterior aim was of course to extract money from the cities, this time in aid of his Hungarian wars. As in the days of their glory, the cities knew how to protect themselves, and how to escape undesirable inquiries by means of subterfuges and evasive answers. Still the first attempt at supervision had been made, and was to bear fruit later.

While matters were in this uncomfortable state, there broke forth the long, terrible strife known to history as the Thirty Years' War. Its causes are to be sought for in those most unhappy differences of doctrinal opinions, which, being rooted in mutual intolerance, a want of fairness of spirit, and of dramatic insight into the needs of divergent mental constitutions, make one man wish forcibly to impose his point of view upon his neighbour, under the conviction that it is the only point of view, and hence the true one. This intolerant and narrow spirit, which more fatally divides individuals and nations than any other form of human folly, had reached its climax in the century of the Reformation, when not only were Protestant and Catholic opposed to one another, but

Protestants were also divided among themselves, Calvinist and Lutheran persecuting each other with an acrimony quite out of proportion to the gravity of the questions at stake.

The details of this most deplorable war fall outside our province, and belong to the history of Germany proper. We can but touch on it as it concerns our League. When hostilities commenced, the Hansa were to realize what even the shadow of a great name implies. Power after power made overtures to the League to make common cause with them. Gustavus Adolphus of Sweden, was the first. As early as 1621, he sought an alliance with the cities, and he counted the more on an affirmative reply, that his enmity to Denmark was shared by the League. But they refused his offer, saying they wished to enter into no unequal bond, assuring the king however, at the same time, that they desired to remain good friends with him, and to continue their commercial intercourse.

The fact was that, seeing the agitated and disordered condition of affairs in Germany, the Hanseatic League hardly felt it wise to take any definite step at this juncture.

Gustavus Adolphus, however, was the more disappointed at their refusal, since he had been led to expect different treatment from them. Since the time he had ascended the throne, his relations with the League had been friendly. An old chronicler tells us how some time before the king's marriage, the "honourable Hansa towns" sent ambassadors to Sweden to conclude a treaty with Gustavus Adolphus about the Protestant religion, and also to treat with him concerning trade privileges. Indeed, the latter seems to have been their chief aim. But as they wanted to keep it secret, says the writer, they professed that they had been sent to congratulate the king upon his marriage. Gustavus Adolphus received them in solemn audience, standing and with uncovered head; no small honour to pay to a confederation of trading towns. Beside him stood his mighty Chancellor, Oxenstjerna. After the king had accorded them a cordial and formal reception, he gave them the traditional presents, usually only awarded to nobles.

Further, he accorded them free board at the cost of the city of Stockholm, as often as they did not eat at his royal table. In order that no mistake might arise regarding quantity, he informed them that in the matter of meat alone, they could count on six oxen, twenty-one fat sheep, one reindeer; and as to drink, on four barrels of good wine, and three hundred and sixty Swedish dollars to cover their other expenses. "This royal treatment mightily pleased the honourable delegates," writes our chronicler, and no wonder, when we remember that the men of the Hansa were famed for the amount they could eat and drink. No wonder, too, that Gustavus Adolphus thought to find in them ready allies, if only in return for his good hospitality.

That the King of Denmark, their old foe, should also have courted their alliance, seems yet stranger. He too, was refused. So was France, who, in 1625, sent delegates to the Hanseatic Diet to sound the members as to her chances of success, in forming an offensive and defensive alliance with these once so powerful merchants.

The most important and strangest offer of all was the wooing of the imperial delegates in the name of Spain, at the Diet held at Lübeck, in 1627. It appears that Spain stood in need of a friendly commercial navy in order to carry on her colonial trade, as well as of a friendly maritime power with which to meet the Netherlands. This idea was in accord with Duke Wallenstein's project to gain empire over the Baltic by means of an imperial navy, thus to surround the imperial crown with a new lustre, and the more surely to hold within bounds the recalcitrant inland princes. It was not from pure ill will or haughtiness that Wallenstein so terrified Stralsund, the town which he besieged so long and mercilessly, nor from pure love of well-sounding titles, that he styled himself "General and Admiral of the Baltic and North Seas."

The two imperial delegates, who appeared before the Hanseatic Diet at Lübeck deigned to speak the quaint formal language that was traditional with the Hansa League. They were begging for a favour, and so deemed it wise to assume no masterful tones. The emperor's word was said to be addressed "to the honourable councillors and other members of the worthy city of Lübeck, regarding it as the head of the most ancient Hansa League." The ambassadors put before the assembled Hanseatic deputies, that the Holy Roman Empire, in its entirety, and the venerable German Hansa towns in particular, had suffered grievously from the restraint on free navigation which had been imposed on them by foreign potentates; and that the German nation had thus the bread taken out of their very mouths. Therefore it was the emperor's earnest and ardent desire to befriend the towns, and to restore the nation to its former reputation and grandeur. A most useful alliance would be proposed to them, and this proposal did not come from a foreign power, but was put forward under the emperor's patronage and protection. The facts were these,—Spain had for some time past declared itself willing to enter into an agreement, that all the merchandise, whether exported from or imported into the Spanish dominions, should only pertain to the natives of the German Empire or to Spanish subjects.

The emperor through his ambassadors admitted that this proposal had at first sight seemed to him somewhat grave, and requiring consideration, but those competent to judge had demonstrated to him, that such direct importation of Spanish and Indian wares into Germany would benefit, not alone the Hansa towns, but the whole of Germany, and would serve to compensate for the privations and sacrifices imposed by the most unhappy war.

The emperor went on to add, that he had ever noted in Lübeck a very true and German frankness and fidelity, and that he did not doubt that Lübeck would carefully consider this proposal, in concert with the sister towns, in order that, after the compact had been duly concluded between the emperor and the King of Spain, it might be openly confirmed with the help and advice of the Hansa towns.

This was the smooth speaking in which the Hansa's imperial masters chose to indulge when it suited their imperial purpose. But decrepit, weakened though the Hansa was, it was not easy to catch it napping. Our wary merchants felt convinced there was some ulterior motive at the bottom of this sudden graciousness, and considered the imperial proposal very carefully and thoroughly. What could it mean, that of a sudden these jealous Spaniards were willing to share the monopoly of their whole colonial trade with the Hansa towns? Our cities feared the Spaniards, even when they came laden with gifts. When we recall, said these traders, the incessant and endless annoyances which our merchants have endured during two centuries while doing business with Spain and Portugal, the arrogant demands, the petty frauds and meanness of the Spanish consuls in the Hanseatic towns, we must confess that this previous knowledge of the character of our would-be allies does not lead us to trust their new, gracious, and friendly offers. They remembered, further, how a certain consul, called De Roy, was never named in their minutes, other than as the "arch enemy of the Hansa towns." They recalled, too, the project of a maritime commercial company (an *Amirantazgo*), proposed some time back by Spain between the Low Germans and Netherlands, which had revealed to the acute Hanseatics that Spain was deficient in ships and in capital, and that its real purpose was to obtain a fleet for itself on terms as cheap as possible. No, decidedly, the Spanish offers were not to be thought of.

Moreover, the Hanseatics very naturally feared an inevitable breach with their Scandinavian neighbours if they accepted. They foresaw, too, that their adhesion to the plan would give the emperor a sort of right to interfere in their commerce and internal arrangements. They had a wholesome fear, not without cause, of being placed under the most Catholic protectorate of Spain, and, looking ahead, thought they beheld, hidden beneath these velvet offers, the claws of the terrible, abominable Inquisition.

The whole project was therefore allowed to remain a project. To the imperial spokesmen were presented respectively four thousand and two thousand dollars, and the Diet resolved to place the proposal *ad referendum*. This meant that it was shelved once and for ever.

Nor did the Diet have cause to regret its decision, for soon after the King of Denmark, at that moment trying to ingratiate himself with them, sent for their perusal letters which he had intercepted. These communications were from the emperor, authorizing Count Tilly to secure the cities of Lübeck, Hamburg, Bremen, Stade, &c. So much for the sincerity of this monarch's vaunted friendship.

And now the war storm long brewing broke over Northern Europe. Germany was to pay heavily for her want of religious unity, or at least the want of mutual forbearance among her people. At first the Hansa towns had hoped that as usual their claims for neutrality would be regarded, but Tilly refused to listen to this, probably owing to his secret instructions from the emperor. All the northern towns had to suffer the full horrors of the war-curse, and they suffered hardly less at the hands of their friends than at those of their enemies. Both proved equally merciless. In order to escape having a military occupation within its walls, Rostock had once to pay 100,000 dollars, and another time 150,000 dollars, Wismar was taxed to the sum of 200,000 dollars; and Hamburg a sum yet higher. Magdeburg's fate was even more sad; it was besieged by the imperial army, pillaged, and given to the flames.

Imperial authority had never appeared so redoubtable to these free cities, or so injurious to their religious liberties and their political integrity. Wallenstein and Count Schwarzenberg even went the length of demanding the Hansa's ships, in order to use them for pursuing the foes of their imperial master upon the high seas, and it is easy to understand how, in presence of an armed force of a hundred thousand men, it was vain for the Hanseatic Diet to object that their deputies had received no instructions which could warrant them in acceding to such a proposal.

The ports of Rostock, Warnemunde, and the town of Wismar were all occupied by the Imperialists, who were also engaged in besieging Stralsund.

The history of this siege and the heroism displayed by this city are among the most notable features in the Thirty Years' War. Wallenstein had rightly judged it as most important for his purpose from its geographical position, and had determined it should be his. As Schiller says in his play *Wallenstein's Lager*, he had sworn—

> "Rühmt sich mit seinem gottlosen Mund
> Er müsse haben die Stadt Stralsund,
> Und wär' sie mit Ketten an den Himmel geschlossen."

This town which, thanks to some succour from outside, succeeded in wearing out the enemy, proved what bravery can do even under the most unfavourable conditions. At the same time the episode throws a fierce light on the low condition into which the League had fallen. In vain did the city of Stralsund appeal to the Diet and to the sister cities for help. It was only after long reflection and many debates that it was decided to advance to this unlucky friend the meagre sum of fifteen thousand dollars, and this at interest of 5 per cent.

These merchants, once princely and noble, at least in their dealings among themselves, had sunk to shopkeepers even in the domestic circle. The fact is, that defeat and terror had paralysed and prostrated them. Instead of making such a firm resistance as they would have done in the past, they had now recourse only to the feeble weapons of tears and entreaties in order to procure some gentler treatment for those of their members who had fallen into the enemy's hands. Most frequently, too, these humiliating steps proved quite futile, and were answered according to the temperaments of the generals-in-chief—brusquely and rudely by Tilly, politely and cunningly by Duke Wallenstein.

Meanwhile matters went from bad to worse for the Hansa towns and for Germany. Even when the empire achieved victories, the people had grown too impoverished and too enervated to profit by them. The story of this long-confused conflict of thirty years' duration is one of the saddest and most depressing in European history.

When in 1648 the peace of Westphalia was at last concluded, it nominally restored calm to the whole northern world, including the Hansa towns. But the League to all intents and purposes was at an end. The peace could restore neither its power, nor its union, and the confederation which seemed to have sunk in deep sleep during the war, awoke from its long repose only to find itself deprived of nearly all its members, and powerless to continue any longer its enfeebled existence.

VIII.

THE SURVIVORS.

Although the peace of Westphalia found the Hansa hopelessly broken, yet it was not until after this event that the various members fully realized their condition. Until then they had anticipated a resuscitation with the advent of political calm. When the Hanseatic deputies had assembled at the Diet of 1628, the last of which an official record exists, they had voted to postpone to a more convenient season all proposals that were brought forward for consideration. This Diet revealed the confusion into which the Hanseatic accounts had fallen. Still even on this occasion various cities pleaded for re-admission into the union. It throws a sad light upon the character of the delegates to read that those of Brunswick, reporting to that city the history of this Diet, should lay great and detailed stress upon the fact that they had not been regaled with the customary wine of honour and the wonted supply of cakes!

All that was achieved on this occasion was that the cities of Lübeck, Bremen, and Hamburg, were charged with the protection of the Hanseatic interests, in the name of all the other cities, so far as such interests could at present be said to be at stake.

Yet another Diet was summoned in February, 1630, at Lübeck. On this occasion there occurred what of late had not been unusual, namely, that no Hanseatic delegates appeared, with the exception of those of Bremen and Lübeck.

It is a picturesque historical invention, but, unfortunately, like most picturesque legends, quite untrue, that on this occasion all the members of the most ancient German Hansa put in an appearance, and in Lübeck's Hansa Saal decreed, in all solemnity, its own dissolution; that, in short, the Hansa was present at its own funeral. As the Hansa never had an actual foundation day, so it had no day of dissolution. As its growth had been gradual, the result of time and circumstance, so was its decay. It had been built up imperceptibly, it passed away almost as imperceptibly.

After the Diet of 1630, and again in 1641, the three cities above named—Lübeck, Bremen, and Hamburg—made still closer their friendly alliance, erecting a species of new Hansa upon the ruins of the old. With great modifications this compact survived down to our own times, and was not dissolved until forcibly rent asunder, as disturbing to Prussian ambition and to Prussian ideas of protective trade. For these cities kept up a species of free trade, while all the rest of Germany was protective, and to this day, though despoiled and shorn of their honour, the cities call themselves proudly the Hanseatic towns. In those days their main endeavour was to save as much as possible from the general wreck, and to try and keep alive the spirit of the League, of which most ambitiously they retained the name. They believed, indeed the other cities believed too, that with the restoration of peace they could establish themselves upon the old foundations.

This vain, daring hope, so common to all who suffer from incurable disease, did not quit them till the conclusion of the peace so ardently desired. This peace inaugurated a state of things incompatible with the commercial tendencies of the Hanseatics, and showed indisputably the futility of their hopes.

Yet with that doggedness or obtuseness which prevents a man from knowing when he is beaten, and which was at all times both the strength and weakness of the Hansa, even after facts had been made plain to them, they still refused absolutely to accept them. They still hoped against hope, to shape the course of events, and as usual Lübeck the energetic was to the front in these endeavours.

After the peace of Westphalia, this city tried repeatedly to organize a Hanseatic Diet in the old style. It was not until 1669 that a number of cities could be found willing to send deputies sufficient to qualify the assembly with the name of a Diet. But many of these deputies came only to announce that their towns would not in future pay contributions to the League, putting forward as their reason either that the war had impoverished them too much, or that the changed manner and course of trade made them doubt as to the continued utility of their union.

The discussions on this occasion were most animated. It was a stormy sitting, but it produced no real result. Too many different and absolutely conflicting opinions were advanced. The only conclusion that was arrived at was the choice of a certain Dr. Brauer, of Lübeck, to fill the honoured post of Hanseatic Syndic.

Vain honour truly, a very sinecure. For our poor old League, already in its death throes, did not survive this Diet. After eighteen sittings had been held it was made manifest that no accord could be arrived at, and the city of Lübeck even doubted if it were worth while to draw up an official report of the proceedings. Respect for ancient usages, however, prevailed, and the minutes were therefore drawn up in all due form. But they had no fact to record, except that the assembly had not been able to arrive at a unanimous opinion on any one point put forward.

Speaking of this final moment, the eminent historian of the League, Sartorius, writes—

"The constituent elements of the League had been united together in silence, and it was also without noise that they were decomposed. No one could be astonished at this end, which for some time past have been foreseen by any intelligent person."

"*Sic transit gloria mundi*" might have been written on its tomb. Its glory had been great and real indeed.

No less a person than the eminent philosopher, Leibnitz, in 1670, advised the imperial authorities, of course without result, to revive German trade by the re-establishment of the Hanseatic towns. The profound indifference of the empire was a fact too great to be overcome. The Emperor Charles VI. even went the length of formally forbidding his subjects to trade with the two Indies by way of England and Holland. At no single princely court of the whole realm was there to be found a sound view of commerce and commercial requirements. In the midst of such apathy and ignorance it was a real piece of good fortune for Germany that, at any rate, the three cities of Lübeck, Bremen, and Hamburg, were allowed to keep their independence.

It was in these cities, then, gradually as trade revived and the disastrous effects of the Thirty Years' War were somewhat overcome, that wealth concentrated itself. Here too was still to be found commercial knowledge, activity, and enterprise, while the old name of Hansa was discovered to have sufficient power left to conjure with. That German industry still found foreign outlet, that it still survived, and proved profitable, was henceforward due solely to the three remaining Hansa towns.

The empire, meanwhile, whenever it did not harry them by attempts at futile restrictions or by foolish criticism of their policy, ignored them entirely. This was always for the cities the happiest course, allowing them free room to act as they, with their commercial knowledge and insight, thought fittest.

But as time went on, and the political state of Germany grew more and more abject, it naturally came about that the Germans grew less and less respected and feared in the foreign markets, the foreign people with whom they had to deal knowing full well that there was no real power to back them. They had to see all other strangers preferred before them and the name of German become a by-word. Indeed they would be scornfully asked what was meant by German, seeing there was no land really so styled, and that the country which once bore that name was split up into a vast number of small principalities. No wonder that this condition of things did not help on German trade. No wonder that under these circumstances the foreign policy of the new League, or rather of the union of the three towns, for league it could not be called, was a policy of weakness, almost of cringing, far different indeed from that of their predecessors, who had played with thrones and deposed kings. Where once they commanded they had now to plead or flatter, and if these methods failed they were driven to observe the mores mundi, to use their own phrase, and let fly silver balls, unlike the heavy balls used in olden times, that is to say, they had to bribe.

After the French Revolution and the European disorders of that time, the Hansa towns by common accord of Russia and France were declared to be perpetually neutral, a gift of doubtful value. The cities were soon made to feel what was meant by owing their existence to aliens.

A little later Napoleon the Great was frequently on the point of giving away the Hansa cities, even before he had appropriated them to himself. In 1806 he offered them as compensation for Sicily, and, according to Lord Yarmouth, would have given them to Hanover if thereby he could have procured the peace with England. Sometime after they were destined by him to serve as the footstool of the throne he designed for his brother Louis in North Germany.

While he was making up his mind they were held by his soldiers, and these days of French occupation were spoken of to their dying days by the burghers in accents of terror. At last, in 1810, quite suddenly and without previous warning, "without due regard and courtesy," as was pleaded afterwards at the Congress of Vienna, Napoleon incorporated the Hansa towns with the empire.

It was well for them that this period was of short duration, for trade was in those days a matter of no small difficulty. Napoleon's mania regarding the continental system had reached its culminating point. Commerce was carried on either by submitting to grave sacrifices owing to the blockade, or by smuggling on a colossal scale. Neither method brought with it prosperity or calm.

Then dawned the memorable year of 1813, and with it came the first check in Napoleon's victorious path. The citizens of the three Hansa towns were among the first in Germany to put on armour and draw the sword for the liberation of themselves and of their suffering fellow-countrymen. Great oppression, happily for mankind and progress, often produces a strong recoil. Enthusiasm knew no bounds; German courage, which seemed dead, was revived.

Alas! it was a false hope. Reaction once more got the upper hand after Germany was liberated from Napoleon's yoke, and it is a question whether the yoke of the native rulers was not even heavier to bear than that of the foreign usurper. It was certainly less liberal.

The three Hansa towns, however, fortunately for them, managed to secure their independence, though not without a struggle. There were not lacking neighbours who gazed at them with covetous eyes, nor others who would have looked the other way had some power appropriated them.

At the Congress of Vienna Lübeck was all but given away to Denmark. But this was more than the Hanseatic delegates present in the assembly could stand. Accustomed of old to lift up their voices boldly, and not to fear crowned or anointed heads, they fiercely denounced this project as a deed of darkness, and appealed so strongly to the consciences of those present, reminding them of the everlasting shame attending a broken word or promise, that they actually succeeded in bringing them round to their point of view. The project was abandoned.

Thus the towns remained virtually free, while nominally attached to Germany, and continued, as of old, as willing, as they were able, to serve their country with the talents that had been entrusted to their keeping. Their flag again appeared on all the seas, their commerce extended in all lands, they even succeeded in concluding favourable trade alliances in virtue of the old Hanseatic firm of "the Merchants of the German Empire."

But, as ever before, they were not backed by the nation or by any real power at home, and now that they were only three towns they could not act as in the days of old, when their number extended across Europe.

But since the many hundred little states of which Germany consisted have been all absorbed by Prussia, and incorporated under the collective name of Germany, even the three Hansa towns, the last to resist and to stand out for their autonomy, have had to succumb to the iron hand of Prince Bismarck and the Prussian spiked helmet. Hamburg still keeps up a semblance of independence, but it is but a shadow, and even that shadow is rapidly vanishing from its grasp. Military, protectionist Germany does not care to have in its confines a town where free trade and burgher independence are inherited possessions. The name of Hansa towns, the title of Hanseatic League, is but a proud memory, one, however, to which modern Germany may well look back with satisfaction, and from the story of the "common German Hansa" it can still, if it chooses, learn many a useful lesson.

NOTE.

Since writing the foregoing, the event, long anticipated as inevitable, has taken place, and the last two cities to uphold the name and traditions of the Hanseatic League, Hamburg and Bremen, have been incorporated into the German Zoll Verein, thus finally surrendering their old historical privileges as free ports. Lübeck took this step some twenty-two years ago, Hamburg and Bremen not till October, 1888—so long had they resisted Prince Bismarck's more or less gentle suasions to enter his Protection League. But they foresaw what the end must be; that his motto was that of the Erl King in Goethe's famous ballad:

"Und bist Du nicht willig, so brauch ich Gewalt."
("And if thou be not willing, I shall use force.")

Still they, and Hamburg in particular, held out nobly, jealous, and rightly jealous, of the curtailment of those privileges which distinguished them from the other cities of the German Empire. It was after the foundation of this empire that the claim of the two cities to remain free ports was conceded and ratified in the Imperial Constitution of April, 1871, though the privilege, in the case of Hamburg, was restricted to the city and port, and withdrawn from the rest of the State, which extends to the mouth of the Elbe and embraces about one hundred and sixty square miles, while the free-port territory was reduced to twenty-eight square miles. This was the first serious interference with the city's liberty, and others followed, perhaps rather of a petty, annoying, than of a seriously aggressive, character, but enough to show the direction in which the wind was blowing.

It was in 1880 that the proposal to include Hamburg in the Customs Union was first politically discussed. It met, not unnaturally, with much opposition among the citizens, and especially among the merchant class, of whom these citizens are so largely composed. Not only did it wound the Hamburgers' pride to see an old and honourable distinction abolished, but they feared, and not without reason, that their trade would be seriously affected by such a step. They were afraid that their city would cease to be the great international distributing centre which it had been so long. Hot and animated were the discussions in the Senate, the House of Burgesses, the press, on docks and quays, in public and in private. But the pressure exercised from Berlin, though in appearance gentle, was firm and decided. How could a single city stand against a strong military empire? In May, 1881, therefore, was drafted a proposal to the effect that the whole of the city and port of Hamburg should be included in the Zoll Verein. This was laid before the Senate, who passed a resolution that the treaty should be accepted, stating its conviction that the inclusion of the free ports in the Zoll Verein would not only be beneficial for the empire, most of whose foreign commerce passed through them, but also would increase the prosperity of the cities themselves. Whether the Senate really held this belief, or whether they thought it wise to profess this opinion, does not appear. The proposal was then sent down to the House of Burgesses. Here it did not find such facile acceptance as among the more aristocratic senators; here no real or professed illusions reigned. For seven hours did the fathers of the city discuss the resolution of the Senate in a sitting that will ever be famous among the annals of the town. The speech made by Dr. Petersen, the Commissioner for the Senate, was most impressive, and it touched the hearts of all his hearers.

He reminded the Assembly that their thousand years' history testified to the fact that the Hamburgers were ever an active, practical, patriotic people, who took life earnestly, caring not only for business and family, but for the common weal. Every good Hamburger has always been ready to sacrifice his feelings and his personal interests for the good of the Fatherland. Let all of them, he urged, even those who could not do it heartily, vote for the measure, in the sure and certain conviction that the "Father City" would flourish and prosper, and increase through the skill, the energy, and, above all, the public spirit of its citizens. Hamburg would still remain the emporium, for the wide world, of the German Fatherland, to which she would be more closely united than ever.

This speech was followed by much and earnest discussion, after which the proposal of the Senate was at last agreed to as an inevitable measure, and Hamburg was included in the Zoll Verein by one hundred and six votes against forty-six.

The details for carrying into effect this conclusion have occupied seven years, and the event was finally celebrated with great pomp, the Emperor William II. coming in person to enhance the solemnity of the sacrifice brought by the burghers of the erst free city for the common weal of the German Fatherland.

As we have said, the step was inevitable sooner or later, and the Hamburgers knew it. The German Empire, so long a fiction, had arisen stronger than ever. It was natural, very necessary, that an anomaly should be abolished which placed the great gateway of foreign commerce outside the customs regulations of the rest of the empire. It was natural for the imperial authorities to desire that their two great commercial ports should be at one with the empire in all respects; that as far as their trade is concerned they should not be in the position of foreign countries, jealously watched by imperial officers lest they might seek to injure the financial interests of the country of which they form a part.

It is too early to know what effect this step will have upon the trade of the two cities, whether it will check or increase their prosperity. The gain to Germany is certain. The gain to the two cities, but in especial to Hamburg, is something less than problematical. Meantime the last and only privilege the three once powerful Hanseatic cities retain is that of being entitled, like the greatest States in the empire, to send their own representatives to the Bundesrath and to the Reichstag.

EPILOGUE.

THE once proud and mighty Hanseatic League is dead now, quite dead. There remains of it only a noble memory, the record of a high and fearless spirit which resisted tyrants petty and great, a spirit which recognized the value of independence, and strove with all its strength to attain and to maintain this boon. We have traced it from its earliest dawn to its recent complete demise; there but remains for us to speak its funeral oration. This is soon accomplished, since whether for men, for nations or associations, if their deeds speak not for them more eloquently than human words, the latter shall avail them little.

The chief title of the Hanseatic League to remembrance is that it was the means of spreading higher culture throughout wide tracts of the European continent, many of them, in those early times, still sunk in utter barbarism; that it introduced Western customs and civilization into all domains of private and social life for millions upon millions of people. This association is a bright spot that strikes the eye, as it looks back across the long, dark abyss of ages past, and we welcome it the more gladly because the bond that held this League together was neither force nor fear, but free will and clear insight into the advantages and necessity of mutual help. To quote the pertinent words of Mrs. Sinnett: "These free cities of Germany rise like happy islands amidst the wide-wasting ocean of violence and anarchy. Not by war and spoil, but by industry, enterprise, and prudent economy, did they accumulate the wealth that enabled them to heal so many of the wounds inflicted on their country by the iron hands beneath whose grasp art, science, even agriculture, by which they subsisted, was perishing. By the unions which the cities formed amongst themselves they stemmed the torrent of violence and anarchy that was threatening to turn their country into a desert peopled by hordes of robbers and slaves; they lent the most effectual aid to the Church in her efforts for the peace and civilization of Europe; yet they held the balance most firmly against the too great preponderance of her power, and rescued the human mind from the injurious subjection which she sometimes claimed as the price of her benefits when society had outgrown the leading strings that guarded its infancy, and felt as a galling restraint what had once been a needed protection. The cities built asylums for the widows and orphans whom the nobles and warriors had made desolate; they stretched out often a helping hand to the poor knight, who was regarding them with envy, hatred, and malice, and all uncharitableness, taking him into their pay as a soldier, and enabling him to get a comparatively honest living, instead of wringing 'from the hard hands of peasants their vile trash,' or filling some menial office at the court of a prince, and picking up the crumbs that fell from the great man's table. Behind their walls and bastions the young tree of civil liberty, which was perishing in the open country, took root and flourished; there, even whilst striving only at first for riches and their peaceful enjoyment, did men learn to prize the blessings of social order, justice, and peace. These cities were not mere aggregations of men within a narrow space, such as may have existed among the most barbarous nations; they were organic bodies animated by a living spirit—a spirit of enlightened intelligence, courage, and self-reliance, which best supplied what was defective in the religious system of the time, and gave a more healthy and manly tone to the character both of individuals and of society. The Church, it cannot be denied, sometimes taught men, in the pursuit of an imagined perfection, to trample on the impulses, and violate the duties of nature; in these little republics, on the contrary, though originally they had only the attainment of temporal good in view, they rose insensibly to higher objects, and not only cultivated the social virtues more effectually, but in their struggle to maintain their place in the world, fought in many instances a more successful fight against the sins of the flesh, through the discipline of the manifold cares of an active life, than the recluse of the cloister, with all his fastings and flagellations. Among the happy influences belonging to these miniature states was the ardent attachment of the free citizens of the Middle Ages to the little spot which they had hedged in from the wide wilderness of slavery around, where the individual, if not of noble birth, was usually the mere helpless victim of arbitrary power. Freedom and honour, the respect of his fellows, the happiness of domestic life, the interest and excitement of active business, the joviality of social intercourse, a thousand ties entwined around him, connected him closely with the city, and even the house of his birth; for in those days it was common for men to live and die beneath the same roof under which they had been born. The merchant regarded his native town with a pride fully equal to that of birth and chivalry in the privileged classes, and little envied, we may suppose, the life of the solitary feudal lord in his castle, or the anxious and dependent position of the courtier. The citizen of a humbler class showed, by parading on all occasions the tools and emblems of his trade with the same complacency with which a soldier displays his sword, or the noble his armorial bearings, that he knew his position and was content with it, and felt none of that weak shrinking from his appointed place in society or uneasy longing after another, which has since been the epidemic malady of the middle classes."

For two centuries and more this guild of merchants made the German name respected in European lands, the German flag respected in European waters. When the empire had fallen to pieces and there was no union, no cohesion left, the Hanseatics remained German and held together staunchly and nobly. Though the time of their existence was brief, yet it was all-important, not only for their own land, but for all Europe.

To appreciate to its full extent the influence exercised upon Europe in general by the Hanseatic League, we must carry our minds back, and compare Europe as it was when the League took its rise, with Europe as it was when the League declined. The Hansa made its appearance in history at a time when barbarism, violence, religious fanaticism, political and civil slavery, and dire intellectual darkness overspread the whole continent, when liberty and industry, as we understand them, were unknown. The constant and active communication kept up by the cities of the Hansa, not only among themselves and with all parts of Germany, but with the most distant countries, awoke and kept alive the intelligence of the people. To the Hanseatics, as to the Italians of the same epoch, was reserved the honour of dispelling the obscurity that reigned in the mental and material world. The Hansa's glory only pales before that of the rival Italian mercantile associations from the fact that its energies were somewhat too exclusively confined to money-getting. Had these communities arisen in a period of literary culture, or among the glorious relics of the art of a brighter age, these cities would have presented several more salient points of resemblance to the republics of Greece and Italy. It cannot, however, be denied that in many of their institutions they improved on the model set by the Italian cities, and this more especially in all matters relating to morality and rectitude. But they were less grand and large in their policy than their Trans-Alpine brethren, and unfortunately for themselves, their commercial maxims were always narrow and selfish. Monopoly was their watchword, their grand aim. And it was largely in consequence of this narrow policy that their ruin overtook them. They perished of that disease whereof corporations are apt to perish, namely, egotism, the centrifugal force which is perpetually tending to rend asunder all human society, and must inevitably do so, when not restrained by some powerful antagonistic action.

It is strange that, while so rich commercially, the Hanseatic League lacked political ambition. Had they possessed it, there is little doubt they might have made themselves independent masters of all Northern Germany. But they seem never to have forgotten that they were merchants. They were held down by petty motives, smallness of views. Here, again, they were unlike the Italians, among whom the trader could develop into the aristocrat, as is abundantly proved by the history of the Medici and other famous great houses. The reason must be sought, no doubt, in the different native temperament of the two nations—the one innately refined, the other rougher and more boorish.

Though the civic pride of the Hanseatics was highly flattered when the kings of the North and the princes of Germany trembled before them, they confined their ambitions entirely to gaining commercial advantages.

Certain it is that the two powers—the Hanseatic and the Italian Republics—each in their respective sphere of action, helped on the progress that has changed the entire face of this hemisphere, and that they did this by no other means than that of their commercial activity.

For this is the great power of commerce, if practised in its best and highest spirit, that it is able to work veritable miracles, bringing into contact the extremes of civilization, enlarging and disseminating ideas, and helping forward towards that universal brotherhood of man, that universal peace and goodwill, which is, and must be, the highest ideal of humanity. Not till war is really rooted out from among us, not till what is for the benefit of one is held for the benefit of all, not until a generous altruism reigns supreme, can mankind be said to be thoroughly civilized. Trade and commerce, though apparently egotistic factors, work strongly towards this end, even though their action proceed merely from motives of self-seeking. War is so serious an interruption to trade that men will seek to avert it, even out of a simple regard for their own pockets. By fair smiling peace, not only traders, but all the world is benefited and made happier. Once let nations fully understand and recognize its incalculable benefits, and even the lowest and most squalid souls will struggle to uproot this remnant of a barbaric spirit which can never evince itself as aught but an evil.

The Hansa uprose in a rough age, and hence had to work with the rough-made methods of its time; but in its time and in its way it did a good work, and posterity cannot withhold from it either gratitude or admiration. Its policy, its laws, its constitution, its commerce, its immense credit, the sway which it once exercised, the able magistrates, merchants, and mariners whom it produced—all these have vanished, unable to resist the torrent of time that engulfs good and bad alike. But its influence and example have remained, while much of its spirit, like many of its ideas and rules, have become incorporated into the general stock of the ideas of humanity.

Of the League itself, it is true there remains only an illustrious name. For Germany, which gave it birth, there remain memories both of pride and regret—memories that should serve as a spur to noble and useful emulation.

"The History of Commerce," says Montesquieu, "is the history of the intercommunication of peoples." The story of the Hanseatic League is an eloquent testimony to the truth of these words.

THE END.

20391398R00152

Printed in Great Britain
by Amazon